WHO IS GOD, AND WHAT HAS HE EVER DONE FOR US?

Why I Believe In Yahweh And His Son Jesus Immanuel, The Christ

David L. Jemison

WESTBOW
PRESS
A DIVISION OF THOMAS NELSON

WestBow Press books may be ordered through booksellers or by contacting:

WestBow Press
A Division of Thomas Nelson
1663 Liberty Drive
Bloomington, IN 47403
www.westbowpress.com
1-(866) 928-1240

Because of the dynamic nature of the Internet, any web addresses or links contained in
this book may have changed since publication and may no longer be valid. The views
expressed in this work are solely those of the author and do not necessarily reflect the
views of the publisher, and the publisher hereby disclaims any responsibility for them.

Any people depicted in stock imagery provided by Thinkstock are models,
and such images are being used for illustrative purposes only.

Certain stock imagery © Thinkstock.

ISBN: 978-1-4497-2980-6 (sc)
ISBN: 978-1-4497-2981-3 (hc)
ISBN: 978-1-4497-2979-0 (e)

Library of Congress Control Number: 2011919086

Printed in the United States of America

WestBow Press rev. date: 6/29/2012

This book is dedicated to YHWH and his son YHWHshua Immanuel, to all of the witnesses of God who will partner with me and get this book into the hands of the people who haven't yet received the love of the truth, and to the millions of precious people who will be saved as a result, at least in part, of this book: to the glory of God.

Contents

PART 3: WHAT IT'S BEEN LIKE, WALKING AND TALKING WITH GOD:

PART 5: THE EXCITING, REVEALING, AND UNDENIABLE, RECORD OF GOD:

PART 6: FROM SALVATION TO REST, FROM REST TO POWER, FROM POWER TO BEARING MUCH FRUIT: (LIFE AND THAT MORE ABUNDANTLY)

PART 7: THE CONCLUSION

Introduction

When the Lord made man, He placed within him a hunger that drives him to search for a power much higher than himself, one that he may refer to as god. Man is smart enough to ask himself the questions, "Who am I? What am I? What am I doing here? And where do I go from here?" Man's life presents to him more questions than answers, questions like, "Why, for what reason, or to do what?" That drive is so great within man that he will pull a god out of his imagination, and worship him. There is a void within man that can only be filled with the one and only living and true God, YAHWEH, the Creator, and Supreme Ruler, of heaven and earth.

Man has always looked up to what has fed into his life, or that which has provided necessary things to him. That is why we sometimes find him worshiping the sun, the earth, the sea, the trees, animals, etc. Then man has a tendency to reverence things that he perceives to be mightier than he, and things that he believes can destroy him. So sometimes we find man worshiping the mountains, volcanoes, thunder and lightning, and again the sea, and the wind. Then man has always had a reverence for things that he does not know, things that are hidden from him.

When Paul went to Mars Hill, in Athens Greece, he found alters to every god known to them. He even found an alter that was dedicated to the unknown god. The god that they did not know was YAHWEH. This book is dedicated to helping all people, everywhere, to find YAHWEH, and to ending their search.

I believe in God; and I believe that if anyone had experienced the things that I have experienced with God, they would believe in Him too.

The things that we believe in are the things that we have some kind of association with. Our beliefs occupy space within our minds, and they send us on a search for those things that are compatible with those beliefs. We long for confirmation. There is a strong resistance to those things that tend to supplant our established beliefs. Therefore, we need to scrutinize those things in which we place our faith. We need to divide those things into different categories.

1. The things that we suppose
2. The things that we think
3. The things that people who we believe in believe
4. The things that we believe
5. The things that we believe in, or on
6. The things that we know to be true
7. The things that are proven to be true, based upon things that we believe, but are not necessarily true. (Built on sinking sand)

We don't see pain, but we have some kind of association with it; so we believe in them. We don't see electrons, but we see what they do; so we believe in them. We can't see magnetism or gravity, but we can see the effects of these on different objects, so we believe in them.

There are two things that are said over and over in the Bible: "Behold," and "He that hath ears to hear, let him hear." The things that we know and believe in, are the things that we have looked for, and have beheld; or the things that we have listened to, and have heard; things that we have come to understand. People's faith is made up of the things that they are hoping, and evidence of things that they cannot see. It's called a belief system. These are things that people depend on, and hope that they are right.

When a couple gets married, they are showing trust in their spouse, and hope that their marriage lasts. When there is a person whom you consider to be your friend, you have in some way, bound yourself to that person; and you are hoping that they will always prove to be a friend. There may come a time when you discover that that person, in whom you have placed your trust, is proven not to be your friend, but instead an enemy.

Sometimes we believe in things that are solid, steadfast, and unmovable; and then again we may believe in things that even from the very beginning, were not very trustworthy. If we had beheld, perhaps we would have seen it; and if we had listened and heard, we would have understood that this thing or person couldn't be trusted.

The chair that looks weak, and that one that you have seen to let others down, and about which you have heard that it has failed to hold others up, is a chair that can't be trusted.

When you believe, and really do believe, in things or people that are untrustworthy, those beliefs stand in the way of your progress, and your true destiny. Therefore, false beliefs are very detrimental to the well being of anyone who holds these false beliefs to be dear to their heart. In your heart is where it all happens. Everything that you see in this world came out of somebody's heart.

If any god is to emerge as the one and only true God, he must meet these criteria:

1. He must be beyond our ability to understand:
2. He must be intelligent, beyond our wildest imaginations:
3. He must not have to give account to anyone:
4. He must transcend every law that there is:
5. He must not be limited by time and space:
6. He must have imagined everything that is:
7. He must have created everything that is:
8. He must know how everything that He created works:
9. He must be able to communicate with everything that He made:
10. 1He must not need help from anything that He has made:

YAHWEH is that God, and it is icing on the cake, for this God to tell us how and when he did all of these things, and to offer us proof of His existence, through fulfilled prophecy, and through miracles, signs, and wonders. And it is nothing short of mind blowing, for this great God to communicate with us, and to enter into agreements with us; thus binding, or obligating Himself, to perform the things that He had promised. This challenges us to prove Him. I believe in the Lord our God, and I believe in His Son Jesus.

The book whose time has come; it's about time:

For many years I have been mindful to write a book that glorifies our Lord. I had even started writing it several times, but I didn't get very far, in writing it.

Now I believe I know what prevented me from completing that book before now. It is because the book was more about me than it should have been.

The Spirit of God has reminded me, that if I am trying to write a book that glorifies Him, then people should not come away, after reading that book exalting me. They should come away being in awe of God almighty. After all, all of the things worth writing about are the things that He has done.

The scripture teaches us in Philippians 2:13 "For it is God which worketh in you both to will and to do of His good pleasure." I might interject here; that it is recorded in Hebrews 11:6 "But without faith it is impossible to please Him: for he that cometh to God must believe that He is, and that He is a rewarder of them that diligently seek Him."

Because there are many different translations of the Bible, I must let you know that all of the scriptural references in this book will be from the Authorized King James Bible.

The reason that I use this version of the Bible is first of all; when it is quoted it is universally recognizable. Secondly, I believe that when people say that they can't understand the King James Version, they are just being lazy; you don't understand any other version either, unless it is revealed to you. Judas saw the works of Jesus with his own eyes, and did not understand. Many of the Priests, Pharisees, and Scribes also saw those works and did not understand either.

Moreover I believe that the King James translators were more capable of being correct in their translations than those of more recent years. Languages of living peoples are living languages, and they change over a period of time.

The people who lived closer to those times are more able to understand the meaning of their words.

I also believe that we must be careful, because **the Word of God** is the most precious gift that the Lord has given to man. It reveals to us the only Living and true God, tells us of our beginning, and establishes a unique relationship with YAHWEH, our God, and teaches us how to have eternal life, and to live with Him. Satan knows this, and is competing with God, and will take advantage of every opportunity to distort the Word of God.

How many English translations are there anyway? Does it really take that many to make the Word of God easy to be understood? As a matter of fact, it causes more confusion. And by the way, we know that some translations were written to change the way people think, and to sway them to the translator's way of thinking.

Many years ago my friend the late Dr. Isaac Green, who had served as treasurer of the National Baptist Convention USA Inc., while he was pastor of the Central Baptist Church in Pittsburgh Pa., pleaded with me, "Jemmie, write those things down. Don't let them die with you. People need to hear those things."

I must write this book because early in my ministry, my experiences with the Lord were so awesome. Yet I had taken them all in stride and kept them mostly to myself. Eventually I began to forget them. I didn't talk about them very much, hardly at all. So much so, that whenever I heard other people, on the radio, or television, tell of their experiences with God, I would say to the Lord, "Lord why don't I have some of those experiences. Then the Lord brought back to my memory all of the things that He had done to me, with me, and through me; and I was ashamed, because I had forgotten.

The Lord be my witness, when I remembered, I realized that of all the things that I heard of the Lord doing in other peoples lives, none of them surpassed the things that He was doing in my life, at least up until that time.

The Lord is not pleased when we fail to give Him the glory.

In Mark 6:31-52, after Jesus fed the 5000 men with only two little fishes and five loaves of bread, and the disciples gathered twelve baskets of leftovers, He immediately, verses 45-46 "constrained His disciples to get into the ship, and to go to the other side before unto Bethsaida, while He sent away the people. And when He had sent them away, He departed into a mountain to pray."

The Lord sent them out on the Sea of Galilee, knowing all the time that there was a terrible storm scheduled to arrive on the sea, just about the time that they were in the middle of the sea. If the storm had not been scheduled, He scheduled one, just for them. The disciples had left before nightfall, but Jesus let them toil all night long, even though He could see them having trouble, until He came walking on the water, and calmed the storm. Jesus was not pleased with them, Mark 6:52 "For they considered not the miracle of the loaves: for their heart was hardened." God forbid that I should not appreciate the miracles and the works of the Lord, lest I should fail to give Him the glory. Our Lord has done great things, and we should not fail to give Him the Glory.

The miracle of birth, bearing fruit after one's own kind, the miracle of multiplying, is no doubt, one of the greatest wonders of all time; the ability of a species, to reproduce itself. That ability is due to a law of nature, a law that was legislated by the Lord God Himself.

Genesis1:11, "And God said, let the earth bring forth grass, the herb yielding seed, and the fruit tree yielding fruit after his kind, whose seed is in itself, upon the earth; and it was so."

Genesis 1:21-22, "And God created great whales, and every living creature that moveth, which the waters brought forth abundantly, after their kind, and every winged fowl after his kind, and God saw that it was good. And God blessed them, saying, be fruitful, and multiply, and fill the waters in the seas, and let fowl multiply in the earth."

Genesis 1:24-25, "And God said, let the earth bring forth the living creature after his kind, cattle, and creeping thing, and beast of the earth after his kind: and it was so. And God made the beast of the earth after his kind, and cattle after their kind, and every thing that creepeth upon the earth after his kind: and God saw that it was good."

Genesis 1:26-28, "And God said, Let us make man in our image, after our likeness: and let them have dominion over the fish of the sea, and over the fowl of the air, and over the cattle, and over all the earth, and over every creeping thing that creepeth upon the earth. So God created man in His own image, in the image of God created He him; male and female created He them. And God blessed them, and God said unto them, be fruitful, and multiply, and replenish the earth, and subdue it: and have dominion over the fish of the sea, and over the fowl of the air, and over every living thing that moveth upon the earth."

Whenever the Lord said let, it was a command to everything that existed, not to hinder, nor even try to prevent it from coming to pass. And when the Lord said to man and woman to be fruitful, multiply, and replenish the earth, and subdue it, that was a command, that empowered them to bear fruit after their own kind, and for it's fruit to also bear fruit, and to fill the earth, and to take command over all living things of the earth. However man is in command under the Lord God almighty.

Thus God is the Law Giver, and the Lord is the first cause. Time is a sequence of events, and time is determined according to the things that the Lord created, and set in motion, according to His laws. Light is the result of electrons and photons, which the Lord spoke into existence, and darkness is blockage of light.

PART 1:
THE LORD SENDS A MESSAGE
TO THE WORLD

Chapter 1

The Origin, Form, and Initial Effect of God's Message.

Let me share with you, the letter from God, and explain how it came to be.

A Genesis experience at Genesis Baptist Church, Sacramento, California.

In 1997 on Mother's Day, I was sitting in the pulpit of the Genesis Baptist Church in Sacramento, California. My wife, Marie, and I were visiting the church. The late Dr. Robert Porter, who was then the pastor of Genesis Church, was preaching the morning message.

Robert Porter was a friend of mine whom I had met in 1975 at JFK Airport. I had joined five other pastors who were members of a team going to Liberia, West Africa, on a Christian campaign to win souls for Jesus Christ.

After getting to know him, I would ask Reverend Porter to preach for our revival each year at the Mt. Olive Baptist Church, in Midland, Pennsylvania. He would also invite me to come and preach at his church, the Shiloh Baptist Church in St. Paul, Minnesota.

In 1977, Reverend Porter and I traveled together again, this time with a team of twelve other pastors on a missionary campaign to Nigeria, Africa. Our team was blessed to see nearly eleven thousand people accept the Lord Jesus Christ as their Savior while we were there. Praise God. I wonder what they have done for Christ, since then. When my wife Marie and I got married in 1995, it was in the Genesis Baptist Church, and Dr. Porter performed the ceremony.

The Lord instructed me to write.

I was sitting on the platform May 11, 1997, and while the man of God was preaching, the Lord spoke to me, not through his preaching, but the Lord spoke directly to me, apart from the sermon, and said, "I want you to write a letter for me to the world." I said that I would. While I was sitting there, and all day long, there was a burning deep inside me. I couldn't stop thinking about what the Lord had told me to do for him.

Pastor Porter had asked me if I would be willing to come back next Sunday and give the morning message. I assured him that I would be glad to. After he and Hazel, his wife, his family, my wife, and I went to a restaurant to enjoy a nice Mother's Day meal, my wife and I returned home to Santa Clara.

The next day, the Lord awakened me early, and His Spirit came upon me, and I began to write the "Letter from God." On the next Sunday I delivered "The Letter from God," for the first time anywhere, when I preached at the Genesis Baptist Church.

I later typed the letter on my word processor. Since then, I have printed thousands of copies of the letter, and my wife and I have distributed them across the country.

Chapter 2

A Personal Letter from God, to Anyone Who Will Receive It

"A LETTER FROM GOD"

My Dear Child,

I call you my child, not because I have fellowship with you nor because you serve me; but because I made you, and I am responsible for you. I am writing you this letter because it is urgent. The time is passing, and the end of this age is near. I love you and don't want you to perish. It is necessary that you understand who I am. If you know who I am, then you can better comprehend what you must do. I am a Spirit, and they who come to me must worship me in spirit and truth.

Before there was a *where* or *when*, I began to create. Creation is the beginning of time, and in the beginning I created the heaven and the earth. I made everything that was made. I made everything that you can see, feel, hear, taste, smell, or detect. I also made the things that you cannot see, feel, hear, taste, smell, or detect.

The inhabitants of the earth had forsaken me, and I had to destroy it by water twice. The second time, I preserved mankind by providing a way for my servant Noah and his family to escape.

I formed my son, Adam, caused him to stand up alive, and placed him in the garden that I had made for him. I intended for him to live forever, be at peace with and have authority and dominion over his world. I put no other burden upon him but that he would believe whatever I said unto him.

I made man a free-will agent with a mind capable of figuring things out and making good decisions, and of coming to good conclusions whenever he considers all things, all of the facts. Then people can come to the knowledge of the truth. I wanted Adam to have the opportunity to decide whether or not to serve me—by his own choice. For this reason, I placed in the garden eastward in Eden, two trees: the tree of life and tree of the knowledge of good and evil.

The tree of life bore fruit that, if a person ate it, could cause the person to live. This one-of-a-kind tree was also capable of revealing the heart of man. The tree was symbolic of the liberty that I intended for man and was accessible, available, and should have been desirable. Adam and Eve were free to, at any time, partake of that fruit and live forever because I had declared it.

I also made accessible unto Adam the tree of the knowledge of good and evil, and I made it pleasant to the eyes. However I commanded Adam not to eat the fruit of this tree. I warned him not to touch it, because the day that he would eat of it, he would die.

I also suffered another voice and opinion to be heard by him, a voice of someone competing with me for Adam's loyalty. I permitted Lucifer, that fallen, rebellious angel to persuade him to rebel against the one who loved him so much and wanted him to live forever.

Although that devil had done nothing for him, Adam believed Satan and Adam, by his actions, was calling me, the Eternal a liar. In Adam's heart, he accused me of deception and fear of losing my glory to him.

Satan had claimed that he would win over my people, become their god, and steal my glory. Satan promised Adam, through his wife, Eve, that they would have the glory that I had enjoyed and that they would no longer be dependent upon me.

What a damnable lie! You all now know that knowing good and evil did not equip man to do the good and shun the evil. Instead of obtaining the glory that I enjoy, he lost the glory that I had freely given him. All have sinned and come short of my glory, and the wages of sin is death.

So I am writing this love letter to you, my child, to let you know that I love you. Although your father, Adam, called me a liar, by his actions; I am giving you as an individual the opportunity to be released from Adam's curse, and to demonstrate that you believe my word and my love for you.

I am giving you the chance to realize and acknowledge that I, and I alone, am the one and only one, living and true God, and beside me there is no other. I had declared—and my word cannot be broken—that the soul that sinneth shall surely die.

Since all have sinned, this is what had to happen; because I didn't want any to perish:

A. Each and every one who had sinned must first die.

B. After each had died, I had to cause them to live again.

> Because sin is not a small thing with me; and because I refuse to let sin go unpunished, I will not eliminate the dying process. My word cannot be broken.

1. Each man must confess that he has sinned: The standard is written in my word.
2. He must accept the responsibility, in full, for his own sin.
3. He must repent with godly sorrow of his sin.
4. He must come unto me that he can be saved.
5. He must ask me to save him.
6. He must hear and believe what I say unto him about what he must do in order to be saved.

In my effort to rescue Adam's race, and yet maintain my own integrity; I decided to join myself unto man by allowing myself to be born as son of man.

This I have no problem doing, since I am omnipresent. My presence is ubiquitous, and I did not have to sacrifice time because I am not subject unto time. I did not have to sacrifice anything I do as God. Because no matter what I do, I am by no means diminished from what I must do.

I caused my Spirit to overshadow Mary during the time of her ovulation, and I fertilized her egg with my own sperm. Nine months later, she gave birth to a man child, who I commanded her to name Jesus; for He and He alone is the one that I have sent to man, to save him from his sins.

Man sinned, and man had to pay for sin. One man had sinned and caused the curse to fall upon all of his offspring. Therefore, one man would be acceptable unto me to represent all humanity, to bring back the blessing of Eternal Life.

One man sinned. One man's death would be acceptable as full payment for man's sin. However, that one man needed to be pure and without sin. Jesus is that man. He is the only provision that I have given unto man, in order to be restored.

There is no other name under heaven, given among men whereby you must be saved, other than the name of Jesus.

My son Jesus did everything that I commanded Him to do; and I am very pleased with Him. He was led to Calvary, allowed them to crucify Him, was buried, and three days later, I raised Him up and gave all power unto Him.

HEAR ME AND HEAR ME WELL!

If you are to be forgiven, if you are to be saved, if you are to be delivered from the bondage of Sin;

You must believe that I am, and that I will reward you greatly for coming unto me.

You must believe that I love you.

You must believe that when JESUS died on Calvary's cross, He was dying for you.

You must believe that He paid for all of your sins in full.

You must believe that I accept His death as full payment for your sins, as though you had died yourself.

When you believe in Jesus, with all your heart, YOU ARE SAVED, right now, and are no longer under the penalty of SIN. You are no longer guilty in my sight: because you believe my word.

This love letter that I am writing to you is the best thing, and the worse thing that can happen unto you. It is the best thing, because I have gone out of my way to show you the depth of my Grace, which is for you, and you have believed my word; and now you are a NEW BORN CHILD OF GOD, and your sins will never again be remembered against you. It is the worst thing because; if my word is not received and believed, there will be no other hope for you. There is nothing else that you can turn to in order to escape the wrath that is sure to come and fall upon all those who believe not my words.

It won't be long before I return to Earth in the person of my Son JESUS: who will take great vengeance upon those who receive not the Love of the Truth. In these last days I am calling on men, women, boys, and girls, everywhere to repent, and come to me; that I might save them.

I, THE LORD YOUR GOD, HAVE SPOKEN THIS; AND I WILL SEE YOU SHORTLY

Overwhelming acceptance of "The Letter from God"

One of the greatest experiences and joys that I have had in life is when I have shared this letter with people where ever I go. I have been doing this since May of 1997, and I can still count the number of people who have turned it down. Most of the people thank me for sharing it with them, even if they have to turn around and come back to thank me.

There have been many reports of people getting saved while reading the "Letter from God." Ironically, the only negative responses that I have received have been from people who are supposed to be saved, some church members; they find fault with a couple of things.

But wasn't it church people who opposed Jesus, when He walked among men? Tell me; since there are two powers in the world, YAHWEH and Satan, do you think that Satan would write such a letter? I leave it up to you, to judge.

Chapter 3

Why should we believe that God still speaks through people today?

One of the reasons that some people, who say that they believe in God, do not believe that the Lord still speaks through people is because, they say that has been done away with: Citing 1 Corinthians 13:9-12. "For we know in part, and we prophesy in part. But when that which is perfect is come, then that which is in part shall be done away. When I was a child, I understood as a child, I thought as a child: but when I became a man, I put away childish things. For now we see through a glass, darkly, but then face to face: now I know in part; but then I shall know even as also I am known."

It has been taught by some, that when the Bible was canonized, and all placed under one cover, that it fulfilled that scripture, as that which is perfect is come.

I must ask you, "Which translation of the Bible best represents 'that which is perfect,' is it the Revised Standard Version, the NIV, the Douay version, the Amplified version, the New American Standard version, The King James version, the New King James version, or which of the many English translations of the Bibles can be described as the "that which is perfect," mentioned in 1 Corinthians chapter 13: verse 10?"

When that which is perfect is come

I submit unto you, that scripture is referring to when Jesus returns, and there shall be a new Heaven and a New Earth, when the former things are passed away.

Revelation 21:1-5 John wrote, "And I saw a new heaven and a new earth; for the first heaven and the first earth were passed away; and there was no more sea.

And I John saw the holy city, New Jerusalem, coming down from God out of heaven, prepared as a bride adorned for her husband. And I heard a great voice out of heaven saying, Behold, the tabernacle of God is with men, and he will dwell with them, and they shall be his people, and God himself shall be with them, and be their God.

And God shall wipe away all tears from their eyes; and there shall be no more death, neither sorrow, nor crying, neither shall there be any more pain: for the former things are passed away.

And he that sat upon the throne said, 'behold I make all things new.' And he said unto me, 'write: for these words are true and faithful.'" This, is what the words "when that which is perfect is come," was referring to.

Furthermore, 2 Peter 1:19-21 says, "We have also a more sure word of prophecy; whereunto ye do well that ye take heed, as unto a light that shineth in a dark place, until the day dawn, and the day star arise in your hearts: Knowing this first, that no prophecy of the scripture is of any private interpretation. For the prophecy came not in old time, by the will of man: but holy men of God spake as they were moved by the Holy Ghost."

In Revelation 1:9-11, it is written, "I John, who also am your brother, and companion in tribulation, and in the kingdom and patience of Jesus Christ, was in the isle that is called Patmos, for the word of God, and for the testimony of Jesus Christ.

I was in the Spirit on the Lord's Day, and I heard behind me a great voice, as of a trumpet,

Saying, I am Alpha and Omega, the first and the last: and, what thou seest, write in a book, and send it unto the seven churches which are in Asia; unto Ephesus, and unto Smyrna, and unto Pergamos, and unto Thtatira, and unto Sardis, and unto Philadelphia, and unto Laodicea."

PART 2:
GROWING UP UNDER THE
SHADOW OF THE ALMIGHTY

Chapter 4

The early foundation, which helped to lead to faith in the Living God

The Lord has made me keenly aware of the fact, that the spiritual foundation that, was laid in my life, is a very strong factor of why I now, so strongly believe in God, and His Word.

A. Part of my foundation that my Mother provided:

The Lord said unto those who were led away captive into Babylon, in Jeremiah 29:11-13 "For I know the thoughts that I think toward you, saith the Lord, thoughts of peace, and not of evil, to give you an expected end. Then shall ye call upon me and ye shall go and pray unto me, and I will hearken unto you. And ye shall seek me, and find me, when ye shall search for me with all your heart."

Looking back over my life, I can now see that the Lord has had plans for me, even before I was born. **I am my mother's first man child**, which is the Lord's, among the covenant people of God: Exodus 13:1-2 "And the Lord spake unto

Moses, saying Sanctify unto me all the first-born, whatsoever openeth the womb among the children of Israel, both of man, and of beast: it is mine."

Numbers 3:11-13 "And the Lord spake unto Moses, saying, "And I, behold, I have taken the Levites from among the children of Israel instead of all the first-born that openeth the matrix among the children of Israel: therefore the Levites shall be mine; Because all the first-born are mine; for on the day that I smote all the first born in the Land of Egypt I hallowed unto me all the first-born in Israel, both man and beast: mine they shall be: I am the Lord."

Since I began writing this book, the Holy Spirit has brought back to my memory, that which my mother, Marie (Dot) Jemison said concerning me, when I was just a lad. I remember her saying that the first boy child was the Lord's, according to the Bible, and that I was her first boy child, and that the Lord was going to bless her boy.

When we were children, we had a big family Bible, which was a Master Art Deluxe Bible, with many pictures of bible characters in it. My Mom would love to open that Bible, showing us the pictures, and telling us about the great Bible stories, of Samson and Delilah, Daniel in the lions den, the three Hebrew Children in the fiery furnace, Abraham, Isaac, Jacob, Moses, Pharaoh, the children of Israel, and the ten commandments. She taught us the Ten Commandments, and to pray the Lords prayer.

I remember that she would tell us that when we reached the age of twelve, that we should join the church and be baptized, so that we would not go to the fiery Hell. She also told us that we needed to be born again. I remember her telling us that her father was a Methodist preacher, and how it was when she was young, and living in the south.

The preachers were circuit preachers, meaning that they would preach at one church on one Sunday, and then travel to preach at another church on the next Sunday. So they didn't have church every Sunday. Those who belonged to the Methodist Church would worship at their Church one Sunday, and would worship at the Baptist Church on the next Sunday; they knew that there was only one Lord, one Faith, and one Baptism. Those who belonged to the Baptist Church did the same thing. They would go to their own church one Sunday, and then to the Methodist Church the next Sunday.

Mom would tell us that she and her brothers and sisters, owned only one pair of shoes each, she being one of twelve children. They would carry them on their way to church, or school, and would stop, wash their feet in the creek, and then put on their shoes, just before they got there.

She said that when they got within a half-mile of the church, you could sometimes hear the people singing and shouting, and they would get excited and begin rushing to church. She loved to sing the song, "The Little Wooden Church on the Hill." I remember the part that says, "When that old-fashioned preacher gave out that metered Hymn, and each heart with the Holy Ghost was filled, the people would be shouting, thank God I can hear them still, in that little wooden church on the hill."

Each time I heard that song sung, it made me wonder what that was like. I never really did get to know, until I traveled to Liberia, West Africa, back into the region, where we had gone on a preaching mission. It was indeed like that then. There was no television, or any great events happening on a regular basis, to occupy their time. So Church was a big deal. Church brought people together, and many of them got the chance to show what they could do, whether it was to sing, dance, or to play the drums, cabasa, or tambourine.

So when preachers came to their little remote community, and Church, all the way from the United States of America, it was a huge event in the community. Even the little dog that came to church was so happy to be there. He would get up and dance around with the people, looking up at our faces, with his little tail wagging, whenever we would get up and sing and dance. I had never seen anything like it before in my life.

When the people would sit down the little dog would go back, and lie down under the pew, until the next song. It occurred to me that even that little dog had more sense than some adults that I knew, back home.

Now that I think about it, I know that my Mother had a lot to do with my foundation, which led to faith in the living God. It's a shame that it would take the writing of this book, for me to really fully appreciate my Mother's contribution to my spiritual life. **I Thank God, for my Mother**.

Exodus 13:11-12 "And it shall be when the Lord shall bring thee into the land of the Canaanites, as he sware unto thee and to thy fathers, and shall give it thee, That thou shall set apart unto the Lord all that openeth the matrix, and every firstling that cometh of the beast which thou hast; the males shall be the Lord's."

My Mother gave me to the Lord, when I was just a child, and when I became a preacher, and then began pastoring a church, She was so proud of her son.

B. Part of my foundation that my Dad provided.

The word says in Psalm 91:1 "He that dwelleth in the secret place of the Most High shall abide under the shadow of the Almighty."

My Father, David Jemison Sr. had found and dwelt in that secret place, and if ever a man abode under the shadow of the Almighty, my dad did. My Dad was and is still my hero. All of my life I knew my Dad as one who loved and lived for God. It didn't matter who you were, if you were around my Father for even a little while, he was going to tell you about the Lord.

My father was a coal miner who operated a cutting machine in the mine. And although he only went to the third grade, engineers came to him to learn more about the operation of that machine.

Dad was a praying man, and many people in churches loved to hear Deacon Jemison pray. Sometimes late at night I could hear my Father praying for all of his children. He prayed so that the shadow of the Almighty would also cover his whole family.

I have no doubt that my father was abiding under the shadow of the Almighty. I could tell it in his walk, I could tell it in his talk, I could tell it in his dedication, and I could tell it in his victories. My father was dwelling in the secret place of the Most High.

Dad would say that, if you have faith in God, you could do anything, go anywhere, and accomplish anything that you put your mind to. And when he would say that, you would have no doubt that he really meant and believed it.

My dad only went to third grade, and had to quit school to go work in the fields with his other siblings. He was one among twenty sisters and brothers, who were born to his mother, who was part Native American, and part Afro American, and of his father, who had fathered one other child by another woman before them, twenty-one sisters and brothers all tolled.

Dad was, I guess just like other boys his age, and among those that grew up in his environment, in the south, in and around Montgomery Alabama. However, when Dad was about twenty-one years old, he got saved in a revival service.

The revival services were about to end, and other people had gotten saved, but not he. One night after the revival service, he prayed "Lord, if you would just save my soul, I will live for you the rest of my life." The next night, when the invitation to accept Christ was given, he got up, went forward, and gave his life to the Lord.

That night on his way home, as the tears rolled down his face, he was so happy, and was still praying to God: "Lord if you really saved my soul," as he was looking up seeing the stars, on that bright and clear night, and seeing and pointing to a certain star, "would you please move that star?" Dad told me that God would move that star. Then he would pick out another star, and God would move that star.

This was an exercise that was to be repeated four or five times, and each time the Lord would move the star for him.

Isn't God good, that the Lord would do this for someone, who needed to be sure that the Living God had saved him, and was in his life?

Praise God, what a Savior! I can truly say that my father lived the rest of his life for The Lord.

I remember my Dad saying one day, "I can get anything that I want. If I know where it is, me and God can get it. All I have to do is take the Lord with me. If you have it, and I need it, God will make you give it to me. I have never asked God for anything that he has not given me."

I remember my Dad also telling me "I'm not afraid of anyone. If anyone tries to do something to harm me or mine, the Lord will turn it back on him. I believe that if someone had chased me up a tree, and out onto a limb, if they took a saw and cut off the limb that I was on, the tree would fall and my limb would stay up."

I don't believe that I've seen anyone chase my father up a tree, but I have seen many trees fall, and my Father was still standing. My Father lived to be ninety-three years old, before he went home to be with God.

We lived in the little coal-mining town of Westland Pa., located just about thirty miles south of Pittsburgh, Pennsylvania. The little town was nestled between two hills on a slope near the western edge of the foothills of the Appalachian Mountains, in what is known as the tri-state area, being close to West Virginia and Ohio.

In our town, everybody knew each other. Parents knew, and recognized the children, and knew who their parents were. All of the men worked in the coal mines, which were owned by the Pittsburgh Coal Company.

In the early days, the company owned all of the duplex homes, in which we lived, as well as the company store: that is until anti-trust legislation was passed, which forbade it. We bought everything at the company store, groceries, furniture, clothes, shoes, hardware, tires, gasoline, kerosene, and would get our cars fixed there.

I remember when they sold gasoline there for as low as twelve (12) cents a gallon, and a loaf of bread cost twelve (12) cents. I find it interesting, that as of April 21, 2005, the price of a loaf of wheat bread is $3.39, and a gallon of regular, unleaded gasoline is $2.69, and has been higher, in Modesto California.

This causes me to think about the scripture in Revelation 6:5-6, which says, "And when he had opened the third seal, I heard the third beast say, Come and see. And I beheld, and lo a black horse; and he that sat on him had a pair of balances in his hand. And I heard a voice in the midst of the four beasts say, a measure of wheat for a penny, and three measures of barley for a penny; and see thou hurt not the oil, and the wine."

Matthew 24:6-8 says, "And ye shall hear of wars and rumors of wars: see that ye be not troubled: for all these things must come to pass, but the end is not yet. For nation shall rise against nation, and kingdom against kingdom: and there shall be famines, and pestilences, and earthquakes, in divers places. All these are the beginning of sorrows."

The third seal represents inflation and famine. The balances or scales are related to commercial trade; a measure is about one quart, the penny is a denarius, and it represents a days wages, when it was written; and wheat, barley, and oil, are considered to be necessities of life; and the price is about ten times what is normal. Does anyone know what time it is?

Not many people owned automobiles back then. My Dad was one of the few people who owned an automobile, back in the forties. I remember that, after they stopped running the streetcars to our town, and even before then, people would ask Dad to drive them down town, to Canonsburg, Pennsylvania, which was a much larger town of over ten thousand people. He would take them, wait for them, and bring them back.

There were three churches in town, the Presbyterian, the Baptist, and the Catholic Churches. The Presbyterian Church worshiped in a fine brick church, at the edge of town, and even had their own parsonage. I suppose, because the Pastor didn't live in town, the parsonage was occupied by the church missionary, Mrs. Partington, who was one of the finest people that I have ever known.

Since the Catholic Church and the Baptist did not have a place to worship in, the coal company let them share a room that was connected to, and under the same roof of a gymnasium, which was later made into a large garage where they kept some of their large trucks, that they used to haul slate. The Catholics would have early morning mass from six o'clock AM to eight o'clock AM, and we, the Baptist Church would start Sunday school, of which my father was the Superintendent, at ten o'clock.

Church services would start at eleven o'clock; my father was the deacon of the church. After a while, they took the building away, and we had no place in which to worship any more.

There was a building in the center of town, which had a lot of ground, and was located on a corner. It was the best property in the town, and had served as the schoolhouse for the first and second grade, before they closed it, and sent those students to the other school building, just outside of town. I have some sweet memories of going to school in that building. If you would stand on the front porch of that school building, you could take a stone, throw it straight ahead, and hit the house where I lived. However, I talked my mother into packing a lunch for me, so that I could eat my lunch with my teacher. She would sometimes let me sit on her lap; and I loved it.

In first and second grade, I had a friend and playmate named Donny; and I would compete with him, to sit on the teacher's lap. Smile!

My father was looking for someway to get another place of worship, and so he went to the principle of the schools, to see if he could use that abandoned school house to have church in. They told him that they would give him the building, but that the land was owned by the Pittsburgh Coal Company. So now, he knew who owned it; and he needed it; so he and God went to the Superintendent of the mines, and told him that his people needed a place in which to worship, and the children needed a place to go to Sunday school. The Super said to him, "Dave I don't know what I can do." Dad replied, "You're the Superintendent, and I know that you can do anything that you want to do; my people need someplace to have church."

Whether it was that day or not, I don't know, but Dad told me that the Superintendent said to him, "Mr. Jemison, I know that you do a lot of running around for your people, and that you don't get paid for it, and you have that big family to take care of; so I'm going to see to it, that you get the property; and I will make sure that you get something for your effort. I'm sure that they don't know how much you do for them.

We will sell the property to you for one dollar, and then we will have a deed drawn up to the church for five hundred dollars purchase price, and they will pay us, and we will pay you for all your labor, it's only right, and if they had to get a lawyer to do it for them, it would cost them more than that."

Today, in 2005, that church, though much improved and enlarged, is still there, and ironically, my Father's Granddaughter, and my niece, is now the pastor of that church. My Dad believed in his God, and I believe that the Lord believed in my Dad.

I am deeply grateful to have known such a man as Deacon David Jemison, not to mention having lived with him, and being fathered by him. **I thank God for my Dad!**

C. Part of my foundation that Mrs. Partington provided

Every summer in our town, the Presbyterian Church would have Vacation Bible School, for two weeks. There were only white people attending their church at that time. As a matter of fact, all the people of color went to the colored churches, and the white people went to white churches. I don't think that anybody thought anything about it in those days.

So Vacation Bible School was for the children of members of that church, and for other white people, and potential members. However, Mrs. Partington, and other decision makers in the church, were not satisfied with that situation. They then decided to have V B S for their own children for two weeks, and then for the colored children for two weeks.

Mrs. Partington would go to all of the homes of the black people in town and personally ask them to send their children. Almost all of the families sent their children, and I remember that we did all that we could, to have perfect attendance. My mom also made sure that we were prepared to get there on time. I loved to go to V B S, and looked forward to going each year.

Every day during Bible School, we had to memorize a Bible verse from the King James Bible.

Most of these verses were salvation scriptures. Mrs. Partington worked with us, and tried to persuade us to live good and clean lives. Many of the songs that she taught us were songs of commitment to God, or invitation songs.

One song that I remember well was; "Come into My Heart Lord Jesus." The song went like this: "Into my heart, into my heart. Come into my heart, Lord Jesus. Come in today. Come in to stay. Come into my heart Lord Jesus."

I remember her, trying to get students to make a decision to accept Jesus in to their hearts, but I'm afraid that I was a little too young, to really understand what she was talking about.

I do believe that she had some influence on the life of every non-Catholic child in town and perhaps on the lives of some of the catholic children also. She was truly a missionary and a servant of God.

Many years later, when I was twenty three years old, on the day that the Lord saved me, and while the Holy Spirit was dealing with my heart, the Lord brought back to my memory all of the salvation scriptures that she had taught me.

When I get to heaven, I want to see Mrs. Partington, and thank her for sowing love, kindness, and the word of God into my heart. It worked. However, I kind of think that she already knows.

Mrs. Partington was dwelling in that secret place of the Most High, and was abiding under the shadow of the Almighty. She chose to extend that shadow to also cover me, and people like me. God only knows the price that she had to pay to make that sacrifice.

Thank the Lord for Mrs. Partington, and the people who supported her.

D. The Questions that troubled me

Before the Lord saved me, there were questions in my mind that troubled me. After I grew up, and got to experience the things that many young men get to experience, such as parties, smoking, drinking, and enjoying the pleasures of these things, it began conflicting with the way that I had been raised.

I would go out and do things; and I enjoyed the things that I did; then I would come home and pray, and I would ask God to forgive me for the things that I did that night. And all the while, I knew that I had already made plans to do the same things, on the next weekend. After a while, this began to get old. I began to see the hypocrisy of what I was doing. What was I doing? Who am I fooling, only myself. I should do one thing or the other.

This God was keeping me from being contented with the life that I was living, but instead of questioning the life that I was living, I began to question God. Is there really a living and true God? If there is, then I should stop doing the things that were wrong, and those things that go against the commandments of God. I should accept Him into my life, and spend my life telling others how I know that God is real, and that they better seek Him, before it's too late.

However, I felt that if there is no living and true God, that I should live any way that I pleased, as long as it didn't harm anyone else, because life is short, and I should enjoy it while I can. I also felt that it would be my responsibility, to prove to other people that there was no God, and that they should live their lives as they pleased. In fact, if I were to discover that there was no God, I would have become one of the most dedicated, atheistic evangelists that you have ever seen.

I would take the responsibility of freeing people of the bondage of false beliefs. But at this time, I didn't know one way or the other. I was agnostic, I just didn't know; and I wasn't satisfied, not knowing. It was too important a matter, to not at least try to find the truth.

Furthermore, I remember that many times people would come to me and tell me about some terrible and sometimes fatal accidents. And I would say to myself; how exciting, why can't I be there sometimes, when those things happen. It's not that I wanted bad things to happen, just so that I could witness it; but if these things were going to happen anyway, I just wanted to be there to see it. How foolish can we be? I didn't know how blessed I was, to never have seen such things.

I guess, God heard my thoughts, and said, "No problem. If you want to see, I will let you see:" Because, several times after that, whenever terrible accidents happened in our area, I was the first, or one of the first on the scene.

I have seen the body of someone whose automobile was rear-ended by a drunken driver, who had been traveling at a high rate of speed. She was a very heavy lady, and her body was split everywhere, having been tossed about twenty-five feet in the air. The other passenger in the car was thrown about one hundred feet in the air, and was still alive. When we turned her over onto her back, we discovered that her hand ripped almost completely off; only the tendons were holding it on, and she was alive, but unconscious.

On another occasion, while coming home late at night from a night club, one of the cars in front of us lost control, turned over, and skidded, upside down, about one hundred fifty feet, into a closed gas station, and came to rest up against the gas pumps. It was a convertible, and was filled with band members, who had just finished playing for a high school prom, and was returning home.

I stopped to see what I could do to help, and while I was feeling for a pulse on one of the victims, who had been thrown from the car, his heart stopped beating. One of the other men, who were trapped in the overturned convertible, was calling out for help. His cries were blood curdling. There was gasoline, spilling out from the gas tank of the convertible, and we were afraid of an explosion and fire.

One of the men had slid along the pavement, and was half in the car, but his head and shoulders were out. He was still alive. When the police came, they tried to pull him out, and he was screaming, bloody murder. They were trying to get to and to help the living, as soon as they could, and they too were worried about an explosion, and fire. The other fellow, who was trapped inside was not to be freed from the wreckage until about an hour later, when the fire department came and pried him out, cutting the metal away from around him.

I don't know if, or how many of these men lived through this ordeal but judging by what I had seen, it's hard to believe that any of them made it. Now, thinking back to that night, I wonder if any of those men were saved, and went to be with the Lord, or if they died and went to Hell. God knows.

On another occasion, while I was on my way to work, there was dust, still in the air, and a car that had hit a bridge abutment, and had been split open, as if someone had taken a can opener around it, and severed it from the frame. I pulled my car over, and ran back to see what I could do.

There was no one in the car, so I looked over the bridge and saw a man who had been thrown from the car and was lying in the creek. I slid down the bank and pulled him from the creek bed. By this time other people began arriving on the scene.

I heard later on that day, on the news, that the man, who was taken to the hospital, was treated and released the same day. I said to myself, somebody up there loves him. His life was a miracle.

On another occasion I heard the news that my cousin, by marriage, was waiting at a bus stop, and a car jumped the curb, hitting her, and pinning her to a wall. She lived, but was completely paralyzed on one side. The thoughts of this troubled me.

E. My search for God, and the truth

As a result of these experiences, I began to fear driving my car, and even walking the streets, for the fear of death. I was even afraid to go to sleep at night, for the fear of waking up in a Christ-less hell. I know now, that this is what is meant by the expression, being under conviction.

I decided that this is not the way to live, so I decided to do research to find out if there was a God or not.

Where would I search? What books would I read? Then I thought; all of the books written about God, Heaven, and Hell, used the Bible as the source. And being someone who likes to go to the source, I decided to go to the Bible to try to find that answer.

When I first started reading the Bible, I started at Genesis Chapter 1. Prior to this, my concept of God was, that He was some white-haired gentleman, who was sitting up in heaven, just watching, and waiting, to see somebody get out of line, so that he could bring down His wrath upon them. It was very hard for me to believe in a God like that. But in reality, I believe that it just shows that I hadn't given much thought to it, I was just feeling my own guilt.

I hadn't gotten very far into the book of Genesis, when I began to believe that the Bible was true, even though many of the things seemed to be incredible.

The idea that the very first man and woman made mistakes, and yet The Lord made provisions for them, was encouraging to me {Genesis 3:1-24}. The idea that the very first child born on Earth, murdered his own brother; and yet God provided some protection for him and his family. {Genesis 4:1-26} This was a surprise to me, but it was encouraging.

The fact that the Lord would get so angry with the wickedness of the inhabitants of the Earth, that He destroyed them, with a world-wide flood, caused me to know that He cared too much for mankind, to allow them to continue in that direction. Yet the Lord chose Noah, described in the Word of God as, "a just man, and perfect in his generations, and Noah walked with God" Genesis 6:9.

I noticed that the scripture did not say that he was perfect, but perfect in his generations. In other words, all of the people in his family roots were worshipers of the Living and true God.

He was not a perfect man, I noted in Genesis 9:20-21, "And Noah began to be an husbandman, and he planted a vineyard. And he drank of the wine, and was drunken; and he was uncovered within his tent." A drunken man is not my idea of a perfect man. As a matter of fact, I found it hard to understand that such a man could have been described as one who walked with God. But the Lord spared him and his wife, his three sons and their wives.

But then I had to notice, that he believed God, and worked on the ark for one hundred and twenty years. Genesis 6:22 "Thus did Noah; according to all that God commanded him, so did he."

Genesis 16:1- 4 says, "Now Sarai, Abram's wife bare unto him no children: and she had a handmaid, an Egyptian, whose name was Hagar. And Sarai said unto Abram, Behold now, the Lord has restrained me from bearing: I pray thee, to go into my maid; it may be that I may obtain children by her. And Abram hearkened to the voice of Sarai. And Sarai, Abram's wife, took Hagar her maid the Egyptian, after Abram had dwelt ten years in the land of Canaan, and gave her to her husband to be his wife. And he went in unto Hagar, and she conceived: and when she saw that she had conceived; her mistress was despised in her eyes."

Now I'm beginning to believe that I know these people. They are acting just like people that I know.

Now Ishmael becomes Abraham's first Son, because his wife was trying to help God to fulfill what He had promised. Isn't that just like people, even though it is wrong to do that? And yet the Lord still blesses Hagar and her Son Ishmael, and promises that, Genesis 16:10 "I will multiply thy seed exceedingly, that it shall not be numbered for the multitude."

Then there is Abraham's deception of Pharaoh, at one time, and Abimelech, on another occasion, by agreeing with Sarah to tell them that she was his sister, thus causing her to appear to be free, to be married to them. And this is the friend of God? Humm!

It seems to me that the Lord loves ordinary people. I can understand Abraham deciding, that since they came there to stay alive through the famine, it didn't make much sense to die trying to keep his wife. That's the way logical, and rational people think. But he was living a lie.

Joseph's father showing him more favor than he did show to the other sons, with the exception of Benjamin, and their jealousy which drove them to get back at their father, by getting rid of his pride and joy, Joseph, reminded me of people that I knew. They did not consider that he and Benjamin were the younger sons; but they did notice that their father had showed more love to Joseph, and Benjamin's mother, because the father loved her more. Rachel died giving birth to Benjamin.

It was also noteworthy to me that the children of Israel, whose name had been Jacob, did not all have the same mother.

Genesis 35:21-26 "And Israel journeyed, and spread his tent beyond the tower of Edar. 22. And it came to pass, when Israel dwelt in that land, that Reuben went and lay with Bilhah, his father's concubine: and Israel heard it. Now the sons of Jacob were twelve." 23. "The sons of Leah, Reuben, Jacob's first-born, and Simeon, and Levi, and Judah, and Issachar, and Zebulon:"

24. "The sons of Rachel, Joseph and Benjamin:" 25. "And the sons of Bilhah, Rachael's handmaid, Dan, and Naphtali:" 26. "And the sons of Zilpah, Leah's handmaid, Gad and Asher: these are the sons of Jacob, which were born to him in Padan-aram."

Now this was the kind of stuff that I could relate to; and these were the Lord's chosen people. I felt that if the Lord chose to make these people His chosen, then to me, what the Bible says about God is believable, and the God of the Bible is reachable, even for a sinner like me.

Sodom and Gomorrah

And then there is the story of Lot, and Sodom and Gomorrah, Genesis, Chapter 19. This passage tells us that two angels came to Sodom, and the city was so wicked, that Lot, not knowing that they were angels, wouldn't think of them spending the night in the streets, and brought these two street people into his home, fed them, and let them spend the night there; and they were strangers. You do know that people, who sleep in the streets, are known as street people, don't you?

Before they had a chance to go to sleep that night, that town being filled with homosexuals, the men of that city surrounded the house, and demanded that Lot would send them out to them, so that they could have sex with them. Lot then, feeling that he was to be the protector of these men, who he brought under his roof for shelter, pleaded with them not to do this thing; but he was outnumbered by far. Then Lot comes up with an idea, which to this day, I can't understand.

He suggests that he has two virgin daughters, which he would send out to them, to do with as they pleased. Now what in the world was this man thinking? If he was so concerned with the safety of these strangers, why didn't he offer himself? Perhaps they had already gotten to him. Now these men were so reprobate in their lifestyle, that they didn't even want the females, they were burning for the men. I know of such a world.

When the angels struck them all with blindness, did they see the light, and turn back? No, the Bible says that they wearied themselves to find the door. To me that was a classic picture of what it was like to be in the clutches of Satan; he won't let you go, and does not care what happens to you.

Then the angels told Lot to gather up his family, and to hurry and get out of town, because they were going to destroy the city. They said that they could do nothing until they were safely out of town. The only members of his family that he was able to take with him were his wife, and his two daughters. And then on their way out of sight of the city, his wife was tempted to look back, and turned into a pillar of salt; because they were commanded by the angels, not to look back, and she did.

Then we have the matter of when, after some time, while they were dwelling in the mountain, the girls devised a plan to get their father Lot, to have sex with them. One was to get him drunk one night, and then lay with him, and the next night the other was to get him drunk, and lay with him. They both did so, and conceived, and brought forth sons. The first son was named Moab, who became the father of the Moabites. And the other son was named Ben-ammi, who became the father of the Ammonites.

By the time I had read these things, I was thoroughly convinced that the Bible was true, that God is real, and is responsible for the Biblical record that I was reading. Nobody in their right mind would invent such a God, tell such a story about themselves, and then say, "We are God's chosen people, and by the way, here are His ten commandments." There is no way that they would do this. **No way!**

The truth is; the God of the Bible is real; He gives people plenty of time, to get it right, even if you have problems. He is willing to work with you; and He really loves people. My research was paying off. I was searching, to know the truth, and I was finding it.

F. Part of my Foundation that Oral Roberts provided

The Reverend Dr. Oral Roberts has played a major roll in my salvation, and faith in God. Someone once asked him; "What is faith?" His answer to him was, "Faith is when the

Lord supernaturally, empties you out of all doubt; and you can't, not believe."

When I was a young man, I got married at the age of eighteen, to my first wife, and the mother of my three children, when she was only seventeen. Because she was a faithful member of the Mount Olive Baptist Church, in Canonsburg, Pennsylvania, and was the secretary of the Sunday school, I joined that church.

I had been baptized at the age of twelve, after joining the First Baptist Church, of Westland Pa., during the annual revival service. I was sincere when I joined, but I really did not know what I was doing, or what to expect from God. It really hadn't gotten to me, about how to be saved. I didn't really know if one could ever consider himself to be saved, while he was still living. My thought was that you could never really know, until after you died.

If you woke up in heaven, then you were saved; if you woke up in hell, then you were lost. If you did not wake up at all, then there was no heaven or hell, you just ceased to be. I trust that this is not the philosophy of many of you who are reading this book, right now. Not only can you know that you are saved; you must know: if you expect to go to be with the Lord.

Prior to joining the church in Canonsburg, I had joined the Friendship Baptist Church in Washington Pa., that is after they took away the place of worship in Westland, and we had no place in which to have church. I remember, when I joined Friendship Church, they asked me if I had anything to say. I said, "If I could only be half the man that my father was, I would be Ok: My father was serving as a deacon in that church, and they loved him.

I began to be active in Mount Olive Church. I joined the choir, usher board, and faithfully attended Sunday school. Later I became the teacher of my Sunday School Class, ages 18-35, and then became assistant Superintendent of the Sunday school, financial secretary of the church, and recording secretary of the trustee board. They made me Vice President of the usher board, and the choir.

The church later voted to put me on trial for deacon, and later began making plans for my ordination as Deacon. Mind you, all this time, I am still not saved, and refused to tell anyone that I was. I had decided that I was not going to let them ordain me before I could say that I was saved, though I still did not know what that was.

I built my Sunday school class up from about five members, to more than thirty-five members, who were faithful about having perfect attendance. Most of these people were members of the church, and some were friends with whom I would party some times. I can't imagine what I was trying to teach. Thank God, we had the Standard Sunday School lessons that we studied from.

One Sunday, I just decided to stay home from church, and told my wife to take our daughter, and go without me. I turned on the television, and Oral Roberts was on, preaching in a Crusade.

There were so many people getting healed that day; and when I saw a particular person get up out of a wheelchair, chills came over me; and goose pimples rose up on my arm like little beads. Later he made an appeal to people who wanted to be saved.

He said, "If you want to be saved, put your hand on the television, and pray with me." I hadn't told anyone that I was seeking the Lord; I didn't want anyone to know. Now I was alone, and there was no one there to see what I was doing; so I had no problem following his instructions. The tears were rolling down my face, and I was expecting the Lord to do something. I expected the Lord to shake my body, to shake the building that I was in, or something like that, but he didn't.

I'll tell you what the Lord did do. From that day on, he placed within me a hunger and strong desire for the Word of God, and after buying myself a good study Bible, I began studying the Word of God, day and night.

I did not stop until I got saved, one year later; and I didn't even stop then. In that prayer that I prayed, I asked Jesus to come into my heart and save me. One year later, He did; but it didn't have to be that long. I could have been saved the moment that I believed on Jesus. **I thank my God for Oral Roberts.**

G. Part of my foundation that Oliver B. Green provided

When I was a young lad about thirteen or fourteen years old, I began to do things that made me know that I was a little different than some of the other boys with whom I grew up.

Many times when they were down on the ball field, playing soft ball, or baseball, I would sit in my room, daydreaming. I would dream of what I wanted my life to be like. I would see myself as a married man, with children, and a loving wife. At this time I didn't even know who that might be.

I would dream of coming home from work; yes, I dreamed of work. I wasn't afraid of work; being the oldest son at home, I had my chores to do. I would see myself coming home, putting on my silk robe, sitting in my favorite armchair, and smoking my pipe, with my wife or my child sometimes coming and sitting on my lap, just like in the movies. Smile!

Well after I got married, I got a chance to live out my dream. However, we did not live in our own house, at that time, but a three room, ground floor apartment, with a large porch, a large living room, with a large picture window. My robe was not silk, but it was a nice one, my chair was comfortable, my wife and my little girl would sometimes come and sit on my lap, I did sit and smoke my pipe, and I felt like I had it made.

We lived next door to the Payne Chapel AME Church, where the Thompson Brotherhood Chorus would practice. One day someone invited me to come and join. And since I had sung in our high school chorus, and was presently singing as a strong tenor voice, in the Mt Olive Baptist Church Choir, I felt that I could add to the chorus.

I enjoyed singing in the chorus, and Bill Thompson, who was the founder and director of the chorus, did an excellent job in pulling out the best in us to produce perfect four-part harmony, acappella, and we sang only gospel music. We traveled and sang at churches all over western Pennsylvania.

We also competed in a talent contest, on Westinghouse television station in Pittsburgh, and got second prize. Had we won first prize, they would have sent us to New York, for the National finals, put us up in the New Yorker Hotel, and given each of us one hundred dollars spending money. There were twenty-two of us, and it was a little girl, about twelve years old who won. I'm sure that it was much cheaper to send her to New York, than to send twenty-two men. The winner of the finals would get money, and a recording contract.

However, it was a great experience, and allowed our families, and friends to see us perform on television.

As a teacher of the adult Sunday school class, I campaigned for members, and built my class up to over thirty-five members. Most of them came because they were my friends. Yet I can't imagine what I was trying to teach those people, most of whom were older than myself. For quite a while, I was able to get away with faking it that is until a couple, who really knew the Lord, came and joined. It didn't take them long to discover that I didn't know what I was talking about, and they said so to some of the class members. When it got back to me, I was upset, and took it personally, but I was quick to admit it to myself, that they were right; I didn't even have a clue.

Because I didn't have a clue, we depended on the comments of those who tried to contribute. This led to very lively discussions, so lengthy that we felt that we didn't have enough time. So we decided to start a weekly Bible study group that would meet every Friday, from house to house. This also helped us to change some of the habits that we had formed, such as partying on weekends.

Most of the people who attended those Bible studies, were not saved, and admitted it. There were two who claimed that they were saved, but I had serious doubts about that. They could not give the reason for the hope that they had within.

It was during this time that we discovered that there were some great Bible teachers on the radio every day. Teachers like Theodore Epps, of the Back to the Bible broadcast, Lester Roloff, from Corpus Christi, Texas, and Oliver B. Green, of the Old Fashioned Gospel Hour, from Greenville, South Carolina.

From these broadcasters, and some others, we learned much, and we were greatly helped in our Bible study.

Oliver Green is, in my opinion, one of the greatest Bible teachers and gospel evangelist that this world has ever heard. He came on the Christian station, five days a week, and taught the Bible, book-by-book, and verse-by-verse. He did this for many years, and when he finished each book of the Bible, he would write a book of commentary on it.

We would never miss the broadcast, and would often discuss what he taught each week, in our Bible study.

Having prayed with Oral Roberts for the Lord to save me, I was being driven to study, and to learn more about God. We faithfully did this for about a year. Then at a particular Bible study, I gave the testimony, that the Lord had saved me that week. To my amazement, Jean Turner, and Floyd Edmonds testified, that the Lord had saved them also that week. There was great joy and curiosity among us that night. In the weeks and months that followed, many more got saved, until all were saved, and more joined and also got saved. It turned out to be a citywide revival, and became the talk of the town.

Transformed, from a sinner to a Saint

The Lord saved me one day while I was at work, and was listening to Oliver Green teaching on the radio. I had brought my radio to work, and didn't miss the broadcast.

I was a cable splicer; I spliced and repaired mine cable, for Carter Brother Cable Repair, in Westland Pa., a little coal-mining town in western Pennsylvania. We would pick up damaged mine cable, bring it to our shop, repair them, and return them to the mines, almost like new. Because the cables were dirty, from being in the mine, we would get very dirty also, by handling it. We would reinsulate the cable, and put it into our cookers to vulcanize it.

This particular day, while Reverend Green was teaching, he said, "For by grace are ye saved, through faith, plus nothing." When he said that I got angry with him, because I knew that it was not quoted exactly as it was recorded in Ephesians 2:8, which does say, "For by grace are ye saved through; and that not of yourselves: it is the gift of God:"

I said to myself, "These preachers make me sick, always adding to the scripture." I had been studying the Bible extensively, and now I am dangerous, because I have a little knowledge. I knew exactly what the Bible said.

I remember that I was standing at my vice, that held the cable ends that I had just finished splicing together, and I was about to carry the splice to the cooker to be vulcanized. It was then that the Lord spoke to me clearly, "He's right." Then the Holy Spirit brought back to my memory, all of the salvation scriptures that I had learned from my youth on up.

"For God so loved the world that He gave His only begotten son, that whosoever believeth in Him should not perish, but have everlasting life." John 3:16

"He that believeth on Him is not condemned: but he that believeth not is condemned already, because he hath not believed in the name of the only begotten Son of God." John 3:18

"Verily, verily, I say unto you, he that heareth my word and believeth on Him that sent me, hath everlasting life, and shall not come into condemnation, but is passed from death unto life." John 5:24

"Verily, verily, I say unto you, he that believeth on me hath everlasting life." John 6:47

And again there was Ephesians 2:8-10; "For by grace are ye saved through faith, and that not of yourselves: it is the gift of God, Not of works, lest any man should boast. For we are His workmanship, created in Christ Jesus unto good works, which God hath before ordained that we should walk in them."

"Yes," I said to God. "That is what you are saying; that if I believe on Jesus as my savior, I am saved. People would ask me how to be saved, and that is what I would tell them, but I would always say; yeah, but there is more. But I was wrong; there is no more. It is just as you showed me; your grace is sufficient."

A week prior to this day, I had committed a sin that I could not forgive myself for committing. So I began reading my Bible, somewhere in the book of John. Then I decided to pray to God, concerning my sin. I said, "Lord, it isn't fair for you to allow me to stoop so low. You know how hard I am trying to live for you:" I had stopped partying, drinking, and smoking; and I was going to Bible study every week. "Lord you've got to help me."

God's hand gives me a hand in understanding

When I got up off my knees, I noticed that the pages of my Bible had been turned. Now the doors and windows were closed, and I was there by myself. The study Bible that I was reading was Moroccan bound, and the pages were Indo paper. These pages do not turn by themselves, and my Bible was well broke in. I looked at where the Bible was turned to; and there was only one group of red letters on both pages. It was opened to 2 Corinthians 12:9; "And he said unto me, my grace is sufficient for thee: for my strength is made perfect in weakness. Most gladly therefore will I rather glory in my infirmities, that the power of Christ may rest upon me."

I had no doubt that God had turned the pages of my Bible; but I didn't have any idea what He was trying to tell me. Perhaps I did have a clue, but the idea seemed too ridiculous to me.

Paul said; 2 Corinthians 12:2-8 "I knew a man in Christ above fourteen years ago, (whether in the body, I cannot tell, or whether out of the body, I cannot tell: God knoweth ;) such a one caught up to the third heaven. How that he was caught up into paradise, and heard unspeakable words, which it is not lawful for a man to utter. Of such a one will I glory: yet of myself I will not glory, but in my infirmities. For though I would desire to glory, I shall not be a fool; for I will say the truth: but now I forbear, lest any man should think of me above that which he seeth me to be, or that he heareth of me.

And lest I should be exalted above measure through the abundance of the revelations, there was given to me a thorn in the flesh, **the messenger of Satan to buffet me,** lest I should be exalted above measure. For this thing, I besought the Lord thrice, that it might depart from me."

That's when the Lord said unto him, "My grace is sufficient for thee: for my strength is made perfect in weakness."

My understanding about this was that God's grace would cover my sin, but this seemed to me, to be too unbelievable for me to accept. But Paul further explains in Romans, Chapters 7 and 8.

My declaration of faith, and my disclaimer

Now that the Holy Spirit had brought these things back to me, I was beginning to see, and to understand the truth about salvation. I said to the Lord, "He's right, it's by grace through faith, and there is no more. I apologize; and right now I receive Jesus Christ as my savior, and from now on, I'm going to live for him. But don't get me wrong; I don't know how strong I will be. But if I understand you right, even if I am weak enough to commit a murder, as long as I believe in Jesus as my savior, I am saved."

Now I wasn't afraid that I was going to kill anyone, but I was sneaking up on my real fear. I said, "And even if I was weak enough to commit adultery, as long as I believed in Jesus, I am saved." I wasn't planning to commit adultery; as a matter of fact I had repented of my sin, but just a week ago I had failed in my trying.

To my amazement, the Lord answered me back and said, "That's right." I did not expect the Lord to reply, but I was just clearing the record about my understanding; it was sort of my disclaimer. Isn't it wonderful that the Lord loves us enough to talk to us, and answer many of our questions.

Now I know that many of you want to know, How did God speak to you, and how did you speak to him, and was there anybody else around, and did they hear it too?

Really, I hadn't given it much thought, before I began writing this book; but when I spoke to the Lord, I don't think that I even moved my lips, I spoke to Him through my mind. And when God spoke to me, I don't think that He even used my ears, but He spoke directly to my mind. However I have absolutely no doubt that it was the Lord speaking to me; I would never have said to myself, the things that He said to me that day. And yes, Don, my buddy that I worked with, was standing at his vice, only about twenty feet away from me, when all of this was happening. He never heard a thing.

Instant Salvation

I remember when I accepted Jesus as my Savior; I was carrying my splice to the cooker, for vulcanizing. I lifted my foot as a lost sinner, and I put it down as a saint; a blood washed, blood bought child of God, a new creature in Christ, with the Holy Spirit living within me. Praise the Lord. My sin was forgiven; Jesus had taken them all away. I could feel that my burden had been lifted, and I could see and understand the things of God, and I was no longer stumbling in the dark. The Lord turned the light on in my soul.

I had committed a crime against God, I had broken His law, and I knew that I was guilty. Sin is a crime against God that is punishable by death. There was an eye witness to my crime, Truth, and he turned me in to the High Sheriff of Glory, who is Death, and there was an APB, All Points Bulletin out on me, I was wanted, dead or alive. It has been said that he always gets his man. Hebrews 9:27 "And as it is appointed unto men once to die, but after this the judgment:"

I had two choices. I could wait until the Sheriff, Death; arrested me or I could turn myself in, and throw myself on the mercy of the court. I decided to turn myself in. I confessed that I had broken God's law, and that I was sorry, said that I wanted to go straight.

I remembered that the scripture said, 1 John 1:8-10 "If we say that we have no sin, we deceive ourselves, and the truth is not in us. If we confess our sins, He is faithful and just to forgive our sins, and to cleanse us from all unrighteousness. If we say that we have not sinned, we make Him a liar, and His Word is not in us."

1John 2:1-2 says, "My little children, these things write I unto you, that ye sin not, and if any man sin, we have an advocate (lawyer) with the Father (the Judge) Jesus Christ (the Judge's Son) the righteous: (the Judges beloved Son in whom He is well pleased)

And He is **the propitiation** (our proxy, and sacrifice) for our sins: and not for ours only, but also for the sins of the whole world." Jesus said, Matthew 5:17 "Think not that I am come to destroy the law, or the prophets, I am not come to destroy, **but to fulfill**."

When I came into God's courtroom, He had a book before Him that had listed all of the charges that were brought against me. Although I had committed many sins, He said that I only had to be guilty of one sin to be found guilty, and worthy of death. Since James 2:10 says, "For whosoever shall keep the whole law, and yet offend in one point, he is guilty of all." and Romans 6:23 says, "For the wages of sin is death; but the gift of God is eternal life through Jesus Christ our Lord."

I was asked, "How do you plead?" Since the Word of God said, Romans 3:23 "For all have sinned, and come short of the glory of God;" I knew that there was no way that I could deny that I was guilty, so I said, "Guilty as charged."

Then God, who was the Judge said, since the defendant, David L. Jemison, has confessed to the crime of sin, this crime caries the penalty of death. So I sentence you to die. Just then my lawyer spoke up and said, Your Honor My Father, We have some other laws on the books that supersede the law of sin and death.

There is John 3:16, Mark 16:16, John 3:18, John 5:24, John 6:40, John 6:47, and Ephesians 2:8, 9, and 10. This is the law of the Spirit of life in Christ Jesus, and it makes them free from the law of sin and death.

Romans 8:1-2 "There is therefore now no condemnation to them which are in Christ Jesus, who walk not after the flesh, but after the Spirit. For the law of the Spirit of life in Christ Jesus hath made me free from the law of sin and death."

Since Jesus cannot lie, every promise that He makes becomes a law, which cannot be broken. The law states, John 6:47 "Verily, verily, I say unto you, he that believeth in me hath everlasting life."

Baptized by the Holy Spirit, into the Body of Jesus Christ

I said to the Judge, "I do believe in Jesus." Then the Holy Spirit took my soul into custody, took me back through time, back to the day and time that Jesus was hanging on the cross; and he placed my soul into the body of Jesus, and there I died with Him, and was buried with Him. Ezekiel 18:4 says, "The soul that sinneth, it shall die." I had sinned, so I died.

1 Corinthians 12:13 "For by one Spirit are we all baptized into one body, whether we be Jews or Gentiles, whether we be bond or free; and have been all made to drink into one Spirit." If we are in the body of Christ, we are there because the Holy Spirit baptized us into it. It was there and then, that I received my new and eternal life, the new creature, which replaced my soul which had sinned.

Now I can say along with Paul, Galatians 2:19-21 "For I through the law am dead to the law, that I might live unto God. I am crucified with Christ: nevertheless I live; yet not I, but Christ liveth in me: and the life which I now live in the flesh, I live by the faith of the Son of God, who loved me, and gave himself for me. I do not frustrate the grace of God: for if righteousness come by the law, then Christ is dead in vain."

Romans 6:3-7 "Know ye not, that so many of us as were baptized into Jesus Christ were baptized into His death. Therefore we are buried with Him by baptism into His death: that like as Christ was raised up from the dead by the glory of the Father, even so we also should walk in the newness of life. For if we have been planted together in the likeness of His death, we shall be also in the likeness of His resurrection: Knowing this, that our old man is crucified with him, that the body of sin might be destroyed, that henceforth we should not serve sin. For he that is dead is freed from sin."

Graduation Day

Galatians 3:23-27 "But before faith came, we were kept under the law, **shut up** unto the faith which should afterwards be revealed. Wherefore the law was our schoolmaster to bring us unto Christ, that we might be justified by faith.

But after that faith is come, *we are no longer under a schoolmaster.* For ye are all the children of God, by faith in Christ Jesus. For as many of you as have been baptized into Christ have put on Christ.

Ephesians 4:4-6 "There is one body, and one Spirit, even as ye are called in one hope of your calling. One Lord, one faith, one baptism, One God and Father of all, who is above all, and through all, and in you all."

That day I was born again, born of the water (the Word of God), and the Spirit of God. The word of God came into my heart, and faith came, then The Holy Spirit came together with the Holy Word of God that was in my heart, a spiritual intercourse took place in my heart, and immediately I was born a new creature in Christ.

My flesh was not born again, but I had a new life that was like the wind, invisible. The Lord adopted my flesh, and owns it, so now I can pray, Abba, Father.

John 3:5-8 "Jesus answered, Verily, verily, I say unto thee, except a man be born of water and of the Spirit, he cannot enter into the kingdom of God. That which is born of flesh is flesh; and that which is born of the Spirit is spirit. Marvel not that I said unto thee, ye must be born again. The wind bloweth where it listeth, and thou hearest the sound thereof, but canst not tell whence it cometh, and whither it goeth: so is everyone that is born of the Spirit."

The born again person is invisible, sinless, and eternal, just like God. That new creature is as Adam was, before the fall. The sins of the old man are not charged to the new man, but they have been charged to Jesus.

1 John 3:9 "Whosoever is born of God doth not commit sin: for His seed remaineth in him: and he cannot sin, because he is born of God."

Romans 4:4-8 "Now to him that worketh is the reward not reckoned of grace, but of debt. But to him that worketh not, but believeth on him that justifieth the ungodly, his faith is counted for righteousness. Even as David describeth the blessedness of man, unto whom God imputeth righteousness without works. Saying, blessed are they whose iniquities are forgiven, and whose sins are covered. Blessed is the man to whom the lord will not impute sin."

Paul said in Romans 10:1-4, "Brethren, my heart's desire and prayer to God for Israel is that they might be saved. For I bear them record that they have a zeal of God, but not according to knowledge.

For they being ignorant of God's righteousness, and going about to establish their own righteousness, have not submitted themselves unto the righteousness of God. For Christ is the end of the law for righteousness to every one that believeth."

Romans 10:17 says, "So then faith cometh by hearing, and hearing by the word of God."

The party of parties

Before I got saved, I would love to go to parties. I would drink beer and hard liquor. I loved to dance, and was the life of the party. After my wife and I got saved, the first thing that we decided to do was to throw a party. I wanted to show people that you didn't have to smoke, drink, cuss, and tell dirty jokes, in order to have a good time. It's good just to get dressed up, and to spend time with people that you love, and eating good food together.

You would be amazed how much fun you could have, just telling stories of your life growing up, etc.

We invited all of the people who we had partied with, along with a few Christian friends. We sat around eating and telling stories. Nobody smoked, cursed, or drank any alcoholic beverages. We just enjoyed each other, and began to know how much we appreciated each other. When the party was over, as our guests were leaving, each of them said that it was the best party that they had ever gone to. I have discovered that usually, it's not the alcohol that brings people to clubs, bars, and parties; but it is people that draw people. It is so important to have other people in our lives. After this party, most of the people who came got saved also. Praise God!

Reverend Oliver B. Green played a large roll in my coming to Christ, and in my getting saved. I thank the Lord for his faithfulness, and sacrifice, to send and to take the gospel all over these United States.

I thank God for Oliver Green.

Chapter 5

Our Bible Study group, and the way that God worked with us:

When we started our Bible Study, we began by selecting a book of the Bible, and studied verse by verse. We would each read a verse or some verses, and then try to explain what it was saying. If anyone didn't agree, we would all discuss it, and try to come to some conclusion about the meaning. I must say that this sometimes led to some very lively discussions, to say the least.

As a result of some of these arguments, someone suggested that we invite some older persons who knew the Lord, to join us in Bible study. I was one of the people who did not agree with this suggestion. We felt that because of the respect that we had for some of the people who were suggested, that we would not challenge anything that they said.

Therefore, we would not keep on digging to know the truth for ourselves, so we did not invite them. My pastor was legally blind, and up in age and not very likely to go out very much. Besides, I felt that he got his chance to teach us every

Sunday. We weren't sure that he would even approve of us having Bible study in the homes anyway.

Sometimes we would use the Sunday school lessons that we weren't able to complete, as a study guide. Then sometimes someone would bring in some correspondence Bible course.

There were times that we would just discuss the questions that were on our minds. And then we were supplied with ample material by the gospel programs that we listened to on the radio. Sometime we would discuss the pastor's message, or the message of some visiting minister.

Through all of this, we learned how to use the concordance and the center references in our Bibles. We also discovered Strong's Complete Concordance, and learned how to use it. Before we knew it, and about a year after starting that Bible Study, the Lord began a revival in our church when He began saving us, until all were saved, and it began to spread throughout the little town of Canonsburg, where Perry Como, Bobby Vinton, and the Four Coins were from.

Then the Bible studies became more exciting than ever. We could hardly wait, to see who the Lord would save next. After a while, we decided to do more than just come together to study the Word; we wanted to do something for people in need. However we did give in church; some of us paid tithes to the Lord.

We decided to bring in the names of people in need, and after hearing from everyone, and after praying that the Lord would direct us to the person that He would have us to help that week, we each would put the name of a person in a hat.

The person whose name that we pulled, would receive from us, either groceries, or cash, if that was the wise thing to do.

I remember one day when Don Carter, my buddy with whom I worked, told me about a fellow that he knew about, and how he lived. I found that what he was telling me was hard for me to believe, so after work, I followed him in my car, and he led me to a place near a closed coal mine.

We got out of our cars and went a little distance from the road, to the old red brick dynamite shack. This was Louie's home. It was a little building that stood about five or six feet tall.

I believe that his name was Louie. He had made a place for cooking outside, and had his few cooking utensils neatly put up. Don called for him but he wasn't home. I found it very hard to believe that there was anyone living like that, especially around where we lived. And yet Louie was so neat. My heart really went out to him.

When I came back to the Bible study group and told them about Louie, they also looked at me in disbelief. When it came time for us to each select a person, and to put the name in a hat, I believe that almost everyone put in Louie's name. They appointed me and two other fellows, to go shopping for Louie's groceries, and to deliver them.

I had a habit of buying good study Bibles that cost about seventy or eighty dollars apiece, to give to the newborn Christians. I would go through the Bible, break in the cover and a few pages in the back, so that it would lay flat.

I would also find many of the salvation scriptures in the Bible and underline them, so that they would be noticed. I didn't know if Louie would know how to use the helps, but the Lord laid it on my heart, to get that Bible and add it with the groceries that we were taking to Louie and give it to him.

It was just getting dark when we arrived at Louie's place, and he was inside the little shack. The little house was so low, that I knocked on his roof, instead of the door. When the door opened there was this little guy with the biggest smile on his face, and he invited us to come in. This little house was about nine by eight feet, and I couldn't stand up straight in it. As we looked through the door, into this little room that was lighted with four little candles, which also served as the heating system, we could see his little cot on which he slept, and all of the rest of his belongings stacked neatly against the walls.

We introduced ourselves to him, and told him that the Lord had laid him on our hearts, to bring these groceries and the Bible to him. He was so grateful, and he showed it. We set the bags of non-perishable goods down, had a word of prayer with him, and then said goodbye, assuring him that we would continue praying for him.

Because this building was snug and tight, he used it for his winter home. In the summer he would move into the old machine shop, where all of the windows were broken out. That following summer, while Louie was living in the old machine shop, the place caught on fire, and Louie perished in the fire. I don't know if Louie ever got saved or not, but I am really glad that we were responsive to the Spirit of God, to do what we did, when we did. Little did any of us know that Louie only had a few months to live. I do believe that the Lord did save him, and I expect to see him when I get to Heaven.

The Untouchables

Our Bible study group became so close to one another that people began to call us the untouchables. I remember once when I was laid off from my job, when my brothers and sisters in Christ heard of it, they brought money to me. Because of their expressions of love through sharing, I lived better during my lay off than when I was fully employed. Between drawing unemployment and their gifts, I had more money than I did before I got laid off. That's how we were; no one had lack.

Now that we were saved, our second favorite meeting place and time was Wednesday night prayer service. This began to be our saving station.

People would come and give their testimonies, and we began to learn and to love many of the old church hymns, being led by our pastor's wife; one of the sweetest people that I ever had the privilege of knowing. It's amazing, that after we were saved, we could now relate to her very well; and we felt a togetherness with her, even though she was old enough to be our grandmother. People who are in Christ, those who are truly saved, are some of the most precious, and loving people in the world.

Chapter 6

The name of Jesus

If the Lord Yahweh were to attach Himself to man, Adams race, then there would be a new species on the Earth, because that had never happened before. Therefore that new person, that new species, would have to have a new and unique name, a name that is above every other name.

Well, I am writing you to let you know; that is exactly what has happened. Christ Jesus Immanuel is that person, that new species of life. That species is so unique, that it had not existed anywhere before; no, not on Earth, nor did it exist in Heaven.

This new and unique person had only existed in the mind of Yahweh, our heavenly Father, because He knew that Adam, His son by way of creation, would fail to lead his race to believe, and to obey the Father, who is the Creator and Sustainer of everything. This was Adam's first experience at living, choosing, and at suffering consequences.

The Lord knew that he would more than likely fail. But if the Lord had not started Adam's race, He would not have been able to attach himself to this people. Adam's race, that first species, had to begin with someone; and Adam is that someone.

One of the great problems of the ages is that the Jewish people, who were God's people, and who were chosen by Him to reveal the one and only true God to the world, to introduce God's Law to the world, and to be the generation through which He would join Himself to man, and thus be born Christ Jesus Immanuel, felt that the Lord's unique and proper name, YAHWEH, was too holy for them to speak.

But this is not what the Lord told them, this is what they concluded on their own, and yet even now I can understand this sense of reverence for that name. I also hesitate as I speak that name. His name is so holy.

There is power in that name, power that I feel each time I say it, I feel it even now. I understand why they felt that they should not be on a first name basis with the one and only true God, who is the Maker and Supreme Ruler of Heaven and Earth.

Perhaps this is part of the reason why blindness in part has happened to the Jewish people. So much is missed because other names were used when referring to YAHWEH in the scriptures, therefore losing something in the translation.

The original Hebrew language does not even have the letter J in it. Then Jehovah is not the Lord's unique and proper name, it is a nickname, given to Him by those who refused to call Him by His real name. Tell me; which is more irreverent, to call the Lord by His proper name which He gave us, or to call Him by a name that we gave Him instead? You be the judge.

People need to feel the power that is in the name YAHWEH, who is the existing one. Say that name. That is the name of our heavenly Father. He is real, and not a figment of our imagination.

In Exodus 6:2-3 says, "And God spoke unto Moses, and said unto him, I am the Lord: And I appeared unto Abraham, and unto Isaac, and unto Jacob, by the name of God Almighty, but by my name YAHWEH was I not known to them." In Psalm 83:18 it says, "That men may know that thou, whose name alone is YAHWEH, art the most high over all the Earth."

The Lord is who He says He is, and not what, or who we say that He is. The LORD exists because He is, has always been, and always will be, and not because we give Him permission to exist, on our terms. I don't think that people have noticed, but that is just the way that many of them think; that is, that God exists the way I believe Him to exist. I am so glad that I serve a God that is all powerful, all knowing, and who is present everywhere, ubiquitous.

YAHWEH exists everywhere at the same time, and in every time, at the same place. My Lord, what a God!

Mary was the juncture at which God began to be with us, among us, our refuge, our way of escape, our dwelling place, our strong tower, our place of rest, our standard who was lifted up. Mary gave birth to this new species, this person who was very God as though He was not man, and very man, as though he were not God. Christ Jesus Immanuel is the first of His kind, but He was not to be the last, thanks to the new birth.

1 Corinthians 15:20-23 "But now is Christ risen from the dead, and become the first fruits of them that slept. For since by man came death, by man came also the resurrection of the dead.

For as in Adam all die, even so in Christ shall all be made alive. But every man in his own order: Christ the first fruits; afterward they that are Christ's at his coming.

John 3:5-8 "Jesus answered, Verily, verily, I say unto thee, except a man be born of water and of the Spirit, he cannot enter into the kingdom of God. That which is born of the flesh is flesh; and that which is born of the Spirit is spirit. Marvel not that I said unto thee, ye must be born again. The wind bloweth where it listeth, and thou hearest the sound thereof, but canst not tell whence it cometh, and whither it goeth; so is every one that is born of the Spirit."

1 John 3:1-2 "Behold, what manner of love the Father hath bestowed upon us, that we should be called the sons of God: therefore the world knoweth us not, because it knew him not.

Beloved, now are we the sons of God, and it doth not yet appear what we shall be: but we know that, when He shall appear, we shall be like Him; for we shall see Him as He is." We shall be like Him.

2 Corinthians 5:17-21 "Therefore if any man be in Christ, he is a new creature: old things are passed away; behold, all things are become new. And all things are of God, who hath reconciled us unto Himself by Jesus Christ, and hath given to us the ministry of reconciliation; To wit, that God was in Christ, reconciling the world unto Himself, not imputing their trespasses unto them; and hath committed unto us the word of reconciliation. Now then we are ambassadors for Christ, as though God did beseech you by us: we pray you in Christ's stead, be ye reconciled to God. For He hath made Him to be sin for us, who knew no sin; that we might be made the righteousness of God in Him."

In John 1:1-4 it says, "In the beginning was the Word, and the Word was with God, and the word was God. The same was in the beginning with God. All things were made by Him; and without him was not any thing made that was made. In Him was life; and the life was the light of men."

John 1:10-14 says, "He was in the world, and the world was made by Him, and the world knew Him not. He came unto His own, and His own received Him not. But as many as received Him, to them gave He power to become the sons of God, even to them that believe on His name: Which were born, not of blood, nor of the will of the flesh, nor of the will of man, but of God. And the Word was made flesh, and dwelt among us, (and we beheld His glory, the glory as of the only begotten of the Father,) full of grace and truth."

Proverbs 18:10 says, "The name of the Lord is a strong tower the righteous runneth into it, and is safe.

Psalm 91:1 says, "He that dwelleth in the secret place of the Most High shall abide under the shadow of the Almighty."

What is His name? When the man was healed at the gate of the temple, which is called Beautiful, Peter explained it by saying, in Acts 3:16; "And His name, through faith in His name, hath made this man strong, whom ye see and know: yea, the faith which is by Him hath given him this perfect soundness in the presence of you all."

And when Peter and John were arrested, and brought before the rulers, elders and the scribes, the record in Acts 4:8-11 says, "Then Peter, filled with the Holy Ghost, said unto them; ye rulers of the people, and elders of Israel,

If we this day be examined of the good deed done to the impotent man, by what means he is made whole; Be it known unto you all, and to all the people of Israel, that by the name of Jesus Christ of Nazareth, whom ye crucified, whom God raised from the dead, even by Him doth this man stand here before you whole. This is the stone which was set at naught of you builders, which is become the head of the corner." This was a quotation from the scriptures, Psalm 118:22.

Acts 4:12 continues, "Neither is there salvation in any other: for there is none other name under heaven given among men, whereby we must be saved."

Power in the Name of Jesus Immanuel

Philippians 2:9-11 says, "Wherefore God also hath highly exalted Him, and given him a name which is above every name: That at the name of Jesus every knee should bow, of things in heaven, and things in earth, and things under the earth; And that every tongue should confess that Jesus Christ is Lord, to the glory of God the Father."

Matthew 12:21 says, "And in His name shall the gentiles trust." John 14:10-14 says, "Believest thou not that I am in the Father, and the Father in me? The words that I speak unto you I speak not of myself: But the Father that dwelleth in me, He doeth the works. Believe me that I am in the Father and the Father in me: or else believe me for the very works sake.

Verily, verily, I say unto you, He that believeth on me, the works that I do shall he do also; and greater works than these shall he do, because I go unto my Father. And whatsoever ye shall ask in my name, that will I do, that the Father may be glorified in the Son. If ye shall ask anything in my name, I will do it."

Before the Lord Jesus was crucified, He said unto His disciples, in John 16:22-28 "And ye now therefore have sorrow: but I will see you again, and your heart shall rejoice, and your joy no man taketh from you. And in that day ye shall ask me nothing.

Verily, verily, I say unto you, whatsoever ye shall ask the Father in my name, He will give it you. Hitherto have ye asked nothing in my name: ask, and ye shall receive, that your joy shall be full.

These things have I spoken unto you in proverbs: but the time cometh, when I shall no more speak unto you in proverbs, but I shall show you plainly of the Father. At that day ye shall ask in my name: and I say not unto you, that I will pray the Father for you: For the Father Himself loveth you, because ye have loved me, and have believed that I came out from God. I came forth from the Father, and am come into the world: again, I leave the world, and go to the Father."

His name is Jesus Immanuel.

The original Hebrew word is [wXwhy lawnmm [.
Transliterated, it is <u>Y@howshuwa</u>` `Immanuw'el.
The phonetic spelling is, Yeh-ho-shoo'-ah Im-maw-noo-ale'

This is Jesus' first and last names. The first name means, from the primitive Hebrew, YAHWEH TO SAVE. And His last name, from the primitive root means, GOD IS WITH US FOR THE PURPOSE OF BEING OUR REFUGE, AND OUR WAY TO ESCAPE, OUR DWELLING PLACE OF REST, or **God, with us, our way to escape.**

You may have noticed that in Matthew 1:23 it says, "Behold, a Virgin shall be with child, and shall bring forth a son, and they shall call His name Emmanuel, which being interpreted is, God is with us."

However, this is a quotation from the Old Testament, Isaiah 7:14, which says, therefore the Lord Himself shall give you a sign; Behold a virgin shall conceive, and bear a son, and shall call his name Immanuel." In Matthew, that name was not fully interpreted.

The book of Matthew, that was translated into English in the Authorized King James Version of the Bible, was not a translation from a Hebrew manuscript; but seems to have been written in Greek, for Greek speaking people. But in order to get the real and complete translation of the name Immanuel, we have to go back to the original, and primitive Hebrew.

Im: means with. The original Hebrew word is; ~[.

The transliterated Word is `im, the phonetic spelling is eem.

'el: means god, and is the transliterated word. The phonetic spelling is ale.

The original Hebrew word is la.

That accounts for the beginning and the end of the name Immanuel; but what do we do with the word, or words ma, and nuw, which are in the middle? This middle part comes from the transliterated word Manowc, which means, flight, refuge, place of escape, and way to flee. The original Hebrew word is ownm. The phonetic spelling is maw-noce.

The word Manowc comes from the primitive particle transliterated word mah, the original Hebrew word is hm, the phonetic spelling is maw, and it means what, how, of what kind, because of what, or for what reason; and also from the primitive Hebrew root word own; transliterated it is Nuwc, and phonetic spelling is noos. It means to flee, escape, to cause to disappear, to hide, and to lift up a standard.

From this primitive root we also get words such as <u>M@ nuwchah</u>, which means rest, or resting place, and the word

Nuwach, which means to rest, settle down and remain, or to obtain rest.

I can tell you now, that Satan did not want us to know our Savior's name, but greater is He that is in me, than he that is in the world.

2 Samuel 22:1-4 "And David spake unto the Lord the words of this song, in the day that the Lord had delivered him out of the hand of all his enemies, and out of the hand of Saul: And he said, The Lord is my rock, and my fortress, and my deliverer; The God of my rock; in Him will I trust: he is my shield, and the horn of my salvation, my high tower, and my refuge, my Savior; thou savest me from violence. I will call on the Lord, who is worthy to be praised: so shall I be saved from my enemies."

The Lord's chosen people, who were chosen by God, to reveal the one and only living and true God to the world, were having some problems of their own. Many of them had a form of godliness, but they denied the power thereof. They were going about to establish their own righteousness, and had failed to submit themselves unto the righteousness of Christ.

Before the birth of Christ, they refused to even say the name YAHWEH. And when Jesus was born, most of them missed that greatest event of all, the day when God came and joined Himself to man. Then when Jesus began His public ministry, John 1:11 says, "He came unto His own," the Jewish people, "and His own received Him not."

And now, even though the early church were all Jews, the one hundred twenty in the upper room, who were the first to be filled with the Holy Spirit, the three thousand who got saved that same day, and the five thousand who gladly received the Lord later, were all Jews.

Even Jesus, said to the woman at the well in Samaria; John 4:22 "Ye worship ye know not what: We know what we worship; for salvation is of the Jews."

It was the priest who paid for the betrayal of Jesus, who was the Lords Messiah, and after His resurrection, it was they who paid for the cover-up. Many of them were out of covenant with the Lord, they had not fulfilled their part of the agreement, and blindness in part had happened unto them. Even to this day, many of them go out of their way to try and prove that Jesus is not the Christ. They do not will, to know the truth.

I thank God that many of our Jewish brothers have received Jesus Christ as their savior, and those of us, who are saved, need to pray for the Jewish people. They have brought to the world, the knowledge of the true God, and provided the conduit, through which the Lord Jesus came into the world.

To my Jewish brothers I say, read the 53rd chapter of Isaiah, and when you pray to God, ask Him, **"Did you have a son, and is His name Jesus?"** If you really want to know the truth, the God who has ears and can hear, has eyes and can see, and has a mouth; and He does speak, will speak to you, and cause you to know the truth.

PART 3:
WHAT IT'S BEEN LIKE, WALKING AND TALKING WITH GOD:

Chapter 7

Rescued from perishing, and living
with a purpose

I was saved in September of 1960, and in September of 1961, the Lord called me, and sent me to preach His Word. I experienced talking to God, and having The Lord to talk to me on the very day that I got saved.

I was married, and we had a little girl, who was the apple of my eye. But I wasn't happily married, at the time. I remember one day being so depressed, that I sat on the side of my bed, with my gun pointed to my own head. I was prepared to take my own life. The strange thing is that I didn't even consider the thought of divorce; it wasn't even in my vocabulary. I never considered it as a second option.

From the time that I was a young boy, even too young to be dating, I would set on the side of my bed, daydreaming about being married, and having a family. I guess the fact that I was raised in a home with both my father and my mother, and my sisters and my brothers, as a family; was the reason why I never considered divorce; I knew nothing else.

The word divorce was not even used in our house, to my knowledge.

I'm grateful to say, that I didn't do it. I did not take my life. If I had, I would have gone straight to Hell. I didn't refrain from taking my life because I was afraid of dying; I was too stupid to be afraid of dying, at the time. But rather, I was afraid of not dying, and becoming as a vegetable, with a bullet lodged in my brain, and having to be cared for by someone, who I thought, didn't even care for me.

Right or wrong, it kept me from killing myself, the two wonderful sons that the Lord would give me later and from sending myself to hell. There are thousands of souls whom the Lord has used me to bring to Christ, and there are those souls who have been brought to a saving knowledge of Jesus Christ, by them. Now I know why Satan was urging me to take my life. He wanted to prevent what the Lord was going to do through my life. This book also, would not have been written, and the thousands of souls that are being saved through this book, may have never have come to the Lord. I thank the Lord that He saved my life.

Now I know; that is just what Satan is trying to do, destroy families, and kill people. I would to God, that I had known then, what I know now.

I believe that my first marriage would still have been intact. It's called spiritual warfare; and the secret is, recognizing the devil, and exposing him; because, when you are in Christ, greater is He that is in you, than he that is in the world.

If you will it to be so, our God is able, to do exceedingly, and abundantly, above all that you think or ask. You cannot defeat what you do not confront, and you cannot confront that which you do not identify. You must determine who or what is the enemy, before you can confront. James 4:7 says,

"Submit yourselves to God. Resist the devil, and he will flee from you." The Bible also says in Deuteronomy 32:29-31, "O that they were wise, that they understood this, that they would consider their latter end!

How should one chase a thousand, and two put ten thousand to flight, except their Rock had sold them, and the Lord had shut them up? For their rock is not as our Rock, even our enemies themselves being judges."

Any man and his wife, who are in Christ, and pulling together, is more than a match for anything that comes against them, because the Lord has already given them the victory. God is for us. Romans 8:31 says, "What shall we then say to these things? If God be for us, who can be against us." Every husband and wife must be in covenant with each other, and the two of them, with God.

A preacher who failed in his resolve

It is very embarrassing and painful to me to confess, that although I have been married for a total of forty-six years, and yet I have divorced three times, and am now in my fourth marriage.

I pray that I have learned something through those experiences. Perhaps I could make excuses for myself, but I choose not to do so. There is one thing that I have come to realize; that there was only one common denominator in each of my marriages; me. I know that if I had been a better me, we might have had the patience to have worked our way through the rough places.

I remember that while I was going through my first separation, I experienced great stress. So much so, that there was a chemical imbalance within my body, and I received burns on my hands, burns from the inside out, which left scars on my hand.

Whenever anybody brought their problems to me, I had to pray over them and then put those problems into file thirteen. I had to totally forget about them; my plate was full. Separation and divorce is a very traumatic experience.

I know that I wouldn't have survived those times, had the Lord not done things, to let me know that He was still with me, and that he was willing to use me. But my word to any Christian couple, who are having marital problems, is this: Marriage was instituted by God, and was designed to be forever. Satan knows this, and he goes out of his way to cause conflict, and to destroy marriages. He knows that if all of the Christian families faired well, and stayed intact, it would be the major cause of this world turning to the Lord God. He also desires to cause the divorced couples to experience guilt, and to carry that guilt around like a heavy weight.

He also knows that the religious community would be some of the first to try to exclude them, from the great work of redemption, branding them as unworthy, except for the bringing their tithes into the storehouse. Their tithes are considered to be first rate.

The Lord has given us the wherewithal to make it in marriage. However marriage is a covenant between a husband and his wife, and both of them need to be committed to keeping their part of that covenant, before God. No one person can do it by his or her self. I was married for twenty five years in my first marriage, for eight years in my second marriage, for four years in my third marriage, and I and my wife Marie have been married for over nine years, and I pray that we will be together for the next twenty five years, or more.

My first wife is the mother of all of my children, and I never ever broke up any marriage in order to be married to another. As a matter of fact, I think, that is one of the most stupid things that a person can do. The person that you marry will always know that you left your wife, or husband, for another person; that makes for a very shaky marriage.

And then again, when things begin to get a little rough, and it will get rough sometimes, that person, who left their spouse to marry you will begin to think, and maybe even say, "And to think that I left my wife, or my husband for this."

Do all that you can to preserve your marriage, and don't wait until things begin to get bad, to start working on it. Think about how you worked on it before you got married. Do things to keep your marriage fresh; and give your spouse some reasons to want to spend their whole life with you, and don't play the martyr, trying to do it all yourself. No one person can make a marriage work; it takes both of you to make it work.

You can tie a dog and a cat's tails together, and you will have union, but you will not have unity. You must communicate, and get your spouse to work on it with you; otherwise, trying will get old pretty quick. You **can** do it. Remember, **God** is on your side.

Chapter 8

Miracles, visions, dreams, and signs and wonders from God

The things that I am about to tell you will not necessarily be in chronological order; but I will speak of them as the Spirit of God directs me.

Many people ask me; why do I believe so strongly in the living God? It's far too late for me not to believe in God now. I have seen too much, experienced too much, and the Lord has done too much for me, and through me, for me not to believe. If after all the things that the Lord has done, things of which I have first hand knowledge, I did not believe; **that** would be incredible.

The things that I will talk about, will not by any means be, the only things that the Lord has miraculously done.

There would be many more, but the Bible says, James 1:5 "If any of you lack wisdom, let him ask of God, that giveth to all men liberally, and upbraideth not; and it shall be given him." This book would be too long, if everything was mentioned, and some things would generate more questions than I could answer.

Tested to the limit

The one thing that stands out most in my mind, of the works of God, is a day that was perhaps the lowest day, and the highest day of my Christian walk with God.

My first wife and I were still very young; I was saved, and in the ministry, and my wife had also professed the Lord Jesus as her savior. It was a habit of mine, to go into the living room, close the door behind me, and spend time with the Lord, in prayer, meditation, and Bible Study. Sometimes I would spend long hours there.

It's amazing how that now, after all these years, and looking back, I can understand very clearly what was going on then. Now I know what I should have been doing then, and was not.

One day my wife came into my prayer room, and began to talk to me. I listened for a while, and then said, "All right honey, now I want to get back to my study, as I sat there in that soft armchair, with my Bible open in my lap. I didn't know at the time, that her interruption of my study time was a cry for help. I should have gotten a clue, when I came home from work one day, and found the door to the living room, taken off the hinges, and taken to the basement.

I was so concerned about my own spiritual growth, and was so in love with God, and Bible study, and the things that the Lord was teaching me, that I didn't take enough time to try to help my wife in her spiritual growth.

I was forgetting that we were supposed to be one, and that I was to be the one to lead my wife in spiritual matters. But when you have a wife that is strong willed, and not easily led, one tends to feel that it is too hard a task, and to see it as a threat to his own spiritual growth; since we know that we have a long way to go to be like the Lord.

Then there is the martyr syndrome, the sense that you are suffering for the cause of Christ, and that you push past everything, in order to reach your goal. I did not know that that goal would lose much of its luster, if I made it, and my wife did not. No longer two, but one flesh; that is what the master said. I have heard that the divorce rate among Christians is equal to that of non-Christians. That tells me that, many Christians have marital problems, and that even though I was a minister of the living God, I was not the only one that was missing the mark.

I believe that this is an area in the Christians life, where there needs to be much understanding, and compassion. This understanding must be taught early in life, preferably before marriage.

My heart really goes out to the man, because the Lord is holding him responsible for seeing that his home is properly led. This is not usually an easy task.

Despite what she said, when she took her wedding vows, he must prove to his wife, that he is worthy of being the leader. Sometimes, he doesn't even know this himself. There is a constant struggle to keep himself under subjection, to the Christ who died for him. It is incumbent upon we men to rise to this task, and with the Lord's help we can do it.

However there is a great need for help, through Christian preaching and teaching. We need to understand, that if we are not successful in doing this, our wives will be that weaker link, unprotected by her covering, her husband. And we know that the enemy, in this case Satan, always attacks the weakest link. We men need to make that sacrifice, to help fortify our wives. Together we stand, divided we fall. A house divided against itself cannot stand. This is why every person should be very prayerful, when selecting a spouse.

I remember that we did not even have family devotions, which was a violation of our Baptist covenant, and which was my responsibility, as the head of my family to see that it happened. Perhaps I thought that, because we went to Bible study, prayer meeting, Sunday school, and Church services; it wasn't necessary.

Anyway, unbeknownst to me, my wife was under an attack of the Devil, and now the Devil was about to attack me, right in my prayer room, with the Bible in my lap. I didn't have a girlfriend; but I'm sure now, that it must have felt like I did, to my wife. When I would go and shut myself in a room, by myself, to be alone with God, I'm sure now that it felt like I had left her alone, to go into another room, and locked myself in with another lover, to do things with that lover that I had never done with her, and yet I was just on the other side of that door from her; but that was part of the problem. I was so close, and yet so far away.

I'm sure that she had noticed how lit up I would be, when I came out from having been shut in with my lover, the Lord God, for such long periods of time.

I can imagine how one might feel, when they are struggling with the things that people do struggle with, especially after they have decided to live their life for God, and to see someone who is very close to you, who is overcoming, that which you have not yet overcome. We men need to learn how our wives communicate, and our wives also need to understand that we men usually don't get it. These words come to my mind; **Help me!**

As my wife stood over me, looking down at me, all of a sudden she lost it, and began beating me with her fist, and

I began singing, "Precious Lord, take my hand, lead me on, let me stand, I am tired, I am weak, I am worn, through the storm, through the night, lead me on, to the light, take my hand, precious Lord, lead me on."

By this time, she had grabbed me by the feet, and was dragging both the armchair and me across the room. Then she stopped, and left the room.

Perhaps that was the time that I should have followed her, to comfort her, and to connect with her, to find out what was really bothering her, and to get her to calm down. But I was in no shape at that time, to help her. This attack was an attack from Satan to try to cause me to discredit my ministry, and my Christian testimony, since I was a strong soul winner for Christ. He was trying to provoke me to react the way I would have reacted, only a few years prior to this time.

The care of a loving Heavenly Father

I was hurt, frustrated, confused, and disappointed. Here I was, a Christian, soul winner, minister of God, in my prayer room, at my prayer time, in prayer, meditation, and Bible study, in my own home, being beaten up by the woman that I loved very dearly. I just could not understand it. Instead of following her, I went upstairs to my bedroom. I was angry, not with her, but with God.

Even while I was on my way upstairs, I was trying to open my mouth, in order to tell God off, ask Him what is this, why is this happening, but all that I could do was groan; Ooooh Lord, over and over. The Lord held my tongue; He would not let me say the things to Him that I was trying to say. And I am glad that He did hold my tongue, because the things that I was thinking to say would have been too disrespectful for the Lord to let me say those things and live. Had I said those things, He would have taken me out, right then.

When I came into my room, I fell onto my face. My head was just a few inches from the far wall, and I was still saying, Ooooh Lord, over and over again.

The Heavenly Vision

The next thing that I knew, I was in this place where there were three steps that extended as far as my eyes could see to my right, and that disappeared into the darkness, to my left. Because of what was to happen next, I surmised that those steps were very deep, from the front to the back, and ascended to a platform that extended the full width of the steps. The steps and the platform were covered with a scarlet colored carpet.

I saw Jesus, seated upon a throne that was on the platform. Somehow I could sense that there was someone seated next to Him, to His right, and to my left, as I faced Him, I didn't **see** anyone there, but I **knew** that someone was there. I could not sense anyone seated on His left.

I could see myself, as though I was somewhere above, looking down at myself, leaning on the first step, and still groaning, Ooooh Lord, over and over. Then Jesus stood up, and came over to the edge of the platform. He stepped down, and stood on the first step from the top, and He fixed His eyes on me.

I don't know why He appeared to me in that way, but I remember noticing, that He didn't look like the pictures that they show of Jesus, and I don't know if it was just for me or not, but I noticed that He had wounds across His forehead, that were caused from the thorns that they had pressed on

His brow. There was still some dried blood caked in His eyebrows. I remembered the scripture concerning Him that said, Isaiah 53:2 "For He shall grow up before Him as a tender plant, and as a root out of a dry ground: He hath no form nor comeliness; and **when we shall see Him, there is no beauty that we should desire Him."**

The Lord Jesus got up from His throne, came towards me, and stood on that first step, just gazing at me, my eyes were fixed on His eyes; and it was like pure energy, pouring from His eyes into me. It was amazing. There were so many thoughts that were flooding my mind, thoughts of some scriptures. I could feel myself being strengthened by Him.

The next thing that I knew, I was back in my room, and when I stood up, I felt strong, very strong. I felt that if Satan was standing before me, I could have knocked him out with one blow. **Hallelujah, what a Savior**. He turned my night into day. He turned my defeat into victory.

Nothing of my circumstances changed significantly, but the Lord had changed me significantly. Now I know Him in a much better way, and I know by experience, that no matter how low you get, the Lord can lift you up.

Andrea Crouch is right, "If I never had a problem, I'd never know that God could solve them. I would never know what faith in His Word could do. Through it all, I have learned to trust in Jesus." I don't know why the Lord loves me so, but I'm so glad that He does. I know that he does good things for many people. I'm not the only one; but **I feel so special.**

Having a Burden for lost souls

From the time that the Lord first saved me, my greatest desire was to share this wonderful truth with others, about the amazing grace, and love of God for us.

The way that the Lord has chosen, to redeem us, was so surprising to me, that I thought that it must be something that would be found to be surprising to others also. I knew that this would be true among my friends, as well as some of the church members, that went to the church that I was attending.

It became an obsession with me, to see to it, that everyone that I knew got a chance to hear the gospel of Jesus Christ, at least one time, and to be challenged to make a decision to receive eternal life through Jesus Christ, or not. Although I made myself a pest to many people, when I knocked on the doors of their homes, to tell them about the salvation that Jesus Christ gives, I am pleased; that it was the cause of many of them receiving the Lord Jesus as their Lord and Savior.

The Lord has always known me, even before I was born, and He knew that after He saved me, that I would be relentless, in my effort to lead other people to God through our Lord Jesus. I believe that this is why the Lord has favored me so. His Spirit within me is, and has been that driving force, that drives me in my quest for souls.

Everybody ought to know, who Jesus is. That driving presence within me makes me valuable to God, and He manifests His presence within me. Sometimes, He even lets me know what He is going to do. I am so blessed; I have discovered the riches of God, and have come to know, that it is mine. He has given those riches to me, and to all who hear His voice.

How blessed we all are, who are the new creatures in Christ Jesus. No longer earth bound, our citizenship is in Heaven, and we are joint heirs with Christ Jesus. Satan is no longer the Prince of the power of the air.

Jesus said in Matthew 28:18-20 "All power is given unto me in heaven and in earth. Go ye therefore, and teach all nations, baptizing them in the name of the Father, and of the Son, and of the Holy Ghost: Teaching them to observe all things whatsoever I have commanded you: and lo I am with you always, even unto the end of the world." Amen.

The Awesome move of God in Canonsburg

The Lord had started something in our little town of Canonsburg Pennsylvania that would turn out to be a citywide revival. Many people there would get saved during this period.

This would serve to be great encouragement to those who were already Christians, and their faith was strengthened. I discovered that the Lord was doing this all over the Greater Pittsburgh area, the people being inspired by the Pittsburgh Experiment.

This was a time when people all over the city, would come together at noontime and pray for the move of God in our state and nation. The Lord God did move mightily during this time.

God, manifested through a Lady

The lady, Kathryn Kuhlman, and her ministry, was largely responsible for this movement. As a matter of fact, she is a contributing factor as to why I believe so strongly, in God today. I believe that, if there was ever a woman of God, it was this woman. The Lord used her mightily; and I don't believe that anyone glorified God more than she did.

Whenever the Lord healed the sick in her services, she insisted passionately, that it was the Lord, and not she, who healed the sick and ailing.

She was so confident of the healing power of God, that she would send those who were being healed, back to the doctors who had diagnosed their sickness, to confirm that healing.

The result was, often the doctors would come to the service, to confirm the healing in person. Praise the Lord God Almighty! When YAHWEH heals, you don't have to worry about, if it is real or not. The WORD of God is truth, and His WORD lives to perform the will of the LORD.

Thrown across the room, onto my face

I don't read many books. I never did, but since I received the Lord Jesus as my savior, I often felt that the time that I took reading the many interesting books, was time that I could have spent reading my Bible.

I also guarded myself from remembering something that I read in a book, and quoting it like it was something that I read from the bible. I regard books about the Bible to be as carp fish, and the Bible to be as fillet; you have to pick the bones out of carp, but not the fillet.

One day in July 1964, someone gave us a book to read, and I told my wife to read it; I didn't want to come away from reading my Bible. After she read it she said, you must read this book; if you do, you won't want to put it down.

The book was "The Cross and the Switchblade," written by David Wilkerson. She was right; after I began reading it, I did not put it down, until I had read the whole book.

While reading it, when I got to the place where David's grandfather said to him, "David, the day that you learn to pray publicly, and specifically, that day you will have the key to power," The very moment that I read the word, power, I was thrown across the floor, onto my face.

I had been sitting in my armchair, leaning back and reading. I did not understand how, if I was rearing back in my armchair, it was possible for me to fall across the room onto my face. That was scientifically impossible.

My center of gravity was located behind my buttocks, and if I could have fallen, it should have been backward; and since I was comfortably seated in a sturdy armchair, it was virtually impossible. It just couldn't happen. There must be, I thought as I lay on the floor, some other explanation.

As I lay there, I began looking around to see if anyone had seen me. My wife was out on the front porch, sitting on the swing, but nobody had seen me. I was so glad that no one had seen it; nothing like this had ever happened to me before, and it was so embarrassing to me.

Then I thought that, perhaps I had a loss of memory, had stood up, started to walk across the floor, lost consciousness, and fallen to the floor.

However, if this is what happened, since I was six ft. three inches tall, and weighed two hundred and fifteen pounds, with only one wall separating the room where I was, from the porch, where my wife was sitting, and the window was open; someone should have heard the sound of my heavy body, crashing to the floor. But she didn't hear a thing.

I was puzzled. What happened? I picked myself up from the floor and sat back in the chair in which I was sitting, made sure that I was firmly and safely seated, making sure that I was leaning backwards, and I began reading again. I began with the previous paragraph that I had read. When I got back to the place, where I had read what David's grandfather said to him, "David, the day that you learn to pray publicly, and specifically, that day you will have the key to power;" BOOM!

It happened again. I was thrown across the floor onto my face the second time. This time I was screaming to the top of my voice: My wife was still out there sitting on the porch, and she didn't even hear me. This time I knew that it was God. I said to the Lord, "What is it? What do you want? I'm not getting up off of this floor until you tell me what you want of me."

I finished reading the book while lying on the floor. I was waiting for the Lord to let me know what He wanted with me. By the time that I finished reading the book, I still did not know.

A preview of future places of ministry

There were in my magazine rack, the latest editions of News Week, and Time magazines. In each of these magazines were two major articles; one of which was the crisis in Nigeria.

In 1960 Nigeria declared it's independence from Great Britain, and in 1963 Nigeria became a republic.

The actions that followed would prove to be very divisive, and led to the secession of the Eastern Region, and the formation of the Republic of Biafra, in May of 1967, and to civil war which would result in an estimated three million people dying, and the capitulation of Biafra in 1970.

The other was the crisis in New York City, drugs, prostitution, gangs, etc. In both cases the magazines had maps showing the divisions of conflict in Nigeria, expressing fears, and the concentration of corruption in New York City.

I asked the Lord, "What do you want? Do you want me to go to Africa? Do you want me to go to New York? What?" I said to the Lord, "Whatever you want me to do I will do it."

When I began to lie on the floor, it must have been about six or seven o'clock in the evening. I didn't get up until about three or four o'clock in the morning, and went to bed. I had to get up in the morning to go to work.

That morning I got out of bed and went to work, still not knowing what it was that the Lord wanted with me; and He had not told me anything. But New York and Africa stayed on my mind.

All day long I listened to the gospel programs that I would usually listen to, the last one being Kathryn Kuhlman. Ironically, that day she announced that David Wilkerson would be at the Syria Mosque soon. I said to myself, "Good, I'll go, and maybe I'll find out what the Lord wants me to do."

When David came to Pittsburgh, and held his youth rally, I was there. I took with me my wife and my young sister in law, Beverly. When David gave the invitation to the young people, to receive the Lord Jesus as their savior, my wife said to her sister Beverly, "what are you waiting for?" She looked at my wife Rose, with an evil look, and said, "What." She repeated her question, "What are you waiting for?"

Beverly got up with a huff, as though she did not want to, and then went forward. By the time she had reached the front, she had already accepted the Lord Jesus as her savior, and began shouting and praising the Lord. I got up behind her and followed her to the front. When she began to praise the Lord, I embraced her, and asked her if she had accepted the Lord as her savior. She said yes and we both began shouting.

Before David had began preaching, he gave a report of the success that Teen Challenge was having in Brooklyn, and Spanish Harlem. He said that they were having no progress in Black Harlem, and asked the people of God to pray for that part of their efforts. I said to myself, "Maybe this is what the Lord was trying to tell me. Maybe I am the one who would help win the lost youth in Black Harlem." I decided to go backstage and talk to David after the service.

After the service was over, I went and talked with David. I told him about the experience that I had while reading his book, and suggested that perhaps his concerns about Black Harlem was the reason why the Lord had dealt with me so. He agreed that might be the case, and invited me to come to Teen Challenge in Brooklyn, stay for a week, and by then both of us would know if I was to stay in New York, or not.

My call into the preaching ministry

I was a minister, licensed but not yet ordained by the Mount Olive Baptist Church, where the Reverend Warren A Mason was the pastor. I was quite active preaching, and had won at least three hundred souls to Christ. Prior to being licensed, I had a desire to become a preacher; I felt that it would give me a greater opportunity to win souls to Christ.

I went to Rev. Mason, my pastor; and asked him, "What do you have to do to become a preacher." He asked me, "Why, **do you think** that the Lord is calling you to be a preacher?" I said yes, **I think** that the Lord is calling me to be a preacher. He said, "Ok, on Wednesday night, in prayer meeting you can exercise your gift."

I didn't quite know what that meant, but on Wednesday night, he had said nothing, so after the prayers and testimonies slowed down, I got up and began talking about the Lord.

I didn't know when to start, and I found out that I didn't know when to stop; and I don't think that I made any difference either.

This was the only time that I would try that, and I didn't bother my pastor about what I thought, any more. A little later I had a dream. I dreamed that I was in a large church, preaching to a large crowd, and everybody was saying Amen.

Then the lights started to go dim, and I began making mistakes. Some of the people began walking out, and the Amens began to be fewer. The lights kept on getting dimmer, I made more mistakes, more people walked out, and the Amens became even fewer. Eventually, everyone had walked out, except for my wife and my mother; and they were saying, in support, Amen, Amen.

When I woke up, I knew that the dream was from the Lord, and I asked Him, "What was that about?" The Lord said to me, "You have enough to start off like a ball of fire, but you don't have enough to last. Study, to show yourself approved unto God, a workman that needs not be ashamed." From that time on I intensified my study. I began studying, every time I could, and as long as I could; I was being driven.

One night, about six months later, on September 11th, 1961, after coming home from a church business meeting, I was so disappointed with my church and the members, and officers of my church. In my opinion, they didn't even act like Christians. I guess that you haven't really been blessed until you have gone to a Baptist Church meeting; Smile. I immediately got on my knees, when I got home, and began telling God about what happened at that church meeting, as though He didn't already know. I just completely spilled out my guts to Him.

When I was finished, I remained on my knees, waiting for the Lord to tell me what to do. After a moment of silence, I was moved to say, "Lord, what would you have me to do?" Immediately, I was carried away in the spirit, somewhere, I don't know where, and I don't know how long I was gone; but when I returned to myself, I was saying, "I'll go."

It was about eleven thirty o'clock, and I knew exactly what I had to do. The Lord had called me to study; and now He was sending me to preach His gospel. After I thought about it for a while, I began to be concerned about what people would think about the way the Lord had called me. They would probably say, "Ah, he just went to sleep, and had a dream;" but it wasn't a dream. It didn't seem to be very impressive to me either.

I had an uncle who was a pastor in Detroit, Michigan, and he said to me that he had a vision when the Lord called and sent him into the preaching ministry. In his vision, he was in a church, and the choir came in robed in white robes, and then a preacher came in wearing a white robe and golden shoes, and he couldn't take his eyes off of those golden shoes.

A man stood by him and said, "Do you like those shoes? You can have some shoes just like them." My uncle, in the vision said, "How?" The man said, "Go and preach the gospel." Compared to this story, my calling seemed so bland. I began asking the Lord to show me some sign, that He really wanted me to do this.

The next day, while at work, and listening to my gospel programs, every preacher preached, or taught about being called into the Christian preaching ministry, ending with Kathryn Kuhlman.

When her program went off, the Lord spoke to me and said, "I know that you are looking for a sign. You will have no other sign; go and preach my gospel."

And so I did. I went back to my pastor and told him that the Lord has sent me to preach the gospel of Jesus Christ. He told me to make my announcement to the church, and he would set a date for me to preach my trial sermon. I thought, why was it so different this time?

Then I remembered, when I came to him the first time, I wasn't sure. I said that **I think** that the Lord was calling me. He knew that I wasn't sure. I thank God, for having a wise pastor.

On Sunday morning, October 1st, 1961, I preached my first and trial sermon, at the Mount Olive Church of Canonsburg, Pennsylvania.

My sermon subject was, "When He seeth the Blood," my text Exodus 12:23. I was confident that the Lord had sent me, and He used me to bring a very forceful, and needful sermon. The church voted to grant me a license to preach the gospel. On Sunday morning, October 15th, Pastor Mason presented me with that license.

Off to New York and to Teen Challenge

On Sunday night August 2, 1964, about a week after talking with David Wilkerson in Pittsburgh, I boarded a bus, to go to New York City, and I arrived there early Monday morning, August 3, 1964.

David had given me the phone number to call, once I arrived in the city, and someone would pick me up at the station. I called, and the person that answered, assured me that someone would be on their way to pick me up. This was my first time in New York, and coming from Canonsburg, I had no idea of how big the metropolis of New York was. If someone had called me at my home, and asked me to pick them up at the bus station, I would have been there five minutes later to pick them up. Therefore, I had no idea how long it would take them to come from Brooklyn to get me; so when my waiting time began to exceed thirty minutes, I began to think that picking me up was not on the top of their list of things to do.

When I was planning to go to New York, I shared it with many of my friends. About three or four times when I shared it, that person recommended that I look up Tom Skinner, when I got there.

I thought to myself, the first time that someone had said that, "What's a Tom Skinner?" I had never heard of him before. They told me that Tom was a great evangelist, who had been a gang leader himself, and who was having great success in the Black Harlem area of New York.

An hour after I had called for someone to pick me up, a van pulled up from Teen Challenge, and I got in to go to the headquarters in Brooklyn, and one hour later, we were pulling up to the back door of the building. **Lord help me**; I had no idea that New York was so big. We came in through the kitchen, and I was introduced to the workers as we entered, and then to the young man named Jim Floyd, who was to be my roommate, while I was there.

It was Monday, an off day, and payday for the team. They had that day to themselves, to do as they wished.

I was led to my room, and began to get acquainted with my roommate. He was a young black man, who seemed to have a look of expectancy in his face, and we got along very well, right from the start.

He said to me, "This is our day off, and I plan to go to Harlem to the Crusade, at the RKO Regent Theatre; would you like to go with me?" I said, "Yes, that's what I am here for. Who is the evangelist?" He said, "Tom Skinner." I was amazed, one week ago, I had never heard of Tom Skinner, but since then several people had told me to look him up when I get to New York; now the first thing that I would do when I got to New York is, to go to a Christian Crusade where Tom Skinner was the evangelist. Remarkable! And it's all part of God's plan. Don't you **love** when that happens?

Off to Harlem and the RKO Regent Theatre

We caught the subway, and went to Harlem, and got off at 125th, the place where there were riots, just one week before. We were early for the Crusade, so we walked around, as he showed me Harlem.

I was carrying my Bible in my hand, and as I walked, there were some people sitting on steps, and just standing and talking. As we passed some of them, I heard someone say, "There goes Tom Skinner."

When I heard that, I wondered what God was doing. Now someone sees a Bible in my hand, and thinks that I am Tom Skinner, a person that I had never heard of, until a week ago, the first day that I am in New York.

As we walked, I saw a man lying on the sidewalk, face down in a pool of blood. I noticed that people just kept walking past. Even those who were sitting on their steps didn't go to see if he was alright. His face was covered with blood, so we called the police and went on to the evangelistic service.

When we arrived at the RKO Regent Theatre, on the corner of W. 116th and 7th, the place where the Crusade was being held, we went in. The Crusade appeared to have been well prepared for, and had the support of many of the local Churches. When I saw Tom Skinner, I began to understand why someone who didn't really know him, might mistake me for him. He was a man of my size and build.

During the first crusade, which was held at the Apollo Theatre, in 1962, there were over 1800 persons present. The Harlem Evangelistic Association, who sponsored the Crusade, was told by the managers of the Apollo Theatre, that the Crusade broke the record for attendance of any single event that had ever been held in their history, beating out competition such as Duke Ellington, Nat "King" Cole, Ella Fitzgerald.

Billy Epstein, Ray Charles, and many other great rock n roll, jazz, and blues performers, each of which drew very large crowds on a given night.

However more people came out to hear the Gospel of Jesus Christ at the Apollo, than to hear any of these. When the week of services were over, 2200 people had come forth and given their hearts to the Lord.

While sitting there in the service that first night, August 3, 1964, at the RKO Regent Theatre, I was still wondering if the Lord means for me to be in New York. When Tom was inviting people to come forward to receive the Lord Jesus as their savior, people came forward. When they stopped coming, I began praying, "Lord, if you want me to be here, please bring more forward;" then more started coming.

Then again when they stopped coming I prayed again, "Lord if you really want me to be here, please bring more forward;" and again, more began coming forward. Then again the third time, when they stopped coming, I prayed again, "Lord please again, if you mean for me to be here, bring more forward;" and again more started coming forward.

This time when they stopped coming, I prayed again, "Now Lord if it is your will that I be here in New York at this time, don't let any more come forward tonight. Then three more people came forward.

Then the Lord spoke to me, "How dare you to ask me to not let any more come forward, just to satisfy your doubts. Where is your heart?" I had to pray for forgiveness; what was I thinking? About 25 souls accepted the Lord on that first day, and I helped to counsel them, and to lead them to Christ. We left after the benediction, and I was assured that the Lord wanted me there, but why? I did not know.

Chapter 9

God ministering through a willing people: Christians organized for the purpose of rescuing the perishing

Each day while at Teen Challenge, we gathered for prayer, several times a day. This particular week, there was a guest evangelist, who shared with us each day, and who would bring the message, when we did street meetings. His name was, if my memory serves me right, Reverend Dodge.

The daily schedule at the center was:

Rising bell at 7:00

Breakfast at 7:30

Dishes and clean up

Personal devotions until 9:30

Group chapel from 9:30-11:30

Dinner at 12:00

Dishes

Prayer

Street work from 2:00 until 6:00 pm, when we ate sack suppers on the street

More street work until 7:30

Back to the Center for evening services until midnight, or to Catacomb Chapel in Greenwich Village for witnessing and soul winning

It didn't take long for me to see and understand, one of the main reasons why the Lord had sent me to New York. It only took seeing the work that Tom Skinner and the Harlem Evangelistic Association were doing in Harlem, and the work that David Wilkerson, and Teen Challenge were doing. But most of all, it was being in prayer with the team, praying for lost souls.

There were wooden floors in the room where we prayed, at the center, and the floor was stained with tears, the tears that fell from the eyes of some of these young Christians, who really had a burden for lost souls. These young people put their lives on the line, each day, in order to deliver those people who were bound with habits, and on their way to hell. When I saw how fervently they prayed, I thought; I'm not even worthy to kiss these young people's shoes.

You see, it was all becoming very clear to me, that when I arrived in New York, there was something wrong with me. ***You don't say David! Smile.*** Aw but I do say. When I had to wait at the bus station for an hour, waiting for someone to pick me up, I was a little angry, because I thought that they were taking me for granted.

Don't they know who I am? Don't they know why I came here? I'm the one that they have been praying for, to help the ministry in black Harlem; my subconscious mind was saying to me. And it was not just a little embarrassing to me when it took us an hour to get to the center. Then when we reached the center, the driver drove around to the back; and I thought; am I not good enough to come in the front door? ***How foolish? Who is this country yokel? Doesn't he***

know that this is New York, and that in the back is where parking for the vehicle is provided?

Looking back and wondering

Now that I look back, I wonder; where did these feelings come from? Perhaps it came from something that was deep within me, things that come from being a black man, in a nation that was predominately white. To be a black man in America, is to be one who is always alert, as to when you are being treated differently.

Like when in high school, when I was a good student in science, and wanted to schedule science courses, and my teacher strongly suggested that I take commercial courses, instead. However, although I don't think that she meant me any good, because the number of students that could take those classes were limited; God was still in control. Satan meant it for evil, but God meant it for good.

Little did I know that I was to become a minister of the Gospel of Jesus Christ, a pastor, teacher, writer, and that I would serve as financial secretary, in our church, even before I was saved, and that I would serve on the budget committee of the Pennsylvania State Baptist Convention, as a preacher.

Or perhaps like after I had graduated from high school, having stared in sports, and having won a partial scholarship from Westminster College; when I went to this man in our town, who owned his own company, for a job; he said that he would give me the job, if I promised that I wasn't going to college.

The irony was, that his daughter was in my graduating class of about thirty five students, and was a cheerleader for our teams; and she was going on to college. I needed a job so badly, that I promised him that I was not going to go to college that year. I did not go to college that year, because I had given him my word. I could not go back on my word.

I remember thinking; "If I was a white boy, would he have made him promise the same thing, or was I again being treated differently?"

This is just a very light sample of what a black man often encounters, while living in the United States. It's like when Dr. Martin Luther King Jr. was assassinated, and this same man said to me, "Well Dave, He was asking for it."

You can't imagine the anger that rose up in me, when I heard him say that; but the word of God says, "Be angry, and sin not. I didn't say a word, although I'm sure that my anger showed on my face. I just held my peace. I remembered that I was a servant of God, and a pastor. Later, after hearing several of Reverend King's sermons, that I was listening to on my radio, in the workshop, he had to come back to me and apologize; "Dave, I didn't know that is what he taught, I'm sorry for what I said.

Oh I pray to God to see the day when we all get beyond that stage of anticipating the worse, simply because it just doesn't happen that much, any more.

Yes, there were some things in me that wasn't right. And also when I was introduced to the workers, I wonder, how was I expecting them to react? They just said hi, I'm glad to meet you.

Too bad David! They did not treat you like the star that you thought you were. I must have been awful bad in God's sight, for Him to throw me across the room, onto my face twice, just to get my attention. At least, I wasn't swallowed by a whale. Smile! And well at least I did not go and sit under a juniper tree, complaining that I was the only one. But then again, there was not an evil queen after me, with a price on my head either. Smile again! Isn't the Lord good?

But these young people, they were the real stars; and yet even they must give the Lord God the praise. If there is any glory, it all belongs to God; because Philippians 2:13 says, "For it is God which worketh in you, both to will, and to do of His good pleasure."

You see, back in Canonsburg, I was a witnessing, soul winning fool. I had determined to be a fool for Christ. But then again, the Lord has not called us to be fools, although the thought is noble; but we are commanded through the word of God, to be wise as serpents, and harmless as doves. And yet the people of Canonsburg had not seen anyone quite like me; even I had not seen anyone like me, someone with a great passion for souls. So many people kept on complimenting me, and some of the wives in our Bible Study group would often say to their husbands, "Why can't you be like Dave?" I didn't like when they would do that, but I believe that some of it was sticking to me; so the Lord sends me to New York, for a head shrinking experience. Thank the Lord; for He cares for me.

Understanding the Baptism of the Holy Ghost

Although I had never spoken in an unknown tongue, I knew that I had been baptized into the body of Christ, by the Holy Spirit, according to 1 Corinthians 12:13, which says, "For by one Spirit are we all baptized into one body, whether we be Jews or Gentiles, whether we be bond or free; and have been all made to drink into one Spirit;" and Galatians 3:27 says, "For as many of you have been baptized into Christ have put on Christ."

Romans 6:3-8 says, "Know ye not, that as many of us as were baptized into Jesus Christ were baptized into His death? Therefore we are buried with Him by baptism into death: that like as Christ was raised up from the dead by the glory of the Father, even so we also should walk in newness of life.

For we have been planted together in the likeness of His death, we should be also in the likeness of His resurrection: Knowing this, that our old man is crucified with Him, that the body of sin might be destroyed, that henceforth we should not serve sin. For he that is dead is freed from sin. Now if we be dead with Christ, we believe that we shall also live with Him."

I also knew that there is only one baptism, according to the word of God, recorded in Ephesians 4:4-6; "There is one body and one Spirit, even as ye are called in one hope of your calling; One Lord, one faith, one baptism, One God and Father of all, who is above all, and through all, and in you all." I knew that I had the right one, the one that put me into Christ; because if you are in Christ, you have been put there by Holy Spirit Baptism. This is the same baptism that John talked about, when he baptized at the River of Jordan.

When John the Baptist was baptizing, Matthew 3:7-12 says; **"But when he saw many of the Pharisees and Sadducees come to his baptism, he said unto them**, O generation of vipers, who hath warned you to flee from the wrath to come? Bring forth therefore fruits meet for repentance: And think not to say within yourselves, we have Abraham to our Father: for I say unto you, that God is able of these stones to raise up children unto Abraham.

And now also the ax is laid unto the root of the trees: therefore every tree that bringeth not forth good fruit is hewn down, and cast into the fire. I indeed baptize you unto repentance: but He that cometh after me is mightier than I, whose shoes I am not worthy to bear: He shall baptize you with the Holy Ghost, and with fire: Whose fan is in His hand, and He will thoroughly purge His floor, and gather His wheat into the garner; but He will burn up the chaff with unquenchable fire."

John was saying to those Sadducees and Pharisees, who came to be baptized of John, that if you are coming to this baptism of repentance, then you need to really repent; because you can't fool God, and by the way; I can't baptize you into the kingdom. But Jesus is coming after me; and He is mightier than I. Not only can He baptize you into the kingdom; He can also baptize you into Hell.

Rest assured that every one of you will be baptized some day. Some of you will be baptized with the Holy Ghost; the rest of you will be baptized with hell fire.

With this, John assures us that water baptism, though it be by immersion, cannot put any one into the body of Christ. Only the baptism of the Holy Spirit can do that; and Jesus Christ is behind this baptism.

The Holy Spirit, the indwelling presence of the Living God

I knew also that I had the Holy Ghost within me. I always knew that, ever since the Lord saved me. As a matter of fact I knew that it is the Holy Ghost, living inside us, who is the new creature that we have become, and which is described in 2 Corinthians 5:17; "Therefore if any man be in Christ, he is a new creature: old things are passed away; behold all things are become new."

2 Corinthians 6:19 says; "And what agreement hath the temple of God with idols? For ye are the temple of the living God; as God hath said, I will dwell in them, and walk in them; and I will be their God, and they shall be my people."

1Corinthians 6:19 says; "What? Know ye not that your body is the temple of the Holy Ghost which is in you, which ye have of God, and ye are not your own."

2 Corinthians 13:5 says; Examine yourselves, whether ye be in the faith; prove your own selves. Know ye not your own selves, how that Jesus Christ is in you, except ye be reprobates?" A reprobate is a counterfeit, or someone who is not saved at all.

Therefore the Word of God makes it clear. If you are in the body of Christ, it was the Holy Spirit who put you there, by reason of Holy Spirit Baptism; and Holy Ghost Baptism is the only real baptism. Also if we are in the body of Christ, the Holy Ghost is in us. When the Holy Ghost comes into us, it is not a watered down version of the Holy Ghost. He comes in with all of His power and gifts. And whenever He wills, He manifests those gifts, severally as He wills.

The Word of God says; 1 Corinthians 12:1-11; "Now concerning spiritual gifts, brethren, I would not have you ignorant. Ye know that ye were Gentiles, carried away unto these dumb idols, even as ye were led.

Wherefore I give you to understand, that no man speaking by the Spirit of God calleth Jesus accursed: and that no man can say that Jesus is the Lord, but by the Holy Ghost.

Now there are diversities of gifts, but the same Spirit. And there are differences of administrations, but the same Lord. And there are diversities of operations, but it is the same God which worketh all in all. But the manifestation of the Spirit is given to every man to profit withal.

For to one is given by the Spirit the word of wisdom; to another the word of knowledge by the same Spirit; To another faith by the same Spirit; to another gifts of healing by the same Spirit; To another the working of miracles; to another prophecy; to another discerning of spirits; to another diverse kinds of tongues; to another the interpretation of tongues:

But all these worketh that one and the selfsame Spirit, dividing to every man severally as He will." The Lord gave gifts to His Church.

It is the Lord who decides who does what, or rather, who He does what through. Paul said in 1 Corinthians 14:2-5; "For he that speaketh in an unknown tongue speaketh not unto men, but unto God: for no man understandeth him; howbeit in the spirit he speaketh mysteries.

But he that prophesieth speaketh unto men to edification, and exhortation and comfort. He that speaketh in an unknown tongue edifieth himself; but he that prophesieth edifieth the church. I would that ye all spake with tongues, but rather that ye prophesied: for greater is he that prophesieth than he that speaketh with tongues, except he interpret, that the church may receive edifying."

God's Word is God's Grace

I knew that there was a legitimate gift of tongues, but I also knew that whatever God had, the devil tries to duplicate. In other words, there is also a counterfeit. Whenever I would come into a service where there was speaking in other tongues, I would pray that the Lord would let me know if it was real or not. As a matter of fact, this was my standing prayer. I did not have to keep on praying this same prayer.

The Lord remembered my request. Each of the times that we gathered together for prayer at the center, there were people praying in the spirit; Not everyone, but most did.

On one particular night, one of the workers was praying in the spirit, and his voice rose above everyone else's; and I began to understand what he was saying in the Spirit. I could hear the words that he was saying in an unknown tongue, and I could also hear what he was saying in English. The Lord spoke to me and said, "Speak out loud in English, what you hear him saying in another language." And so I did. I did not have to wait until he completed a sentence, in order to interpret what he was saying. I was speaking, just a few words behind him.

When he finished, and the service was over, I went over to him and asked, "Did you know what you were saying, when you were speaking in another language?" He said no. I began telling him some of the interpretation of what he was saying. The one thing that he was saying, that seemed to stand out, and that still lingers with me until this day is, "**The Word of God is despised; and God's Word is God's Grace.**" I had never heard anyone else say that, and I don't recall seeing those words, so arranged, in the Bible; but it certainly is in perfect harmony with what the Bible teaches. Every thing that we have has come through Gods word. John 1:1-3 says; "In the beginning was the Word, and the Word was with God, and the Word was God. The same was in the beginning with God. All things were made by Him; and without Him was not anything made that was made. In Him (the Word) was life, and the life was the light of men."

In the beginning, God spoke everything into existence. Even the food that we eat, is the offspring of that which God spoke into existence, in the beginning. It was made by the

Word, and is made of the Word of God. Every time that we eat, we are eating a form of the Word of God.

When the Hebrew children were wandering in the wilderness, and God sent them manna from heaven, it was the word of God that sustained them for forty years. There are no gardens in the sky. How then can one reject the Word of God, when we cannot even exist naturally, without His Word. The Word of God is the greatest gift that the Lord has given to man. And we become empowered to a greater and abundant life, through His Word of promise. God's Word ever lives to produce the things that the Lord has promised.

The vision of burning in Washington D.C.

On another occasion, one young man told of a vision that he had seen the night before. He said that he saw the White House, and there were billows of smoke, rising above the White House. He said that he didn't know what it meant, but he knew that God was revealing that something was going to happen.

On April 3, 1968, Dr. Martin Luther King Jr. was assassinated, in Memphis Tennessee. While watching the television coverage of the riots and fires that followed the Prophet King's death; I saw on the news, smoke rising up behind the White House, and since it was in the foreground, my first thought was, that it was coming from a burning White House. It was just like he had seen in the vision.

As a matter of fact, the Lord had revealed to many of his people that something big, was about to happen, even before the deaths of each, John F. Kennedy, and Martin King. When Martin King was killed, I was pastoring a little church, located in a little town along the Monongahela River; the

First Baptist Church of Gallatin Pa. I was also broadcasting, teaching the Gospel of Jesus Christ, once a week, on the Canonsburg radio station, WARO, which had a potential audience of five million people, at that time.

"When God says burn baby burn"

One Sunday about three weeks prior to the assassination of Reverend King, the Lord inspired me to preach a sermon at First Baptist, entitled "When God Says, Burn Baby Burn." I had recorded it on my new Stereo Tape Recorder, and when I went home and listened to the tape of that sermon, I was moved.

The Lord inspired me to buy time on the Pittsburgh radio station WAMO. This was the station that most of the young people in the Tri State Area listened to. They played Rhythm and Blues, Rock n Roll, most of the day, every day. I obeyed the Holy Spirit, drove into the Pittsburgh radio Station, paid for an hour of radio time, and left the tape with the engineer, to be played on Monday, April 8th, 1968.

On the day following the death of the preacher, and civil rights leader, the station covered the news. For the next three days, the station was in mourning, and played only Reverend King's sermons, and Gospel music, in memory of Doctor King. The mourning period ended Monday afternoon, April 8, 1968, just in time for my scheduled sermon, "When God Says, Burn Baby Burn," to be aired. Many young people, all across America, had been running through the streets in protest, and setting fires while shouting, "Burn Baby Burn."

When I preached that sermon in our church, I didn't quite know why the Lord gave me that title. But then again, I couldn't see into the future, I didn't know that the preacher would be killed, I did not know that people would be rioting, burning, and looting, I didn't know that the Lord would tell me to put that sermon on the most popular rock n roll station in the Pittsburgh area, and I did not know what day that I should schedule for it to be played. I didn't know; **but God did**.

There were many people, who had been waiting for three days to hear their favorite Rhythm and Blues songs; but when the mourning period was over, the first thing that they would hear was, David L. Jemison, preaching "When God Says Burn Baby Burn." For the next hour they heard Hell fire, and Brimstone preaching, coupled together with a passionate invitation to receive the Lord Jesus as their Savior.

Then immediately after the invitation, Alexander Martin, the disc jockey for the station, played an invitation song; "You're Going to Fool Around and Lose Your Soul." Nobody but God could have planned this, and have been so accurate, and timely. **Praise God. What a Savior!**

Ministering in Catacomb Chapel

For two evenings in a row, after doing street meetings, I went with David's Mother and part of the team to Catacomb Chapel in Greenwich Village. It was called Catacomb Chapel, after the catacombs in Rome Italy, because to enter, we had to go down some steps, below the street level.

There were tables situated around the room, as though it was a restaurant; and we the workers would share refreshments, such as cookies and Kool-Aid with those people who would come into the chapel from the street above. We would share the Word of God with them, and try to lead them to Christ. I was told that this chapel had been open for about one year, and only one soul had received Jesus Christ as Savior, as of August 1964.

This location was chosen in order to reach the beatniks, gays, prostitutes, pimps, and drug addicts, who gathered there from all over. I can imagine that whenever life started to get boring to them, they would come into Catacomb Chapel, to have some fun with the "holy weirdoes."

One evening when I was working there, a young man came in for that very reason, with two beautiful girls, one on each arm, and sat down at my table. I ordered some refreshments for them, and then asked the young man, "Are you saved?" He said to me "no." I asked him, "If you die without Christ in your life, don't you know that you will go to hell?" He said to me, "Hey Preach, I want to go to hell, because everything that I like will be there, all the wine, whiskey, and these fine girls." I turned to the girls, and said, "I didn't know that you ladies were planning to go to hell." They both answered at the same time, "No, no, not me."

I then turned again to the young man and said, "If there is any whiskey, and wine in hell, it would too hot to drink, and if there any beautiful women there, they would be too busy, and too much in torment, to do you any good. Son, you need to be saved." He replied sharply, "But I want to go to Hell."

I, then said to him, "Be my guest." He said, with an element of surprise, "Whoa Preach, I thought that you were supposed to save me." I said "no, I'm supposed to help you go where ever you want to go. You said that you want to go to Hell; then go. And if you want, I will show you how to make sure that you make it there, I wouldn't want you to be disappointed, because God is doing everything that He can to make sure that you miss Hell, and make Heaven."

Proverb 26:4-5 says, "Answer not a fool according to his folly, lest thou also be like him. Answer a fool according to his folly, lest he be wise in his own conceit." That young man came to Catacomb Chapel to have some fun with the servants of God, but his fun backfired on him.

When he left, he left thinking that those religious nuts aren't as dumb as he thought they were. Too bad that he didn't know that we have a source for wisdom. James 1:5 says, "If any of you lack wisdom, let him ask of God, that giveth to all men liberally, and upbraided not; and it shall be given him." We can go to God for wisdom as often as we need to, and the Lord will never rebuke us for coming to Him for wisdom too often, and he will give it to us, every time.

Another fellow came and sat at my table. When I began to witness to him, and tried to win him to Christ, he said, "There is no Hell." I said, "Oh but there is." He said, "No, there is not." I said again to Him, "Yes there is, and I can prove it to you." He said, "You don't know that, How can you prove it."

I said unto him, "I'm not a betting man; but I'll bet you a thousand dollars that there is a Hell." He asked, "How can you know that?" I asked him, "Is it a bet? Lets shake on it." He then reluctantly shook my hand; and then quickly said, "Now, how are you going to prove it?"

I said, "We'll just wait and see. I'm living a good life; I like what I'm doing; I have peace of mind, and a purpose for living.

If I die, and find out that there is no Hell, and that life just ends, like you said; at least I would have died happy, having lived a fulfilled life; and I have lost nothing. But if you die, and find out that there is a hell, you will have Hell to pay, with no chance of being rescued, throughout all eternity, away from the presence and grace of God. And all through eternity, you will remember this day, the day that you had a chance to be saved, and you would not.

That alone, would be torment enough to be Hell. And believe me, you will remember, and you will be able to see me in the arms of the Lord, and will know what you missed."

When this young man left, he wasn't so sure that there was not a Hell; at least he wasn't so sure that he was willing to bet his life on it.

God gives a Word to a young man named Stanley

Then there is Stanley, one of the major reasons why the Lord sent me to New York in the first place. Stanley was a young, clean cut Jewish man; and he came in and sat at my table, on the first day that I served at Catacomb Chapel. I began to witness to him, and found him to be sincere, and honestly curious. He told me, "I know that those Pharisees were pricks back then, but if I was to accept Jesus as the Messiah, and my Savior, my family would disown me, and disinherit me." I said to him, in the words of the scripture, Mark 8:36; "What would it profit you, if you gained all of your inheritance, and it was millions, and you lost your own soul?"

When it seemed that I would not be able to get him to make a decision to receive Jesus as Savior that day; I asked him, "Stanley, do you believe in YAHWEH?" He said, "Yes." Then I asked him, "Do you believe in, and do you read the Old Testament, the book of Isaiah?" He said, "Yes." I asked him, "Don't you really want to know if Jesus is the Messiah or not?" He said, "Yes I would" I said unto him, "Stanley, when you go home tonight, I want you to read the fifty third chapter of Isaiah. And then I want you to pray to YAHWEH, and ask Him, Lord, did you have a Son, and is His name Jesus. If you sincerely ask Him, and you really want to know; He will tell you. But you should settle this tonight; because you don't know the day nor the hour that you will die, or when the Lord Jesus will return for His Church.

Every day that you put it off, you take the risk of dying, and going to Hell." He said, "I know; but I will do that when I get home."

I prayed a prayer with him, that the Lord would open his eyes, show him the truth about Jesus, and to save him. With that, he excused himself, and left the Chapel.

The next day I was back at Catacomb Chapel, and Stanley came in. He was limping; and I said to him, "Stanley, what happened to you?" He said; "I was hit by a car." I said, "Man, you could have been killed. What did I tell you last night?" He said, "Yeah, that's right. Isn't that Ironic?" I said, "Ironic my foot, the Lord is trying to tell you something. Did you do what I told you to do last night?" He said, "no." I said unto him, "Stanley, stop taking chances, do what I told you to do, if you really want to know. And you don't have forever. Now tonight when you get home, read the 53rd chapter of Isaiah, and then pray to YAHWEH, and ask Him; Did you have a Son and is His name Jesus? The Lord will let you know."

This was my last day to be in New York, and since the chapel was not as far from the bus station as it was from the center, and my bus was leaving late that night, going back to Canonsburg; my bag was packed, and I had it with me, at Catacomb Chapel.

Before I left that day, David and I talked. He told me what to expect from Teen Challenge, if the Lord was to lead me and my family to come back. He knew that it would be a big decision for my wife and I to make. However, I kind of believed in my heart that I had already received what the Lord wanted me to receive, and I had done what the Lord wanted me to do, while I was in New York. I believe that there are three major reasons why the Lord so dramatically sent me to New York.

God's Purpose for sending me to New York

1. I had a big head, when I went to New York; and the Lord had to show me that it was unmerited. He used those youth to give me a head shrinking experience.

2. I believe that the Lord wanted to inspire me to do greater things in his name; and in order to do that, He had to put me among some of His servants, who were inspired, and doing great things for the Lord, people with a vision. If you want to be inspired, you have to be around inspired people, who are doing something in the name of the Lord. David Wilkerson, and Tom Skinner, were certainly, very inspired servants of God; and I was blessed for the time that I had spent with them.

3. I know that the Lord loved Stanley so much, and that He sent me to New York to plant that seed in Stanley. I know that the Lord had provided me with the missing link, that information, and inspiration, that would make the difference in his life.

Right after we closed the chapel that night, they took me to the bus station, where I boarded the bus and went back home to my family. The Worlds Fair met in New York City, in 1964, and 1965; and I attended it with my wife, and her younger brother Lawrence. We stayed at Sloan House while we were there. One day I decided to go to Catacomb Chapel, to see David's mother, and the other workers.

When I came in, the first thing that I noticed, was Stanley, seated at one of the tables, with a Bible open on the table, and he was leading another person to Christ.

You can't imagine how blessed I was to see this young Jewish man, saved and unabashed, winning souls to the Lord Jesus Christ.

When he finished, I went over to him and embraced him. I asked him, "What happened? How did you get saved?" He said, "I went home and studied the Prophets." What a blessing! And to think that the Lord let me come back to see it. When I think of it, it was worth all of what the Lord put me through, just to see Stanley saved; and who's to say, how many souls Stanley would bring to Christ. **The Lord God Almighty be praised; there is none like Him.**

The Baptism of the Holy Ghost, and the gift of tongues

When I returned home from New York, in 1964, I remember thinking about one of the young workers at Teen Challenge asking me; "Do you have the baptism of the Holy Ghost?" I said, "yes." He then said; "With the evidence of speaking with other tongues?" I said, "no." He said, "You've got to get it." I said, "Get what?" He said, "The Baptism of the Holy Ghost, with the evidence of speaking with other tongues." I replied; "I have been baptized by the Holy Ghost, into the body of Christ, according to 1 Corinthians 12:13; Why do I need to speak with other tongues?" He said; "So that you will have power." I asked him; "Power to do what?" I already knew what the scripture said. He said, "Witnessing power, power to witness." I asked him; "Do you have it?" He said, "yes." I asked him, "Are you a witness for God?" He said, "Yes."

Then I asked him; "How many souls have you won to Christ?" He said, "There is this fellow that I have been witnessing to, and I expect that it won't be long before He gets saved."

I said unto him; "I was saved in September of 1960, and I have won more than 300 souls to Christ." I said unto him; "In Acts 1:5, Jesus said, For John truly baptized with water; but ye shall be baptized with the Holy Ghost not many days hence. And in Acts 1:8 He said; But ye shall receive power, after that the Holy Ghost is come upon you: and ye shall be witnesses unto me both in Jerusalem, and in all Judea, and in Samaria, and unto the uttermost part of the earth.

There is only one baptism of the Holy Ghost. The Holy Spirit and the Holy Ghost are one and the same.

1 Corinthians 12:13 says, "For by one Spirit are we all baptized into one body, whether we be Jews or Gentiles, whether we be bond or free; and have been all made to drink into one Spirit." Don't try to divide the body of Christ. Not all Christians speak with other tongues.

1 Corinthians 12:27-30 says, "Now ye are the Body of Christ, and members in particular. And God hath set some in the church, first apostles, secondarily prophets, thirdly teachers, after that miracles, then gifts of healings, helps, governments, diversities of tongues.

Are all apostles? Are all prophets? Are all teachers? Are all workers of miracles? Have all the gifts of healing? Do all speak with tongues? Do all interpret?" The answer to each of these questions is obviously, "no." Chapter 12:31 through Chapter

13:1 says, "But covet earnestly the best gifts: and yet show I unto you a more excellent way.

Though I speak with the tongues of men and of angels, and have not charity, I am become as a sounding brass, or a tinkling cymbal."

Every born again Christian, without exception, has the Holy Ghost. There is no salvation, apart from having the Holy Spirit, which is the Spirit of Christ. The Lord wants all of us to relate to each other, according to the Gospel of Jesus Christ.

Wanting all that God has for his people

Having had this experience with that young man, and having just returned home, with my experiences still fresh in my mind, I reflected back on this while praying to God one night. I said to the Lord; "Lord there is so much misunderstanding among the people of God, concerning the baptism of the Holy Spirit, and the manifestation of the gifts of God.

I know that I have your Spirit in me, and I know that I have power with you, and that I am a soul winner; but I want to feel free to teach the truth about Holy Ghost and the gifts.

If I say the things that I need to say, people would probably say, the only reason you are saying that, is because you do not have it. So Lord give me this manifestation of your Spirit, the gift of tongues, so that when I teach about it, I can say like Paul, I thank God that I speak with tongues as much as you all.

While I was praying, I began praising the Lord; and while I was praising Him, this new and beautiful language began to flow from my lips. It was flowing so simply, and easy, that I was moved to ask the Lord; Is this it? I don't want to embarrass you. The Lord said, "Yes this is it, and you will not embarrass me.

This is between you and me." I remained on my knees, praying in an unknown tongue, for about one and a half hour; then I went to bed.

You know not what you ask

By then it must have been about 1, or 2 o'clock A M. While I lay awake in bed, I was still very excited; and I said to the Lord, "It's not enough, I want to see you." Immediately the Lord spoke to me and said; "Get up, and go downstairs to the living room, and you will see me there." I jumped out of bed, ran to the hallway, and began to run down the stairs; but I didn't know that a person could think about so many things, in such a short period of time; because, from the time that I reached the top of the staircase, to the time that I reached the bottom of the stairs, my thoughts were so strong, that my run had turned to a slow walk.

And fear had gripped my heart, so much so; that I had closed my eyes so tightly, that my upper eyelids turned inside out. I had to take my finger to set them right again.

One of the things that I had thought about was the scripture that said in Exodus 33:20, "And He said, Thou canst not see my face: for there shall no man see me and live." My God, what had I done? What possessed me to ask for such a thing? I thought that my heart would stop beating. When I reached the foyer, with my eyes closed, I reached for the side of the doorway leading to the living room.

When I came into the room, all of my energy left me, and I dropped to my knees, and then fell upon my face. I immediately took my arms, and looped them above my head, so that my face was completely shielded. I didn't want to see anything.

I was terrified at the thought of what might happen, if I opened my eyes, and saw the Lord.

All of a sudden, it became very clear to me. I had been on an egotistical high, and I was pushing it to the limit. My request wasn't about God; it was all about me. I began to recognize it then; I had been there before, and the Lord had to straighten me out that time also. With my eyes still tightly closed, and with my face shielded, I said to the Lord, "Lord, it is enough, I understand now. I have seen you, every time that I saw a soul miraculously saved, drug addicts, and alcoholics lives dramatically changed, I know that it was you, and I can see you in those things. Lord, it's enough; I understand now."

I'm not sure how long I lay in that position, unchanged; but after a while, I began to peep through a little gap, between my two arms, to see if I could see any light. I did not see any other than the light coming in from the foyer.

A little later I got up enough nerve to scan the floor. I was looking for some feet, like fine polished brass. I remembered what John had said about Jesus' appearance, when He appeared to him in a vision, on the Isle of Patmos. Revelation 1:14-15, "His head and His hairs were white like wool, as white as snow; and His eyes were as a flame of fire; And His feet like unto fine brass, as if they were burned in a furnace; and His voice as the sound of many waters." I didn't see any feet, and so I felt that it was safe to get up.

Again I said to the Lord, "Lord, I understand. I don't need to see you. Thank you; I'm going to bed now. And with that, I got up, and went upstairs, and went to bed, like I had good sense.

To this day, I thank God that He responds to our prayers, no matter how silly they may be, but still takes the time and uses that opportunity to help us to learn from it. **Praise God, for His mercy.**

Chapter 10

The Emerging of a Gospel Preacher servant of God: The beginning of "GOOD NEWS EVANGELISM" of Canonsburg

The members of our Bible Study group started a non-profit Christian Organization, named "GOOD NEWS EVANGELISM", for the purpose of enlarging our capabilities to spread the gospel of Jesus Christ, by radio, and the printed word, and so that people who were led to help support our work could deduct those gifts from their income taxes, and in order for us to take advantage of more favorable mailing privileges.

One of the things that the Lord inspired me to do after returning from New York, was to write a gospel tract, entitled *"SAVED,"* which was published in September, 1964. This tract was designed to explain why people needed to be saved, and how to be saved.

After I finished writing that tract, which was designed to be printed in three colors, and with different size type, the Lord told me to order 50,000 copies. I had no idea how many fifty thousand was, or what that many copies would look like. The tract was eight pages, including the front and the back, size 4x5 ½", stapled book form, to be printed on polished paper; and it needed to be printed offset, one color at a time.

At the time I didn't have two nickels to rub together, to spare for this order. This was in 1964, and the cost was $600.00. I didn't have any of it; I went ahead and ordered the fifty thousand tracts, believing that by the time that they were ready, I would have the money to pay. The man called me one day and told me that he had 10,000 copies completed, and that I could come and pay for them and pick them up.

I was able to pay him $200.00 at that time; but I was amazed how many 10,000 copies were. It was more like I had imagined that 50,000 would look like. However, when the printer had completed the entire 50,000 copies, the Lord had provided the rest of the balance in full. Our God will provide for His work.

Good News Evangelism had gotten our non-profit mailing stamp, had purchased envelopes, and had acquired phone books from all of the major cities in the U.S., and some not so major cities and towns. When we came together, we would assign a person to a particular city or town that week, and they would pray over the phone book of that town, that the Lord would direct them where to send the tracts, and we would randomly select names from the telephone books.

Some people would be responsible for stuffing the envelopes with the "Saved" tract, and the cover letter, and for sealing them. Using this process, we sent the "Saved" tract all over America.

One day my sister in the Lord, Jean, who had gotten saved the same week that the Lord saved me, thought of her sister Doris, and decided to send one of the "Saved" tracts to her. We had been praying for Doris to be saved. We even took her to a service in Pittsburgh Pa.; that had been announced on the radio, and that was preached by someone that we knew little about, only that we heard him preach on the radio, and liked what he had to say. We hoped that she would get saved. She did not at that time, but had been fairly receptive.

Doris said, When she received the letter in the mail, and saw what was in it, she got angry, and threw the tract onto the bed; but when it landed, the word Saved was on the top. She walked out of the room, and then came back. Seeing the tract laying there, and the word Saved standing out, she picked it up and started reading it. Then she threw it down again, but the word Saved was still on the top.

She walked out of the room again, and when she came back, she picked it up again, and began reading it. I don't know how many times that she did this; but finally she read all of it, then dropped to her knees, and invited the Lord Jesus to come into her heart, and He did. **Praise God, what a Savior.**

One day we all went to Pittsburgh, and stationed ourselves on the busiest corner in the city, where Gimbals, and Kaufman's department stores were located; passing out the Saved tract.

It didn't take long to discover that after they read some of the tract, that some of them would throw them down onto the street. About one third of them did this, so we had someone to go and retrieve most of them. We deliberately left some of them, because we knew that some people would come along after we were gone, and would pick them up, and perhaps be saved.

This is exactly what happened in a town in West Virginia. The person who picked it up, wrote to us, requesting us to send her more, so that she could distribute them.

It wasn't until 2004, that I discovered the reason why so many people threw those tracts down, including Doris. One morning while I was laying in my bed, the Lord spoke to me and told me. He said that it was because of some of the words that was in the tract.

On the first page, there is a place where it says "I know that you want to throw this tract away, but that wouldn't change things. The TRUTH would win out anyway." The Lord said to me that, when I said in the tract, "I know that you want to throw this tract away," I had suggested that throwing it away was an option. He said, "Your words live, and have Power." Wow! I never thought of that.

One evening when we were having Bible Study in my home, I shared it with those who came.

Then a sister asked me, "Did you change it?" Lord have mercy, it never occurred to me to change it. You can see why we need each other. The next day I changed it. It now reads in that place, "The Lord has inspired me to write this tract so that you will know the truth; and so that the TRUTH will make you free. The people of God need to know that our words have power.

Amazing conversions

Then there is the conversions of Leroy, and Margaret. Leroy Lovell was a nice looking, hard working, young man, who tells of being beaten with a buggy whip, as a kid, but didn't cry. Pete, as we lovingly called him, and which was a mild mutation from P, which was short for his nickname

Peewee, was a tough young man who did not back down from anyone. He had no problem throwing down a drink or so either.

One night Pete came to the Church on watch service night; that was New Year's Eve. We would gather at the church at ten o'clock, sing, pray, give testimonies, and hear a sermon from our pastor. At 12:00 midnight, we would all try to be on our knees praying to God and thanking Him for letting us see a new year. This night after midnight, the pastor closed the service, and dismissed us.

But James Anderson, who is another preacher that was licensed by the Mount Olive Baptist Church to preach the gospel, said "I don't feel like leaving, is there anyone else who would like to stay with me?"

Now the church had been almost full, and everyone stayed, except for a couple who was setting in the last row near the door, and had left before they could hear Jim's request. So we went into worship again.

During this time of worship, the pastor's wife, a sweet and precious woman, prayed and called Peewee's name out, and asked the Lord to save him. Later in the service Pete got up, and with tears running down his face said, "Nobody has ever called my name out in prayer before, and Mrs. Mason prayed for me. I know that I need the Lord in my life."

So that night Pete accepted the Lord as his savior, and from that day began to walk with the Lord. Every time that you would see him after that, he had his Bible in his hand. The whole town was amazed at Peewee's conversion.

After Pete got saved, we started to work on his wife Margaret. One day when two of us went to witness to her, she said to us, "Get out of here with that stuff, I don't want to hear it." But we were continued in fervent prayer, for her salvation. We knew that if she got saved, it would make it a lot easier for Pete, in his walk with the Lord.

Pete was good with his hands, and sort of a Jack of all trades, and they had bought a house, that needed to be refurbished, and he remodeled it for their home. He had completed it, and asked the Bible Study Group, if we would come and dedicate his house unto the Lord. We gladly said that we would.

That evening, when we came to his house, Margaret told us one of the most amazing stories that any of us had ever heard. She said, "When I got up this morning, I was feeling good, and I wanted to hear gospel music, so I turned on the record machine, and put on gospel music.

I was in the kitchen, preparing for you guys to come tonight; and I just felt good, I don't know why, but I did." Pete's house sat on the side of a hill, and was located on the lower side of the street. If you came in the front door, you would be in the living room, and immediately to the left was the staircase, leading downstairs to the kitchen.

Margaret continued by saying, "There was a knock on the door. I said who's there. The person answered and said, It is the Lord. I thought that it was one of my neighbors having fun with me; so I said, Well, come on in. I heard them come in, and I heard their footsteps coming down the stairs, and when they reached the bottom, I saw no one. Then I felt something came over me, and I began shouting. I shouted all over my kitchen." "I am saved," she said, "Jesus came into my life today."

Needless to say, when we heard her testimony, we all began shouting and praising the Lord.

Even now, while I write this, I am again filled with the Holy Spirit, and I can hardly see to type, because of the tears falling. What kind of God is this that we serve, that He should make a house call, to save one precious soul. I don't know, and I don't understand, but its enough to cause me to want to serve Him for the rest of my life. Who wouldn't serve a God like this?

My ordination as Assistant Pastor

In a church meeting at the Mount Olive Baptist Church, on Vine Street in Canonsburg, the members of the church voted that they ordain me to be Assistant Pastor of the church. So on Friday night, March 20, 1964 at 7:00 PM, I was ordained. The Reverend Warren A. Mason was my pastor.

In preparation for ordination, I had to study Hiscox's Directory for Baptist Churches, and I had to know the twenty Articles of Faith, by memory; and be prepared to provide some scripture that supports each article. I had been prepared by the Reverend Rucker, who was the former Pastor of the Nazareth Baptist Church, after his retirement from the pastorate.

Actually, he had prepared me in 1961, before I became a minister, and when I was on trial for deacon. He was strict, and went beyond the norm for deacons preparation. He required that we knew the Articles of Faith, verbatim; so when my ordination for the ministry came up, I already knew them. The church had voted to ordain me as deacon, and my pastor asked Reverend Rucker to prepare me for my examination.

Before the church could ordain me as deacon, the Lord called and sent me into the preaching ministry. I didn't know whether I should let them ordain me as deacon, after my call into the ministry, so I talked it over with my Father-in-law, who was serving on the deacon board in our church, and who was one of my greatest fans. He followed me everywhere, when I would preach. He said, "No son, the Lord has called you to a higher calling." So I would not let them ordain me as a deacon.

The reason why I wondered about it was, strangely enough, in our church as an ordained deacon, I could serve communion, and even baptize people, but as a licensed preacher, I could neither serve communion, nor baptize people, unless given special permission by the church. I thought that being an ordained deacon would eliminate that limitation as a minister; then the only thing that I would not be permitted to do, is to marry people. But that is not the way that it worked.

Whenever one of our churches would consider the ordination of a licensed minister, that church would vote to call a counsel together to examine the candidate, and to advise them as to the propriety of ordaining the candidate. This is to guard against false brethren being unawares brought in.

And since the Articles of Faith, are articles of agreement, concerning basic beliefs believed to be taught by the Word of God, and since it is the practice of ministers to work closely together, the clergy needed to guard against someone with different beliefs, coming into the denomination, and trying to make it into another denomination; God is not the author of confusion.

I don't even think that this is Christian to do so. As the Word of God says in 1 John 2:18-20, "Little children, it is the last time: and as ye have heard that antichrist shall come, even now are there many antichrists; whereby we know that it is the last time. They went out from us, but they were not of us; for if they had been of us, they would no doubt have continued with us: but they went out, that it might be made manifest that they were not all of us. But we have an unction from the Holy One, and we know all things."

Our church invited some of our sister churches, to come and form the council to examine me, and to advise the church as to the propriety of ordaining one David L. Jemison to the gospel ministry of Jesus Christ, and adjoining themselves to me, as brothers in the Baptist ministerial fellowship. The council consisted of 10 messengers from 10 different churches. Reverend W. D. Petett, who was serving as the Moderator of the A.U.B.A. (Allegheny Union Baptist Association), which was an association of over 150 Baptist churches, presided over the council. The council examined me, asking me questions concerning Bible doctrine.

The Spirit of the Lord was upon me, and I did very well during my examination; and I felt no nervousness at all. My catechizer was the Reverend W. T. Foster, Pastor of the New Hope Baptist Church of Lincoln Hills Pa. The Holy Spirit prevailed throughout the whole procedure.

The Reverend Haywood Robinson Jr. who was the Pastor of the Nazareth Baptist Church, of Washington Pennsylvania, preached the ordination sermon. He preached from the subject, "What Does He Preach?" And His text was Jeremiah 22:29, "Oh earth, earth, earth, hear the word of the Lord."

After such a message, I could not hold back the tears; for a charge to keep I have, and a God to glorify, who gave His Son, my soul to save, and to fit it for the sky.

Prayer was offered by the Reverend P. H. Johnson, and the charge to the minister was given to me by the Reverend G. L. Bowick; and my Lord, what a charge it was. The presentation of the Bible and the Hymn book was given to me by the Reverend Clifton Ruggs. The Reverend V. Simpson extended to me the Right Hand of Fellowship. The Church, still rejoicing, dismissed the council, and we received the benediction. It was a night that was God ordained. I shall never forget that day.

Spreading the Good News

Good News Evangelism was working fervently, to bring people, all over these United States, to a saving knowledge of Jesus Christ. Later I made arrangements to begin broadcasting the gospel, each Saturday morning, on radio station WARO.

I continued teaching the Bible on the air until 1969, when I was called to be the pastor of the Mt Olive Baptist Church, in Midland Pa. There was a knoll which prevented the station from being heard in the Midland area.

In 1967, a facility became available for sale, with about 28 bedrooms, the Pine Lawn Home Sanitarium; and I thought that it would make an excellent place for helping troubled youth. While we were praying about it, The First Baptist Church of Gallatin, Pa. called me to be their pastor; I told them that I would pray about it, and let them know within two weeks. I felt a strong urge to go and help this little church out; but I wasn't sure. I said to the Lord, "I don't know what you want me to do. I know that I am not pastoring anywhere, and this church needs a pastor, and I believe that I should accept, and you have not said yes to our purchasing the property for troubled youth.

If you don't want me to accept this position, let me know, or stop me." With that, I began making plans for my installation.

My wife played piano, and had taken lessons from Jimmy Phillips, the pianist for the Kathryn Kuhlman Foundation; and she played piano for the Youth Choir at Mt. Olive Baptist

Church in Canonsburg, and those young people were like our own children. As a matter of fact, they called her Mother.

When I told her that I felt that I should accept the offer, and what my plans were for installation services, she said that she was not going with me; and since we would be commuting to the church, if I went I wouldn't be leaving her behind. Besides, when the choir said that they wanted to go with me, I told them that they would have to stay where they were. I had not yet told the church that I would accept, so I thought that this was God's way of stopping me.

I reminded my wife, "Those people sat in our living room, and said that they wanted a family man. I'm not going to go down there by myself; they are expecting a family man, with his family. I'm going to call them and tell them that I won't be coming." When I picked up the phone to call them, she took my arm and pushed the phone back down into the cradle, saying to me, "You better go on, you know that the Lord wants you to take the church." I asked her, "Did you change your mind, are you going with me?" She said, "no." I said, "Then I'm not going either."

And with that I picked up the phone again, to call them. Again, she put her hand on top of mine, to force the phone back into the cradle.

I began to be so frustrated; I left the room, and went into my daughter's room, just to be alone. As I walked through the door, the Lord spoke unto me and said, "Since when have you given yourself to serving Satan, you know that I want you in Gallatin." I said, "Ok Lord, I'll go."

Then the Lord showed me a vision. There was this kid who fell from a building, onto the sidewalk, and I saw the ambulance come and take the child away. Then I was standing in a church, and some people came in, and rolled a casket to the front of the church. After they left, I went down the isle, to the front of the church to see who was in the casket. When I got there, and looked in; I saw that it was my daughter lying in that casket. I said to the Lord, "I said that I am going, what's this for?" The Lord replied, "If you don't obey me, I'll hit you afar, and then move up to you."

I immediately went to the phone and called the chairman of deacons, and informed him that I was accepting the pastorate; and that there would be a letter from me confirming my acceptance. I also told him that my wife may not be with me, and if they wanted to change their minds, I would understand. He said, "No, we want you, the people have fell in love with you. Sure, we would prefer to have your family too, but if not, we want you." So I began making plans to go and serve as pastor of the First Baptist Church of Gallatin Pennsylvania. Praise the Lord, when I assumed the position of pastor, my wife was with me. People often think that whenever there are visions, and prophesies, they are nice and always good news; but I have found that many times the Lord is revealing some awful things, to consider.

As an eagle stirreth up her nest

Deuteronomy 32:11-12 says, "As an eagle stirreth up her nest, fluttereth over her young, spreadeth abroad her wings, taketh them, beareth them on her wings: So the Lord alone did lead him, and there was no strange god with him." So the Lord began to wean me, teaching me to follow Him.

I had served as the assistant Pastor of the Mount Olive Baptist Church, in Canonsburg, until the Lord told me to get up, and get out. I turned in my resignation, and gave them four months notice, reminding them that they would have to get someone to help Pastor Mason. I'm sorry to say that I had been spiritually wounded by my pastor.

One day in the course of my service as Assistant Pastor, I went to the Pastor and said, "Rev. Mason, we have not had a revival at our church for a long time, do you think that it is about time for one?" He said, "You know what I told you boys," referring to Rev. Anderson, who had moved to California, and myself, "go ahead and plan it, but be sure that you get the church to vote to have it; they will be the ones who will have to support it." I assured him that I would.

We only had church meetings once a month, and I felt that if the church approved it, we should be able to proceed quickly from there. Trying to be prepared to proceed from there, I called a pastor, one who I knew was known and respected by our Pastor, and the congregation; the Reverend George Bowick, one of the most respected pastors in the Pittsburgh area, and he was my mentor, I learned much from him, and there was much about him that I wanted to emulate.

I told him that we were planning to have a revival, and I told him the week that I thought that we would have it, and asked him if the church chose him to be the evangelist, would he be available that week, and would he be willing to do it. He said yes.

On church meeting night, I presented the plan and the time frame to have revival services at our church, without telling them who the evangelist would be. The church voted to have the revival as planned. After the vote, I told them that I had spoken to Pastor Bowick, and that he would be available, and be willing to come if we chose him. They all agreed that he would be an excellent choice; so they voted to ask Rev. Bowick to be the evangelist for the revival. I contacted him, and he came and preached the revival. We all had a good time, and a man who was an alcoholic in our town got saved during the revival. It was a success.

The next time that we had a board meeting, Pastor Mason got up and said to them, "Brethren, Rev. Jemison went out and got a preacher to preach a revival, and I knew nothing about it." I was shocked. I didn't know why he was saying that. I was waiting for one of the officers to get up, and remind him of the church meeting, and what happened there, but none of them did; and they were all there when it happened.

I couldn't believe what was happening. I stood up and said, "Reverend Mason, I guess I was wrong. I'm sorry, and it will never happen again. With that I walked out, and went downstairs into the basement; I didn't want to break down and cry in front of all of them; so I went downstairs, so that I could let it all out.

They thought that I had gone home, and I heard them upstairs, those who could not stand up, and speak up for me, were now speaking up and saying, "I didn't know that he had done that, as though they had had a bad case of amnesia. And these were Christians, and good friends of mine.

From this time on, the Lord kept on saying to me, get up, and get out. I had a dream, in which I saw myself, trying to get into Mt Olive Church, and could not. The Lord spoke to me and said that you will be in the wilderness for three and a half years, and then I would come and be the pastor of Mount Olive Baptist Church.

After I resigned, some of the members came to me and asked me to reconsider. Some even said, "I don't understand the Lord telling the Shepherd to leave the sheep;" because I was preaching at Mt. Olive, in Canonsburg every Sunday morning.

I told them, "I can't tell you now, but in three and a half years, you will understand. I thought that the Lord meant that in three and a half years, that I would come back and pastor my home church; but instead 3 ½ years later, to the month, I was called to become the Pastor of the Mt. Olive Baptist Church of Midland Pa. So during this three and a half years, I would be shunned by churches who knew me, and would not even invite me to the pulpit, as they would usually do; this was because I had told the Lord that I was not going to preach at any church that already had a pastor, but only at the churches that were without a pastor, and there were about sixteen of those in the area at the time.

I asked the Lord, "What is happening, why am I being shunned by these churches?"

The Lord said unto me, "I did not send you to preach in vacant pulpits. I sent you to preach where ever I send you." I said, "Yes Lord, I will preach every time I get the chance."

From that time on; the door was opened to me, and I was preaching almost every Sunday and sometimes two and three times a day. I even preached in churches of other denominations.

Little things mean a lot

However, little things mean a lot. And yet, what seems to be little, may prove to be a tremendous thing. Many valuable things come in small packages. I would tell you of a time, before I was called to pastor in Gallatin. There is a little town, along the Allegheny River, just on the edge of the city of Pittsburgh Pennsylvania, Sharpsburg, where there was another Mount Olive Baptist Church, which was without a pastor also.

I was invited to come to preach at that church one Sunday morning. They were worshiping in an old building that they had recently moved into. I was in the pulpit preaching, and they were sitting on the edge of their seats, listening to every word, and I was about to give the invitation to discipleship.

Just then, a bat came down from the attic; the trap door had been left open by someone. As he flew low over the peoples heads, they were ducking, and he kept on swooping and they kept on ducking. I said to them, "This is just the work of the devil;" in the meanwhile, I hated bats, couldn't stand them, they made my flesh crawl. I told myself, "David, if that bat comes at you, you can not duck."

Just then the bat flew to the back of the church, and turned around, coming straight down the center aisle, headed straight towards me; and I said again to myself, " David, whatever you do you can't duck;" and just when he was about five feet in front of me, I ducked, and it was all over but the shouting.

Then I thought to pray, out loud. I said "Lord, you've got to do something about that bat." And as soon as I prayed that prayer, that bat flew back out, the same way that he came in. But it was too late, the people were cracking their sides laughing.

I dismissed the people, and said to myself, "Oh well, I guess that I can forget about being called to this church. But I learned a valuable lesson that day. When you have a problem that you can't solve, glorify the Lord by praying. He will hear and answer prayer.

I tried to solve that problem by being strong, but after prayer, God proved to be God, by answering prayer. I had a problem, the Lord solved it, when I asked Him to do it.

Even if I had not ducked, that would not have solved the problem; the bat would still be there. (Use the force Luke) Smile! The Lord God, YAHWEH is the force. Greater is He that is in you, than he that is in the world. In this world, we are going to have problems; but problems is why miracles come. If I never had a problem, I'd never know that God could solve them, I'd never know what faith in His Word could do. Through this problem, I have learned to trust in God's Word. Ask, and you shall receive.

Touch not mine anointed

When I was Assistant Pastor of the Mount Olive Baptist of Canonsburg, my Pastor was in his eighties, and was legally blind. He was not completely blind, but blind enough to be declared to be legally blind. One day the chairman of the trustee board, and the chairman of the deacon board, came to my home, together. They said that they wanted to talk with me. They said that Reverend Mason was old, and unable to pastor any more, and that they needed a young man to lead the church; and asked me if I would be willing to become the pastor of the church.

I told them no. I said, "The only way that I would consider becoming their pastor is, first, I would have to know that Pastor Mason had resigned, without being forced to resign, second, he and his wife must be allowed to stay in the parsonage, and third, The church would have to continue paying him a salary. That is the only way that I would consider it.

But my advice to you is, if you think that you need a new pastor, you need to pray to the Lord; because if the Lord is unwilling to move an 85 year old man from the pastorate, you don't stand a chance of being successful. My advice to you is, leave that man alone."

They then got up and the deacon said, "Well I'm glad we had this talk." The trustee said, "You'll be hearing from us." I knew the trustee well, and I knew that he would not leave it alone.

One week after their meeting with me, that trustee was dead. The Word of God says, Touch not mine anointed, and do my Prophets no harm. The Lord means what he says. Beside all this, the church had grown, and was stronger than it had ever been under the present circumstances. It's not the pastor that makes a church strong, it is the God in the pastor and His body, the Church.

God heals my car

Early in my Christian life, I drove a 1953 Oldsmobile 88. I was having trouble with it, so I took it to the mechanic, and left it with him. He said he would look at it and tell me what was wrong, and what it would take to fix it. When I came back, he had taken the head off the engine and looked into it. He said to me, "Your car is not worth fixing, it would take more to fix your car, than it would to buy a newer car."

I asked him, "How long do you think I can drive it?" He said, "I doubt if you can even get it home." I knew this man, and believed that he was a knowledgeable, honest and fair mechanic. He didn't even charge me for what he had done; but I didn't believe him. He said that I would have no power going up hills.

There was a hill, inclined about 20 or 30 degrees, just outside his shop, so I decided to test it there. I could not make it up the hill. Thank God, there were no hills inclined any more than 10 or 15 degrees, between his shop and my home, so I was able to make it home, where I parked it in the lot right across the street from where I lived; and for a week I had to hitch a ride to work with my buddy, with whom I worked.

One night that week I was in a church service, and after the sermon, the guest preacher asked us to write down on a piece of paper, what we wanted the Lord to do for us; so I wrote, "My spiritual growth in the Lord." That was a safe request. Who is to know whether the Lord did it or not? There is not much chance of failure there. Isn't that what we do with God? We try to make it as easy as possible, for him to answer our prayers.

Oh to believe in a Great God! YAHWEH is able to do exceedingly, and abundantly more than we ask or think. Dare to trust Him. Then the preacher asked us to bring our requests with us, and he would pray with us, and we would agree together.

Before he got to me, I decided to live dangerously; I decided to ask the Lord to do something for me that I really needed, not that I didn't need to get strong in the Lord; but my greatest need at the moment was, I needed my car fixed. Lord, heal my car. I didn't get a chance to write it down, but I prayed it from my heart.

The next few days, I still rode with my buddy to work; I had tried to drive my car, but the problem was still there. Later it was time to get groceries, and I decided to take a chance and drive the car to the grocery store, since there were no major hills between my home and the store. When we got there, I discovered that I had left my wallet at home, so I left my wife to shop, while I went back for my wallet.

As I was going back, I noticed that I didn't have much gas in the car, and I didn't want to take the chance of running out of gas, so I stopped at the service station, and bought a couple gallons of gas. While there, I decided to check my oil level; it was down a quart.

About a month before, I had bought a can of Bardall oil additive, to put in the engine, when the level was low enough to add. So instead of buying oil, I used the Bardall to bring the level up.

Glory be to God, as I drove out of the gas station, my car was purring like a kitten; and it purred like that for sixteen months, and I never had to take it to a mechanic again. I only had to put gas, oil and coolant in it, for sixteen months. In less than a week, the Lord healed my automobile.

Did you notice that when it was sick, I called it a car, and after the Lord healed it, I call it an automobile? Smile! I never had any more trouble with it until I was able to buy a new car; and even then it was not the same problem. That time, it was the transmission. If we give the Lord a chance, He will do great things for us. Just trust Him. Little things mean a lot.

Chapter 11

The Church hungry for revival, and preacher Anointed to serve: Beginning ministry in the Ohio River valley

I had served there in that church for two years, when I was called to the Mount Olive Baptist Church, of Midland, Pennsylvania, to be their pastor, full time. I had not been looking for a church, but I had called them to see if they would consider hearing a minister friend of mine, since they were without a pastor.

The chairman of deacons said yes, and then asked me if I would come and preach for them some Sunday morning also. I said that I am pastoring, and I don't like to be away from my church too much. He pressed me to give them a fifth Sunday; preachers often take the fifth Sunday off from the pulpit.

Then I said, "Well I'm due a Sunday off, but I don't take off on the fifth Sunday, because when the congregation knows that I won't be there, and that we would have a guest preacher in my place, some of them stay home; so when I would not be in the pulpit, only the deacons would know it in advance.

So I agreed to come the Sunday after Reverend Anderson, my friend would be there. When he went there, he told them, "You wait until you hear the preacher that will be here next Sunday." When he told me what he said to them, I said, "Are you nuts? I have a church; why would you do that?"

After I preached for them, they asked me to come back, but I told them that I didn't want to leave my church in the morning again, that soon. So they asked me to come and preach for them in the afternoon. I said that I would.

They scheduled Jim, to come again that morning, and I was to be there in the afternoon. But the weather began to get foul, and I was concerned with getting there safely and on time, in the snow. Wisdom told me that I shouldn't take that chance.

There was another church in Midland, which had no pastor; so I called the chairman of deacons, of the First Baptist Church, of Midland, and asked him if they needed anyone to preach for them on that same Sunday. He said that they did not have anyone scheduled yet, and would be glad to have me to come to preach for them that Sunday. So I was scheduled to preach at First Baptist Church in the morning service, and to preach at Mount Olive Baptist Church that afternoon. At First Baptist, they announced that on Monday, they wanted people to be present at church meeting, for the purpose of choosing a new pastor.

After morning service the chairman of deacons took me to dinner, and asked me, "How would you like to become our pastor?" I said, "You all are having a meeting tomorrow, for the purpose of calling a pastor, your minds are already made up; and your people don't know me, I'm a stranger to them." He said, "They seemed to like you quite a bit." And then he began to tell me what they were offering the preacher that they would call. When I heard what it was, I said, "There would be no problem there, but I'm sure that the people have made up their minds already." The next day they voted to elect a pastor; and placed my name in nomination, along with three others. My name came in second, to a preacher who had already turned them down once.

That afternoon I preached at the Mount Olive Baptist Church, which was less than two blocks away. After the service, the officers asked me if I would come back, and preach a week of revival services at their church. I said that I would.

The church would seat about two hundred people, including the choir stand and the balcony; and by Wednesday night of the revival service, you couldn't buy a seat, and there were chairs in the isle. I asked them to leave the front row on the right side open for those who were anxious to receive the Lord Jesus as their savior. This is what the folks down south would call the mourners bench.

When I gave the invitation to the lost sinners, to come and give their lives to the lord, five teenagers came forth. I went down from the pulpit, and asked each of them why they came forth; they each replied, "I want to be saved."

I told the congregation to carry on, while I took them back to the study.

One by one they all received the Lord Jesus into their hearts, with tears streaming down their faces; and declared that they were sure that the Lord had saved them. I led them in a prayer of thanksgiving; and they followed me back to the front of the church. I had them to stand and asked them to tell the congregation what the Lord had done for them. One by one they told the church that the Lord came into their lives, and saved them; and before they could finish, they all began shouting and praising God. The church then just exploded with shouting and praise.

After a long while, I started to sing a song, thinking, that it would bring back order in the service; but nobody was even paying attention to me.

I don't think that they even noticed when I started or when I stopped. I couldn't even hear myself sing. When I looked down to the anxious seat, I noticed that the five who had just gotten saved had moved, and made room for nine more teenagers, that came forward to be saved. I came down again from the pulpit and asked each of them why they came forward, they each with tears streaming down their cheeks, blurted out, "I want to be saved." I said unto them, "Follow me." As I led them to the study, I said to the congregation, "Church, I don't know what the Lord is doing; but I like it, carry on."

While I was back in the study with the young people, I could hear the people singing, shouting, and praising God. Then I heard a loud sound just outside the door, which sounded like someone had fallen from the balcony.

A moment later the door to the study opened, and there was this teenage girl, brought by a couple of deacons, who said, "Here's another one Rev." I asked her also, "What did you come for?" She said, weeping out loud, "I want to be saved, I don't want to go to hell."

A little later there was another sound, as if one was falling down the stairs from the balcony. Later someone told me that another teenage boy ran down the stairs from the balcony, and ran straight to his mother, and said to her, "Lord have mercy, Mama, something is up there in that balcony." There sure was, the Holy Spirit was all over that church that night. He was there to save and deliver people. It was a troubling of the waters, and the Lord was in it. The rest of the week was to be more of the same. When the week was over, thirty two people had come forward, and given their lives to the Lord.

The thing most remarkable during the one week of revival, was the affect that it had on the young people. From the time that the Lord saved them they were very visible in the services, expressing their joy, by shouting, and praising God. One particular person comes to mind; a young sixteen year old girl named Valerie, who was about the size of a minute, and who was in the youth choir. She would jump and shout, until she passed out. The deacons would carry her out to the vestibule, or the study until she came to. Then she would come back in, glassy eyed, and would get back into the choir again. It wouldn't be long before Valerie would be shouting again; and again she would pass out; and again they would carry her out. She was really enjoying herself in the Lord.

During this revival another pastor, Pastor Ross of the New Hope Baptist of East Liverpool Ohio, asked me if I would come to East Liverpool, and preach revival messages at their church. I said that I would be glad to. So before the revival services were over in Midland, he made the announcement at the Mount Olive Church, that two weeks later I would be preaching revival services at their church.

When the revival services started at New Hope, the Lord continued doing the things that He had done in Midland. About sixteen souls would come to the Lord in those services, and it became apparent that revival had come to the Ohio valley. On our way to East Liverpool for the first night of the revival, as we had to go through Midland to get there, we saw three young girls, hitch-hiking to the revival in East Liverpool Ohio. I was very fearful for them, and stopped to pick them up. One of them was Valerie.

The Young people of Midland joined the young people of East Liverpool, to form a Community choir to sing during the revival services. The seats in the choir stand were folding chairs, and the young people continued their shouting ways, in New Hope also. There were times that they would shout so that there was no more than three chairs left standing; and they would carry some of them out after they passed out, among which was Valerie. I would love to see her come back in, glassy eyed, and with a smile on her face, wearing scared hair, as though she had received an electrical shock. It was revival for me, just to see the Lord working with the Young people that way.

The call to pastor Mt. Olive Baptist Church

As soon as they legally could, the members of the Mt Olive Baptist Church voted to call me to Pastor their church.

The Lord had already let me know that they would offer the call to me, and that it was His will for me to leave my church in Gallatin, and accept the position as Pastor of the Mount Olive Baptist Church of Midland. However, when you have pastored a people, you have a tendency to get very close to them; and leaving them is a painful event.

The one thing that allows it to be also a pleasant event, is the knowledge that it is the Lord's ministry, and that it was He working through you. I knew that I would be leaving First Baptist, but the Lord would not be leaving. There was a lot of sadness when I announced to the congregation, that I would be leaving to accept another church.

They planned a farewell service for me at First Baptist, and I announced it at Mount Olive. Mount Olive planned to surprise me, and chartered a bus, and came to Gallatin to be in that service. It really just added to the sadness of the members of First Baptist.

One woman, who was usually very sweet, and kind, came to me and said; "If you're going, just go. You are just like all the rest of those preachers; you're only going for the money." This struck me to my heart; I thought, "I have pastored this people for two years, and she doesn't know me any better than that?" Yet I knew that she still loved me, it was just her way of expressing her own sense of loss, at my going. And then again I knew that this was coming from her subconscious mind, which tells her, preachers are only in it for the money.

I'm sure that this is what many people think about the servants of God, his preachers; and I know that there are many preachers that are in it because they consider it to be their vocation, and are in it for the money.

But the man of God, is only the servant of God; and pleasing the Lord is his greatest joy; and he often suffers great hardships, and makes great sacrifices to do the will of God. I told this dear woman; "Sister Gray, I'm not going for the money, but because it is the will of God that I go; and if I were not to obey the Lord, I would be in trouble with Him. Furthermore, I am actually going to have a cut in pay, in order to go there. I and my wife will both be quitting our jobs, and we will have to sell our house that we had just bought four years ago, in order to pay off our bills, so that we can live on my small salary, that they will be paying me."

This was in 1969; and when Mt. Olive met to call a new pastor, they were unanimous in electing me, but they had four abstentions, four people who chose not to vote at all.

And when I came that church to accept the call, these four people came to me and told me, that they were the four who had abstained from voting. They said, "We abstained because we were not in favor of the pay package that the deacons had included in the motion. They wanted to pay you $60.00 a week; and we thought that if they offered you that small amount of money, that you would not accept the call. You have a family, and you need more money than that to live on; but we're so glad that you accepted."

I had met with the officers of the church, and agreed to accept the charge for $60.00 a week, and to live in the parsonage, which was next to the church, with the utilities being paid by the church, on the condition that they would raise my salary within ninety days of my assuming the duties of the pulpit. They agreed.

However, when the ninety days had almost expired, and when I had heard nothing about a raise, I had to bring it up. Then the Chairman of Deacons said; "Did we say within ninety days? I thought that we said after ninety days." I asked, "How many years after ninety days?" They then met, and suggested to the church that they would raise my salary to $90.00 a week. The church voted in agreement.

I needed time to sell my house, and I had given a three-month notice to my job, that I would be quitting, and told them that I would be going to Midland to be in full time ministry. During my last week on my job, I was wondering how the Lord would provide for my family; then I got a phone call from Pastor Byers, of Library, Pennsylvania. He said that he had scheduled two weeks of revival services at their church, to start next week, and Dr. Isaac Green was to preach it, but he has had death in his family, and had to fly to Dallas, Texas.

He asked me would I help them out, and come and be the evangelist those two weeks. I told him that I would be glad to. I went, and we had a glorious revival; souls were saved. At the end of the services, the pastor handed me an envelope, with a check in it for $550.00. I said, "Thank you Lord. The very first week of my full time pastorate, you have shown me how you are going to take care of me and my family. Now I know, that church will not be my source, but You are my source." In all of my time of serving the Lord, I have always had my needs met. My God is faithful.

The Lord is truly faithful, you can depend on Him. When I worked for Carter Brother Cable Repair, for fourteen years; their idea of vacation was, a week off, with two and a half day's pay. Needless to say, I and my family didn't have much of a vacation, at any time of our marriage.

But after one year of pastoring at Mt Olive in Midland, I was able to take my family, in my brand new car, and go for three weeks vacation to California, and down to Mexico, and back. We were even able to go to see Grand Canyon. The Lord even opened the door for me to preach the Morning message at the church that was pastored by Dr. Byrd in Los Angeles. Dr. Byrd was at the time the president of the California State Baptist Convention, and the Vice President of the National Baptist Association of America. We visited that church on missionary meeting night, where he asked me as a visiting pastor, if I had anything to say. I stood and said a few words, and sat down. This pastor, who had never laid eyes on me before, asked me to come back Sunday morning, and preach for them.

As we left the church that night, one of the people who we went there with told me, "I was shocked when he asked you to come and preach Sunday morning. He doesn't do that for anybody." But it was God ordained, I came back and preached, and the love offering that they took up for me was such a blessing to me and my family, on our vacation. This was only half of our vacation and journey, we had to get back home, and I had already started to tighten up on the budget. The love offering from that church was such a great blessing. It was a God send.

Now I was able to relax, and we were able to enjoy ourselves completely. I was even able to fly down into the Grand Canyon, in a helicopter, on our way back. This was our second trip to the Grand Canyon. When we serve well, serving God pays well.

The Lord will not let us beat Him giving. Nobody provides like our God provides.

Prove me now herewith saith the Lord

Malachi 3:8-12 is a record of the Lord's own words, "Will a man rob God? Yet ye have robbed me. But ye say, Wherein have we robbed thee? In tithes and offerings. Ye are cursed with a curse: for ye have robbed me, even this whole nation. Bring ye all the tithes into the storehouse, that there may be meat in mine house, and prove me now herewith, saith the Lord of hosts, if I will not open you the windows of heaven, and pour you out a blessing, that there shall not be room enough to receive it.

And I will rebuke the devourer for your sakes, and he shall not destroy the fruits of your ground; neither shall your vine cast her fruit before the time in the field, saith the Lord of hosts.

And all nations shall call you blessed: for ye shall be a delightsome land, saith the Lord of hosts." Tithes and offerings is the way the Lord supports His work, and feeds His servants, as well as the poor; and those who tithe to the Lord YAHWEH shall be greatly blessed.

One day when I came home to my wife and told her that we were going to have some company that week; She said, "Where are we going to get the food to feed them? We don't have any meat in this house; How are we going to feed them? I thought you said that if we would tithe, that the Lord would open the windows, and pour out a blessing; I don't see my needs being met." I said, "I didn't say that, the Lord did; I was just quoting Him, and I do see my needs being met."

She said, "Do you have any money to buy some?" I said, "No, I just have about five dollars, and I'm going down to the store to buy me a steak to eat." I used to love to eat steaks.

I left right out and went to the store, and picked up a steak that cost less than four dollars. When I came to the check out counter, one of the members of our church was there. She said, "Reverend Jemison, I'm so glad to see you. I've been meaning to do something for you and your wife for some time now. Go and get whatever you want, and I will pay for it." I said, "No, I'm not going to do that." She said, "Then wait right here and I'll do it. Don't leave." When she came back, she had all meat in the buggy, enough to fill two bags. She paid for them, and then shoved them to me, and said, "God bless you."

When I got home, I went to the kitchen and took the meat out of the bags, and spread them all over the table. Rose looked at me and said, "I thought that you didn't have any money." I said, "I didn't." She said, "Well where did all of this come from?" I said, "Well you had to open your mouth and say that you didn't see your needs being taken care of, so God had to show you that He was taking care of our needs."

Then I told her of meeting the member at the store. God never fails, and He is a very present help in the time of trouble. Oh, how I love the Lord. He has done so many things for me.

If God makes a promise, He will do it. So arm yourselves with His promises. His promises are His gifts to us.

The vision of an arc of fire

Pastor Herman Gore Sr. was the evangelist for the revival services at the Sixth Mount Zion Baptist Church, in Pittsburgh, Pa. Pastor Gore was a very spiritual man of God, who walked closely with God. He was the Pastor of Christ Southern Mission Baptist Church, of St. Louis, Missouri, and Christ Second Baptist Church, of Long Beach, California, at the same time. He would spend six months in St. Louis, and the other six months in Long Beach. Whenever Reverend Gore would come to Pittsburgh, people would come from all over the tri-state area to be in the services.

On one particular night, I was among many pastors seated in the pulpit, as he preached. There were more than thirty preachers present at that service, sixteen of which were up on the platform.

When the service was over, a friend of mine named Evelyn Carter, who had been sitting over on the right side of the church, came up to me and said, "Did you see it?" I said, "See what?" She said, "There was an arc of fire over the seven of you ministers who were seated in the middle. The Lord said that you seven were to be His firebrands." I hadn't seen any arc of fire, and I didn't quite know how to take what she said, or what that meant.

Then another fellow, who had been sitting on the opposite side of the church came up to us, and said to me, "Did you see it? There was an arc of fire over those of you who were sitting in the middle of the pulpit." I had to go and look up the meaning of the word firebrand. Webster's dictionary describes it as,

1. a piece of burning wood, and
2. A person who stirs up others to revolt or strife.

Evelyn Carter was a servant of God, who traveled around, sharing the word of God. Some times while traveling to preach, I would run into her at the airport, and she would be going somewhere else to teach the Word of God, at some conference or something. I always admired her commitment to God. I saw her as a woman who was sold out to God. Evelyn was often a guest on the PTL television program, with Jim and Tammy Baker. On the show, she was affectionately referred to as "Rev. Ev."

Let God be true, and every man a liar:

Now looking back over my life, I can say that prophecy has come true, as far as I am concerned. For example, the Lord has been leading me to urge the Christians everywhere, to correct an error that the churches had made, concerning the crucifixion and resurrection of Jesus.

The Lord would have me to tell the world, that each time that we acknowledge "Good Friday" as the day that Jesus was crucified, it is an insult to Him. Jesus was not crucified on Friday, but instead, He was crucified on Thursday. Jesus prophesied several things concerning His death, and His resurrection.

1. Matthew 12:39-40 "But He answered and said unto them, An evil and adulterous generation seeketh after a sign; and there shall no sign be given to it, but the sign of the prophet Jonah: For as Jonah was three days and three nights

in the whale's belly; so shall the Son of man be three days and three days in the heart of the earth."

2. John 2:18:21 "Then answered the Jews and said unto Him, What sign showest thou unto us, seeing that thou doest these things? Jesus answered and said unto them, Destroy this temple, and in three days I will raise it up.

Then said the Jews, Forty and six years was this temple in building, and wilt thou rear it up in three days? But He spake of the temple of His body."

3. Jesus said in Luke 9:22, "The Son of man must suffer many things, and be rejected of the elders and chief priests and scribes, and be slain, and be raised the third day."

4. John 10:17-18, "Therefore doth my Father love me, because I lay down my life, that I might take it again. No man taketh it from me, but I lay it down of myself. I have the power to lay it down, and I have power to take it again. This commandment have I received of my Father."

5. John 12:32-33 "And I, if I be lifted up from the earth, will draw all men unto me. This He said, signifying what death He should die."

There is no way that you can count three days and three nights, from Friday afternoon to Sunday morning; and when we say that He was crucified on Friday, we are saying, in essence, that Jesus is a false prophet, who could not even predict His own death accurately. And we know that He cannot lie.

When whatever you believe is in conflict with what we know Jesus said, play it safe, and go along with Jesus; you will understand later where you were wrong. If the Church is telling the world to confess their sins and repent, shouldn't the Church do the same. Read Second Chronicles 7:14, "If my people, which are called by my name, shall humble themselves, and pray, and seek my face, and turn from their wicked ways; then will I hear from heaven, and will forgive their sin, and will heal their land. It is the highest form of evil, to call Jesus, our only way to the Father, a liar.

The Word of God says, Romans 3:4 "God forbid: yea, let God be true, but every man a liar; as it is written, That thou mightest be justified in thy sayings, and mightest overcome when thou art judged."

Every Jew knows that every time that there is a Passover, the last twelve hours of that day, from 6:00 O'clock AM, to 6:00 O'clock PM, is the time of preparation for the first day of the Feast of the Unleavened Bread, which is a holy convocation, during which no Jew is to do any servile work; in other words, it is a Sabbath Day, every time: See Leviticus chapter 23.

The Bible says in John 19:14, "And it was **the preparation of the Passover**, and about the sixth hour: and he saith unto the Jews, Behold your King!"

John 19:31 says, "The Jews therefore, because it was the preparation, that the bodies should not remain upon the cross on the Sabbath day, (for that Sabbath day was a high day,) besought Pilate that there legs should be broken, and that they might be taken away."

These passages clearly show that the Sabbath that was being referred to was the Passover Sabbath; and it was a high Sabbath, because the Passover Sabbath immediately preceded the regular weekly Sabbath. Whenever this happens, it is called a high Sabbath. There were two Sabbaths, back to back. It doesn't take three days for one Sabbath day to pass.

Let us stop calling Jesus a false Prophet, by saying that He was crucified on Friday, instead of Thursday; because if He was crucified on Friday, and He rose from the dead on Sunday morning, then His prophecy that He would be in the heart of the earth, three days and three nights would have been false; and Jesus, the TRUTH, can not lie. Lets insist on getting it right. Let God be true, and every man a liar.

People of God rise up, and stop putting up with false teaching; the Word of God is the only authority. And stop saying, I don't know, I'm just glad that He rose.

Don't you know that if Jesus was wrong in His prophesy, then He would not have been without blemish. And a mark on Jesus would also be a mark on the Father, because the Father spoke from Heaven and said, Mark 9:7 "This is my beloved Son: hear Him."

And Jesus said in John 8:28-29, "When ye have lifted up the Son of man, then shall ye know that I am He, and that I do nothing of myself; but as my Father hath taught me, I speak these things. And He that sent me is with me: the Father hath not left me alone; for I do always those things that please Him."

And Christians should not be celebrating Easter, which is a pagan holiday which occurs in April, and during which people would sacrifice to Eastre, or Ishtar, the spring goddess of fertility. That is where the rabbits, which lay eggs come from; these are symbols of fertility. But rather, the children of God should be celebrating Resurrection Day, the day that our Lord rose from the dead.

Now we can see how the Jew and the Gentile both need each other. The Gentile Christian has been adamant in preserving the weekly position of the resurrection, Sunday; and the Jew has been adamant in preserving the order of the Passover, and the Feast of the Unleavened Bread. With the two of them together, the truth concerning the crucifixion and the resurrection of Jesus our Lord is preserved.

As the song goes, "We are one in the Spirit, we are one in the Lord, and we know that our unity will soon be restored, and they'll know we are Christians, by our love, by our love, and they'll know we are Christians, by our love, by our LOVE.

Last chance to be saved

The week of July 10, 1977, the Central Baptist Church, located on the corner of Wylie and Kirkpatrick streets, in Pittsburgh, Pa., held a street meeting in the lot of a closed gas station, located right behind the Church. I, and a couple of other ministers were invited to be the team who would work together to evangelize this center-most place in the Hill District of Pittsburgh. We would take turns preaching; each night there would be a different preacher, and we would all serve as counselors, to instruct those who responded to the invitation to discipleship.

One night I went around the area and approached those persons who were curious enough about what was going on, to come near the fence, around the station, but not curious enough to come inside. I had the "SAVED" tract that I would pass out.

I approached this young man and offered him the tract, which he refused to receive. I asked him if he knew where he was going when he died. He said I guess I will go to hell. I said to him, "It doesn't have to be that way; Jesus died for you, paid for your sins, so that you won't have to go to Hell." He said, "That stuff is not for me." I pleaded with him until he walked away.

That night, after everyone had left and gone home, and the gate was locked; that same young man was shot to death, on that very same corner. The Lord loved him enough to schedule a street meeting on that corner, just so that this man would have a chance to hear the gospel of Jesus Christ, and be saved, and he would not. He was curious enough to come near and listen, but not decisive enough to receive the greatest gift in the world, when it was made available to him.

If he had known, that it was his last two hours on the earth, would he have received the Lord as his Lord and Savior? Many of you are saying to yourselves, "I surely would." However, if you are not saved, right now as you read this, how do you know that this is not your last two hours to live. You don't. The Word of God says that Now is the time, Today is the day of salvation. You must respond to the love of God. Make your move now. The decision is yours. You must want it; you must want to be saved, and know that every minute that you spend without Christ; you run the risk of going to Hell.

Two nights later, I was doing the same thing, passing out tracts and talking to those who would not come in onto the lot; and I approached a young woman, who was also resistant to the gospel. I pleaded with her to come and receive the Lord as her Savior.

I told her that we don't know the day or the hour that we might die; and then I told her about the young man that I had pleaded with, only two hours before he was shot to death on that very same corner. She said angrily, "That was my brother." And then she hurried away. I prayed that she would get the message, and be saved.

On another night a young lady along with many more, responded to the invitation, and came forth. I took them aside and began to lead them to Christ. Most of them were getting it, the concept of salvation being the Gift of God; but she was having a hard time with it. She said, "Nobody gets anything for nothing." I reached in to my wallet, looking for a dollar bill; I had none. Then I looked for a five, and found none; then I looked for a ten, I had no ten either. I only had a twenty dollar bill, but I couldn't stop now.

I held the twenty in my hand, and said to the young woman, "Do I know you, and have you ever done any thing for me, do I owe you anything?" She said, "No." I said to her, "I am giving this twenty dollar to you; it is a gift to you from me.

Now for you to have this gift, what do you have to do?" She said, "Just reach out and receive it." I said, "That's right, so take it." She reached out her hand and received the twenty. I said, "See how simple that was; Jesus is offering us everlasting life the same way, and we receive it by simply believing on Him; and when we do, just know that we have everlasting life." She sat there, still holding the twenty in her hand. I asked her if she understood, and she said "Yes, here's your money." I said, That is not my money, I gave it to you. It is yours now."

She said, "I can't take your money." I said, "Well you can't give it back to me; it's yours, and I will not take it back." She began to cry, and received the Lord Jesus as her Savior.

When the Pastor, Dr. Isaac Green, tried to schedule her for baptism, she told him that she was a prostitute that she was living with her pimp, and if he knew what she had done, he would kill her. Pastor Green scheduled baptism at a time convenient for her, since she would have a hard time coming to church, because her pimp wouldn't allow it. That brave soul came and was baptized. Later the Lord delivered her from the clutches of that pimp, and she became a member of the Central Baptist Church of Pittsburgh. Our God is so faithful, and so able. Praise the Lord!

Chapter 12

Supplanted, from the east coast to the west coast, in order to expand in ministry: Beginning ministry in the state of California

Before leaving Midland, Satan tried to kill me, as I came out of my house, on my way to one of our home Bible studies that were held at different times, and in different places, in Midland, and in East Liverpool. When I stepped on the edge of my concrete porch to descend the three steps, I was unaware of the ice that had formed, due to the freezing rain that fell during the night.

My feet slid forward in front of me, and I flew through the air, falling to the walkway below. My head hit the concrete walkway, missing the last step by only one or two inches.

Had my head not cleared that last step, I would have been dead with a hole in my head. Satan formed this weapon against me, but it did not prosper, because the Lord carried my body far enough to miss that step. How grateful I am to the Lord.

After pastoring Mt Olive Baptist Church for nine and a half years, with my marriage on the rocks, I was led by the Lord to resign as pastor, and to move to Modesto, California. I had been prayerful about where I was to go from Midland. There were three places that I was considering, Atlanta, Georgia, Philadelphia, Pennsylvania, or somewhere in California.

A friend of mine, whose church had split, and who had gone and started another church, asked me to come to California, and be co-pastor with him in Modesto, California.

I told him that I wouldn't come to be co-pastor, but I would come to help. I don't believe in co-pastors; anything with two heads is a freak, it is not natural. I do believe in Senior Pastors, and Assistant Pastors. So I said my farewells to my parishioners, family, and friends, and left for California. My former wife worked as a manager of a Super Market, and had already bought another house.

On my way to California, January 15, 1979, before I had even gone 10 miles from the Pittsburgh hotel, where I had spent my last night, the highway was icy, and the traffic was beginning to bunch up and get close. The Lord spoke to me in the car, and told me to slow down, and get in back of that crowd, because something is about to happen. I did what He told me to do, and within one minute, all of the cars in front of me were out of control and spinning.

I even had to leave the highway, riding along an embankment, in order to get around them, without being a part of it. The Lord steered me safely around it all, without a scratch, though a bit shaken for the ordeal.

Again Satan had formed this situation, in order to kill me; but it did not prosper. The Lord, my God delivered me to safety.

When I arrived in California, I stayed with my friend, in his five bedroom house, and preached and helped with the duties of the church, since the Pastor had another job, which demanded some of his time.

I had a few hundred dollars in my pocket, had no job, no income, no pension, and I could not collect any unemployment, yet the Lord provided for me, and I was even able to help with buying groceries.

God had raised friends for me, back east, who knew my situation, and would send me money from time to time.

I needed a job, so I went to the unemployment office, to see if they could assist me in finding a job. I wanted to demonstrate to them that I was not afraid of work, even though I just came from full time ministry.

The first job that they offered me was a job delivering phone books. You haven't been blessed if you didn't see the spectacle that I made, delivering those phone books. I didn't even own a pair of blue jeans. Here I am, driving a 1978 Oldsmobile 98, fully loaded, wearing a three piece suit, going door to door, with an arm full of phone books. I have to laugh, even now when I think of it.

Looking for a job

Before I had left Pennsylvania, I had gotten a name of an executive with Prudential Insurance, and told to get in touch with him when I got to California; so I went to Prudential, and applied for a job. I took their test, and got an interview, and was told that I had the job that I was to go to Sacramento for six weeks training, and what my starting salary was to be.

When I went home I was thinking that I needed, and would be worth more money than they were offering, for the position. So I put it to the Lord, "Lord, if this is the job that you have for me, then you will have them pay me more money. If they don't agree to pay me more money, then it was not your will for me to have this job." Then I called the contact number of the executive whose name I had been given. He said, "Ok, I'll look into it.

When I came back to meet with them as scheduled, the woman told me, "You won't be happy with us." So they withdrew the offer. There was no negotiations or any thing. So I told myself that it wasn't the Lords will that I worked for them. When I think of it I strongly feel that it was the Lord who lead me to put it to the test. Why would I, who had delivered phone books, and who didn't even have a job, refuse to accept the pay of a legitimate job, unless the Lord had led me to do so. I lost that job before I could work one day. People asked me, "Have you lost your mind? It's a job." Even I began to wonder, if I had done the right thing. (Lord help my unbelief.)

One day while talking with Annie, my youngest sister, she suggested that I try the telephone company. She was a Supervisor with AT&T, in Pennsylvania.

So I went to the employment office of Pacific Bell Telephone Company, and told them that I wanted to apply for a job. They said, "We are not accepting applications, at this time." I said, as I was leaving, "Oh well, it was worth a try. My sister who works for AT&T, back east suggested that I try here."

The woman said unto me, "Oh, you're a referral, come on back, we can let you fill out an application." The referrals have about a two to three week's advantage over those other applicants, when they start taking all applications.

At least once a week, I came back, to see if they were hiring yet. It got so that all of them in the employment office were pulling for me. One day when I came in, they told me that they had some jobs available, and scheduled me for an interview.

When they interviewed me, they asked me which job would I like, Installer, Lineman, or Splicer. I didn't know anything about the pay scales, so since I had been a Splicer back east for 14 years, I accepted that job.

As I left the office, those in the outer office asked me, "What job did you get?" I said, "the Splicer job." One of the women got upset. She said that her fiancée, who works for the company as an installer, had applied for that job. I discovered that it was the highest paid job out in the field, at that time. I was the last Splicer that would be hired in that district, for three years.

Again the Lord had favored me. Ironically, the starting pay that I would receive, was exactly the same as the pay that Prudential had offered, the training period was also six weeks, and the training was to be in Sacramento, California.

However the Lord gave me peace in accepting the job, for which I gave Him praise. I had two more tests to pass though, before the job would be mine; the medical, and the stress test.

Years ago, when I worked as a splicer back east, I got a hernia, that was so severe, that it doubled me over in pain. The doctor diagnosed it as a hernia, and said eventually I would have to have surgery. Then made out a prescription for a hernia belt that I wore all the time, until the Lord healed me. I had prayed many times for God to heal me, and one day he did. When I filled out the medical questionnaire, I put down that I had had a hernia. So when the doctor who had examined me asked me when I had surgery to remove the hernia, I replied, "I didn't have surgery." He asked, "What happened to it?" I said, "I prayed, and God healed me." He asked, "Does it ever bother you?" I said, "No." He said, "I'm going to have to examine you again, and take X-rays."

So he did. After he finished, he shaking his head said, "You're right, you don't have a hernia now. All I can see is a little fatty tissue that shows that you had previously had one. You pass. How does that make you feel? I said, "Great." Praise God! He is so good to me.

After I had worked for the company for about one year, my salary doubled over night, and I received $5000.00 retroactive pay, because of wage credit. Before the contract that was in force when I was hired to work for Pacific Bell, they would give people credit for the time that they had spent doing similar work, which meant that they would receive pay that would reflect that credit.

Normally, it would take a Splicer five and a half years to receive the maximum level of pay, receiving incremental raises, every six months.

But when the company agreed to that current contract, they decided to take it out, and opted to not offer wage credit any longer. So it was not in force when I was hired.

A year after I was hired, the company decided to put the credit for service clause back into the contract. It had not been bargained for by the union; the company just decided to put it back in on their own, **just for me**. Smile! I applied for it, and got it. Beside all this, I loved my job, and usually could work all of the over-time that I wanted. I leave it up to you to judge, was it the Lord who led me to turn down that other job, and to accept the one with Pacific Bell? You be the judge.

In March of 1980, I married Ollie Mae, who was a member of the Progressive Baptist Church, and after we were married, I joined her as a member of thee Progressive Church, where I served as an associate minister. I would often lead people to Christ, after they responded to the invitation.

One Sunday, the preacher asked all the people who were not saved to stand up. Some of them did; then he said to them, "Come on up here to the front." And as one young man, who just happened to be my Brother in Law, was coming, the preacher said to the congregation, "Isn't it great that this young man is coming to be saved." Then he sent him to go with me to the back room, to be led to Christ.

When we got in the room, I asked him, "Jerry, did you come to be saved?" He said, "No, I just came up because he told us to come, I didn't want to be disrespectful." I said, "I thought so, but if you are ready, you can be saved today." He said, "I plan to be saved some day, and I feel that it is not far away, but I am not ready today. I'm a little upset because I feel that I have been tricked, now I am too embarrassed to go back out there. I wasn't the only one that stood up, but I am the only one who came forward; I guess they knew what to expect."

How revealing those words are. What does the sinner expect, when he comes to your church? tricks, con artists, liars, or crooks. What do they expect to find.

Wouldn't it be grand, if they expect to find, a people with unswerving faith in the power of the living God. I told him that he didn't have to go back out there, until the service was over, and I would wait with him. I prayed for him and we left together after the service.

An immediate answer to prayer

I got in my car, and while driving home from church, November 15, 1981, I was so angry about what was going on; I said out loud, "Lord, you've got to get me out of this place."

One half an hour after we got home, I received a phone call from the Moderator of the St John Baptist Association. He said, "Rev. Jemison, Sister Sallie, who is the President of the Women, and widow of the late Reverend Sallie, called me from the Rock West Baptist Church in Tracy.

She said that the young minister, who had been there for only one year, has just resigned, today; and they will need a preacher for next Sunday. I told her that I would call you, to see if you would be interested."

I said, "Yes indeed, I am interested." He said, "I will have her to call you. You see, her husband was the founder of that church, and he pastored there for many years." I assured him that I would wait for her call, and thanked him for recommending me.

I got a call from Sister Sallie, and also from the Chairman of Deacons. So on the next Sunday, November 22, 1981, I preached the morning message at Rock West Missionary Baptist Church in Tracy California. My subject was, "Which Way To Heaven;" and my text was found in Acts 2:37-40, Acts 16:25-31, and Matthew 19:16-22. After that service, they asked if I could come the next Sunday, and so I did.

On November 29, 1981, when I came back, I preached the message, "How Big Is God?" My text was Joshua 1:1-9. After that second time, they asked me if I would come back again the next Sunday, three Sundays in a row.

By this time I began to be suspicious, that they were planning on calling me to become their Pastor. I was a bit troubled by that, because the Lord had told me that the name of the next church that I would pastor was Good News Missionary Baptist Church, although I knew of no church that had that name. I agreed to come back for the third time. Moderator H. F. Dean warned me that they had asked him to come to Tracy, after his morning service. He said, "Jemison, I think that they want to call you, and they want me to moderate the meeting."

I came to Tracy for the third time, December 6, 1981, and preached the message, "New Ways to Do Better Things." My text was found in Mark 2:1-12. It was right; after that service, they asked me to excuse myself from the sanctuary, because they were going to have a meeting, but not to go too far.

I left the sanctuary, and they voted to call me as their Pastor, and then called me back into the sanctuary, and informed me of their decision. I told them that I was pleased that they wanted me to be their Pastor; but there was a problem with me accepting the call. I said, "The Lord has already told me the name of the next church that I would pastor, and He has given me a program for that church. He told me that the name of the next church that I would pastor would be Good News Missionary Baptist Church."

Someone said, "Maybe He meant that you would do that, sometime in the future." I said, "No, He said that it would be the name of the next Church that I would pastor. And that church would have to agree to the program that He gave me, Project Seventy." After some discussion, someone asked, "Can't we change the name of the church to Good News?"

After further discussion, that is exactly what they did. They voted to change the name of the church, from Rock West Missionary Baptist Church to Good News Missionary Baptist Church; and they also voted to adopt Project Seventy.

I believe that this speaks volumes for Sister Elorise Sallie, the widow of the late Reverend Sallie, who founded and pastored that church for more than thirty years, and gave the church it's name.

She showed much grace, agreeing to the name change; She could have kept it from happening. God bless Sister Sallie. In January 1982, the church's name was changed to Good News, and for the next three years the church grew, both spiritually, and numerically.

Celebrating the Passover, Crucifixion, and Resurrection

In 1984, during Passover week, we decided to celebrate the Passover on the same day that it would have fell during the week that they crucified our Lord Jesus, which would be Wednesday night, beginning at 6:00 o'clock PM. We had made plans for a lamb to be slain, and his blood was to be smeared onto the lintel and the doorposts of the church, where we would be shut in, eating unleavened bread and bitter herbs, along with the roast lamb.

After midnight, I would lead a procession out of the church into the park just across the street from the church.

I would then leave the main body of the church, and take with me the twelve members of our project seventy missionaries a little farther into the park, where I would leave all but three of them, and those three and myself would go a little farther into the park; and finally I would leave them, and go farther by myself to pray.

All the while, I would have been recalling to the people, how it happened on that night of the Last Supper.

How it happened the week that Jesus died and rose again:

1. Passover celebration 6:00 PM Wednesday to 6:00 AM Thursday morning.

   A. Jesus ate the Passover with His disciples

   B. Jesus and His disciples crossed over the brook of Cedron into the garden of Gethsemane, and prays:

   C. Jesus is arrested, and brought before the High Priest, was falsely accused, beaten, and denied three times by Peter.

2. Preparation for the Passover Sabbath, which is the first day of the Feast of the Unleavened Bread, 6:00 AM Thursday morning to 6:00 PM Thursday evening. See Leviticus 23:5-7 (counted as the first day)

   A. The chief priests and the elders of the people took counsel against Jesus to put Him to death:

   B. He was led bound, and brought before Pontius Pilate the governor.

   C. Jesus tried before Pilate, found innocent, but sentenced to be crucified.

   D. Jesus was delivered to the Roman soldiers, who stripped Him, mocked Him and beat Him.

   E. Jesus is crucified, there was darkness from 12 noon to 3:00 PM, the approximate time of His death, when He laid down His life.

   F. Between 3:00 PM and 6:00 PM, Jesus' body was taken down from the cross, and buried in the new tomb of Joseph of Arimathea.

3. Passover Sabbath, or the First Day of the Feast Of the Unleavened Bread, from 6:00 PM Thursday

evening to 6:00 PM Friday evening. (counted as the first night, and the second day)

4. Regular weekly Sabbath Day, from 6:00 PM Friday evening to 6:00 PM Saturday evening. (counted as the second night and the third day)

5. The first day of the week begins at 6:00 PM Saturday night; the night ends at 6:00 AM Sunday morning. (counted as the third night)

   A. Jesus rose this night, just before morning, and during the third day, or within 72 hours of His burial. See Matthew 28:1-2, "In the end of the Sabbath, as it began to dawn toward the first day of the week, came Mary Magdalene and the other Mary to see the sepulcher. And behold, there was a great earthquake: for an angel of the Lord descended from heaven, and came and rolled back the stone from the door, and sat upon it."

6. Dawn of Sunday, the first day of the week at 6:00 AM on Sunday morning.

The Prophesy of two different earthquakes

On Wednesday, April 18, 1984, I was in my car driving to work in Turlock, California; and a voice spoke to me and said, "There will be an earthquake Tuesday." Nothing like this had ever happened before, so I didn't know what to make of it.

I knew that there was no one with me in the car, but I looked around to see anyway. I thought that it was the Lord who spoke, but I was troubled by what I had heard. "This is Wednesday," I thought, "We will know within one week, whether these words came from God or not. This is not an estimate, and we have small earthquakes all the time.

If this is from God, there will be a significant earthquake, in our vicinity, on Tuesday of next week; there is no wiggle room here, either there will be or there won't be an earthquake, and we don't have long to wait to see if it is true or not. I'm not telling any one this. I'm not going to embarrass myself, or the church." But I did tell it. I told my buddy Dennis, with whom I worked, what I had heard in the car, on my way to work.

When he heard it, he said, "What have you been smoking Dave?" I laughed and said, "I know, but that is what I heard, and I said that I was not going to tell anybody, but here I am telling you." Dennis said, If I were you Dave, I wouldn't tell anybody else."

In my mind, I agreed with him. But I felt that I was between a rock and a hard place, because if it was God who told me that, and I knew that I had not imagined it, then He told it to me for a reason. If He told it to me, then I am to glorify Him by telling it. Yet it wasn't like many of the prophesies that I had heard that were so nebulous that you wouldn't notice if they came true or not, or there was no given time frame, so that all that you had to do is wait until there is some significant earthquake, and then say "That was it."

This was either a time for me to glorify the Lord by telling it, within a week of it happening, or a time to embarrass myself, by predicting an event that would not happen. I thought, "What is God doing, and why is He doing it?" All day long my thoughts troubled me.

That evening at 6:00 PM we began our celebration of the Passover, and commemoration of the crucifixion and resurrection of our Lord Jesus. The blood of the lamb was on the lintels and doorposts of our Church, and we were all inside. We ate bitter herbs, unleavened bread and roast lamb.

After eating we went back into the sanctuary, and began singing, praying, and testifying to the goodness of the Lord.

While the members were testifying, I was sitting by myself, along the right wall, and again that voice spoke to me, "There will be an earthquake Tuesday, and many people are going to die." This time I was pretty sure that it was the Lord speaking.

However, due to the exactness of the prophesy, I felt that I needed to be absolutely sure; so I said to the Lord, "Lord, I believe that it is you speaking to me, but I want to be sure; I don't want to embarrass you or myself, so if it is you, please let Sister Dorthy Wilson be the next person to give her testimony." The very next person to give their testimony was Sister Dorthy Wilson. I said, "Lord it is you, and I will tell it."

After a while, I got up and told the church of both occasions that the Lord had spoken to me, and of the fleece that I had put before him, for assurance that it was He that spoke to me.

The Morgan Hill 1984 Earthquake

The members just looked at me as if to say, "I think that our pastor has gone too far now; there is no way for him to get out of this, if it does not happen."

But on Tuesday April 24, 1984, there was an earthquake that measured 6.2 on the Richter scale, at the time, but later upgraded to a 6.4, with the epicenter located at Morgan Hill, California, not very far from our church in Tracy.

When the people came back to the church on the Sunday after Resurrection Day, many of them said, "Pastor, the next time that you tell us that the Lord has told you something, we will believe you. By the way, Has He told you anything else?" As I stood in the pulpit that Sunday, I said to them, "Church, I thought that this was one prophecy, spoken twice; but it wasn't. The Lord sent and told us about this earthquake, that we would know that the next earthquake would surely come. Only one person died in this earthquake.

There will be another earthquake in the Bay Area, on a Tuesday, and many people will die. He sent this earthquake as a warning, that the next one would surely come."

While living in East Palo Alto, I had a problem with my income taxes, and had made arrangements with the IRS to pay them, on a schedule; but they broke the agreement and seized the money in my bank account, and took my pay, leaving me with nothing.

I was so angry, angrier than I had ever been. I called a friend, Sister Margaret Tookes, who lived back east, and who had been a member of the Mount Olive Baptist Church, in Midland Pennsylvania. She said, "How are you?" I said, "Angry!" She asked, "What is the matter?" I said, "These people make me sick. They think that they can get away with anything, because of who they are; but they don't know who my God is.

The IRS took my money, after I had made arrangements to pay them in payments. But in Matthew 16:19 Jesus said, And I will give unto thee the keys of the kingdom of heaven: and whatsoever thou shall bind on earth shall be bound in heaven: and whatsoever thou shall loose on earth, shall be loosed in heaven; and I'm binding this, and when God gets through them, they won't know what hit them." Margaret said, " I'm going to pray too."

So I began to pray, while she was still on the phone, "Lord, you see what they have done to me. I'm bringing this matter to you and I am binding it in the name of Jesus Christ, and I'm asking you to take care of it; and please do whatever you deem necessary to do, that they may know that you are God, and you are God all by Yourself. There is none like you, and they can't treat your people just anyway. Amen!" And Margaret said, "Amen!"

The Loma Prieta 1989 Earthquake

It was Tuesday, October 17, 1989, and within a minute of finishing my prayer, the earth began to tremble beneath my feet, and then the floor began to shake, and I jumped up out of the chair that I was sitting in, and that was just in front of a sliding glass door, to move away from the glass, that I feared would shatter.

I said to Margaret, while I was seeking shelter, "We are having an earthquake, and I'm going to hang up and leave the building." She said, "Please don't hang up, because if you do, we won't be able to get in touch with you after the earthquake for a long time, and we won't know what happened to you." I said, "All right but I'm moving into the hallway for protection.

The books are flying out of the bookcase, and dishes are flying out of the china closet; My God this is a bad one; I know that some things are going to be down, somewhere. I can hear sounds, like the sound of nails being pulled out of boards. My God, why doesn't it stop, its still going on. I know that some of these buildings will be down. It has finally stopped, I'm ok, and I'm going to hang up, and get out of this building now." So I hanged the phone up, and ran out into the parking lot, expecting to see some of the buildings in our apartment complex to have been collapsed. But to my amazement, they were all standing. I said, "Thank God."

It wasn't until then, that I remembered that I had just finished praying that angry prayer. It was the Loma Prieta earthquake, which was originally measured at 6.9 on the Richter scale, but later upgraded to 7.1, during which 63 people died, more than 3,500 were injured, and over 100,000 buildings were damaged, and initially, over 12,000 people were made homeless. The Cypress Freeway collapsed, as well as a section of the bay bridge.

I realize now that it was all a set up. This was the other earthquake that the Lord had said would happen, during which many people would die; and again, it was on a Tuesday, and at a time when the entire world would be watching. Just as the World Series began, the earthquake struck, with all the world watching.

To make sure that I would not miss it, the Lord let them do to me what they did, knowing all the time, what I would do about it. I'm very slow to anger, and when I do get angry, I try to sin not. The Lord knew that I would pray, and that He would answer with an earthquake. He knew that I would call Margaret, and that she would be a witness, so that everything could be established with two witnesses.

John 8:17 says, "It is also written in your law, that the testimony of two men is true." Deuteronomy 19:15 says, "One witness shall not rise up against a man for iniquity, or for any sin, in any sin that he sinneth: at the mouth of two witnesses, or at the mouth of three witnesses, shall the matter be established." The second prophecy came true, just like He said it would; and the Lord made sure that I did not miss it, and that it was witnessed by another Christian.

It wasn't until many years later that the Lord showed me that the first time that He told me that there would be an earthquake Tuesday, that He did so on the seventy eighth anniversary of the 1906 earthquake, to the minute. The 1906 earthquake happened on Wednesday, April 18, 1906, at 5:12 AM Pacific Standard time.

The Lord spoke to me on Wednesday, April 18, at about 6:12 AM Pacific Daylight Saving time, which is precisely the same time. I was to begin work at 6:30 AM that day. On the day that the Lord spoke to me, I had no idea of what day, or at what time that the 1906 earthquake happened. But isn't it amazing, that the Lord can and does predict when earthquakes will happen, and could it be that He even causes some of them to happen?

I find it interesting that there was an earthquake, when Jesus died, and there was also one when He rose from the dead. When Paul and Silas were in jail, at midnight, while they sang songs and prayed, there was an earthquake, and they and all of the other prisoners' stocks were loosed. **What a mighty God we serve!**

From Good News of Tracy, to Second Baptist of Modesto

In 1984 I was led to resign as pastor, because I felt that the people had stopped following, and were trying to lead. I gave a four months notice, and called for a month of prayer. We had already scheduled a revival service, with the Reverend Robert Porter as the evangelist. During the month of prayer, I traveled twenty five miles each way, every night from Modesto to Tracy and back, to be there in prayer for our church.

To my dismay, only about one third of the members showed up to pray for the church, and some of the leading members of the church stayed home.

Had the members shown me that they were willing to work with their pastor to build up the church, I was willing to withdraw my resignation. Because of the no show, the resignation stood. My wife and I left this church and went and joined the Second Baptist Church of Modesto; and Good News called a minister that I had ordained to serve with me there as one of my Assistant Pastors, Reverend B. Edwards.

When we joined Second Baptist, the church had just gone through a split, and most of the members had left the church, and acquired another church building, and called a pastor, and seemed to be doing quite well.

In Second Baptist Church, you could probably throw a stone into the church, and not hit anyone; there were just that few people there. After serving there for a year with Reverend Clark, the pastor, people started joining the church, and even most of the people, who had left and started another church, came back, and asked the church's forgiveness.

Each Sunday, for quite sometime, there were no less than ten people joining the church. It wasn't long before the church was full.

There was a job surplus on my job, and I was forced to accept a job with the company, in the bay area. I tried as hard as I could to find a job on the list of available jobs, on my side of the San Francisco Bay; but because of my low seniority, I was forced to accept a job in San Francisco.

When I looked the jobs over, I saw that there were multiple openings in several locations, and in one location there was only one opening. I asked myself, "Why is that?" I surmised that in the places where there were several opening, that the people were trying to get away from there; and in the place where there was only one opening, it was because the people had more than fifteen years of seniority, because that is where they want to be. They never left that location willingly.

So I put in for that job, and got it. It was maintenance splicing. I had spent six years as a Construction Splicer. I put new cables together and connected them to the existing cable, and to the central offices. I loved the work that I did, but I had thought that I would have been working for the company for only about three or four years; and then I would be pastoring full time, but not so.

Maintenance Splicing in San Francisco, I found to be a very pleasant thing for me. My jobs would sometimes require me to be in as many as ten different places, in beautiful San Francisco, in the same day. Sometime I would be at Fisherman's Wharf, then I would be on Knob Hill, then I might go to Golden Gate Park, then from there, perhaps down along the ocean front. Then sometime I would be in part of China Town.

One of the most memorable places that I have been was up on one hill, on the street where I had to work at the De Wilt mansion, which had been reportedly sold to Jim Willingbourg, who purchased it for more than four million dollars, and who planned to earthquake proof the mansion for another four million dollars. The neighbors were the Getty family.

The De Wilts, who were Dutch royalty, had owned the De Wilt mansion. This mansion was sometimes used in movies. Then there was the excitement of being held up, because they were shooting a movie in the city.

One day while working in Golden Gate Park, when I picked up my trouble ticket for the defective circuit; my trouble led me to the headquarters of the Park police, who were mounted policemen.

I was having a hard time isolating the cause of the problem, and I had to go inside to ask one of the officers if he knew where the termination point was for that building. He was only partially dressed, and he couldn't say where it was.

I drove out to the main street to that termination point to get a reading, and to put a tone on a clear line. I got up in my bucket and lifted myself to the splice and terminal to work.

After I entered the splice, I heard all kinds of sirens going off, and several police cars and fire trucks, were rushing into the park, where I had just come from. I said to myself, "Oh Lord, I must have set off an alarm; I better go and let them know." I closed the terminal and splice quickly, got down and jumped into my truck, my heart was pounding. "What are they going to say when I tell them that I am to blame?" I said to myself, as I drove back into the park.

I saw that all of them were parked around the building that I had just left, with all of their lights flashing. "Boy I have really done it now," I thought. A policeman stopped me and I leaned my head out the window of the cab of my truck and said, "Officer, I think that I may be the cause of what has happened."

He quickly stepped back and reached for his gun. And with his hand still on his gun, he said, "What do you mean?" I knew that this could be bad, but I didn't think that it would cause me to be shot over it. I said, "I am working on some of the telephone lines, and I may have set off an alarm." He said, "No, you didn't do anything." I asked him, "What happened?" He hesitated, and then he said, "An officer has been shot." "My God," I thought, "an officer has been shot, and here I come confessing; it's a wonder he didn't shoot me."

I was glad that I wasn't shot, and I was glad that I didn't cause them to come.

But when I think of it, I would rather have been the cause of the trouble, than for it to have been what it was. A man was killed. One officer had accidentally shot the other. One had just bought a gun and was showing it off. The gun went off and the bullet went through the other officer's head, and killed him.

When I got there the officer who had done the shooting was sitting on the side of the building holding his head in his hands. The officer who got shot was the same officer that I had asked directions from. To think that only about fifteen or twenty minutes earlier, I was in that building, talking to the man that had just got shot. He had been in such a great spirit, and suddenly he is dead. When I drove away, I was just hoping that he was saved.

The joy of commuting, from Oakland to San Francisco:

When the company had first sent me to San Francisco, they provided temporary living for me for up to 45 days. I chose to live in Oakland, at a motel, which was cheaper, but not bad, and which was near some nice restaurants. Also, it was closer to my home in Modesto.

When I would go home on weekends, I wouldn't have as far to go. To get to work, I had to travel over the Cypress Freeway to the San Francisco Bay Bridge, which I would cross to get to my job in San Francisco.

No one had prepared me for that first Monday morning commute, from Oakland to my job during rush hour traffic.

This country boy thought that he would lose his mind in that crazy traffic. My stress level was off the charts.

On my second day commuting into the city, I rear-ended someone, just before getting onto the bridge. I was still driving my 1978 Oldsmobile 98, and when the woman got out of her car, to see if there was any damage, when she saw my car, she grabbed her neck. I asked her if she was all right; she said, "My neck hurts." We both looked at the damage, and there was none. I knew that she was faking an injury, because I hadn't hit her car that hard.

I had to ask the Lord's forgiveness for what I did next. I told her that I didn't have any insurance, and asked her if we could drive to the other side of the bridge, and settle up, before the police came. She said that she didn't have any insurance either, and agreed to get the information on the San Francisco side of the bridge. So we got back into our cars, and I followed her to the other side.

As soon as we could, we pulled over to the side of the street, and exchanged information. I told her to go to the doctor, and get checked, and if there was any expense, I would take care of it. And so she went her way, and I went my way. I never heard from her again; but I had lied, because I knew that she was lying. I did have insurance, but I didn't want her taking advantage of me.

It was times like this that I was glad that we are saved by grace. If it was by works, I would have missed it then, because of my lie. I don't condone lying, but this time, the wisdom that I had asked God to give me was kicking in. A liar puts a truthful person at a disadvantage, because they don't mind lying, and will lie as much as they need to, in order to get what they want.

Again, the Lord was good to me, because rent in San Francisco is so high; but a member of Second Baptist Church, who was also a cousin to our Pastor, had a sister who lived in the city. That sister was living in a two bedroom co-op apartment, and had just undergone open heart surgery, and needed someone to stay with her, just in case something happened. Furthermore, the little extra money would help her.

The complex was on the corner of, Gough, and McAllister. I was able to get that room, having the use of the whole apartment, for only $225.00 a month. I checked the apartments just across Gough, and they were renting a one room apartment for $1200.00 a month. The Lord was really blessing me; I could stay there thru the week, and then go home for the weekend. Since we were still paying a mortgage on our home in Modesto, I counted this low rent to be a blessing to me, and financially feasible.

Two inches from dying

Early, one Monday morning, after having been home with my wife over the weekend, and while I was up preparing to drive into the city, to go to work.

There was a strong earthquake. It felt like some great giant had taken our home, lifted it up from the foundation, and was shaking it. I took cover, and warned my wife, who was still in bed to take cover.

After it was all over, I checked all around the house, and everything was still intact. I am very sensitive to earthquakes, and was very shaken by this one. I drove into the city, to my job.

When I got there I got into my truck and drove to my first job assignment. I parked my truck, which was an aerial lift truck, in a place where I could reach the pole mounted termination point. I got out and set out my safety equipment, to form a safety zone around my work area. I put on my hard hat, got up into the bucket, and lifted myself to the terminal. I found my cable problem, fixed it, and began to come down.

On my way down, something knocked my hard hat off, and it fell down onto the street below. I looked up to see what it was that had knocked my hat off; and I was shocked to see that it had been knocked off by the trolley wire, that I had parked beneath. I must have been so shook up from that earthquake, that I had paid no attention to where I had parked.

The rim of my hat was no more than two inches wide, and that trolley wire got under the rim of my hat as I was coming down, and knocked it off. I came within two inches of dying. If that wire had touched my skin, I would have died. As a matter of fact, if any part of my boom or bucket had touched it, I would have died. Our trucks are not insulated, and the voltage in those trolley wires is too great for the tires on the truck to insulate.

Any voltage greater than 400 volts, would work its way down through the carbon in the tires, and would go to ground, blowing out the tires. I would have been dead. God, and God alone kept me from dying that day, but he let my hat be knocked off, so that I would know how close that I came to death.

And to make matters worse, one of the most beautiful women that I had ever laid my eyes on, was across the street when it happened. She slowly glided across the street towards my hat, bent over and picked it up; and by the time that I had lowered my boom, and set it down in it's cradle, she was looking up in my face, and handed me my hat. I thanked her and she said, "You're very welcome." and walked away.

Just then, I said to myself, "My God, if Satan can't kill me, he tries to get me through temptation.

But you better believe that I was really thanking God for sparing my life that day. If I never had a problem, I'd never know that God could solve them.

And all of these dreams, visions, miracles, signs, and wonders, has my God worked, and many more. His care is constant.

Chapter 13

Being contagious for God and having something worth catching

The salvation of God is a communicable disease. In Jeremiah 20:8-9 the prophet says, "For since I spake, I cried out, I cried violence and spoil; because the Word of the Lord was made a reproach unto me, and a derision daily. Then I said, I will not make mention of Him, nor speak any more in His name.

But His Word was in my heart as a burning fire shut up in my bones, and I was weary with forbearing, and I could not stay." But in Jeremiah 20:11 he says, "But the Lord is with me as a mighty terrible one: therefore my persecutors shall stumble, and they shall not prevail: they shall be greatly ashamed; for they shall not prosper: their everlasting confusion shall never be forgotten."

When we **repent** of our sins, and **receive** the Lord Jesus as our Savior, it does not mean that the world will be kinder to us; on the contrary, they will often be meaner to us than ever before; but the Lord will be kinder to us. As a matter of Truth, He will provide for us, and will protect, and fight for us. The Word of God says in Romans 8:28, "And we know that all things work together for good to them that love God, to them who are the called according to His purpose."

Romans 8:31 says, "What shall we then say to these things? If God be for us, who can be against us?"

So we, who are on God's side, have the assurance that the Lord is on our side. He did not say that we would not have any problems, but He said that we would have tribulations, but that we are to fear not, for He has overcome the world.

After His resurrection, and just before His ascension into Heaven, our Lord declares in Matthew 28:18-20, "All power is given unto me in heaven and in earth. Go ye therefore, and teach all nations, baptizing them in the name of the Father, and of the Son, and of the Holy Ghost: Teaching them to observe all things whatsoever I have commanded you: and, lo I am with you always, even unto the end of the world. Amen." The one who goes with us, Jesus, has all power in his hand.

In other words, He is able to control every power that might be formed to be against us, both in heaven, and in earth. Therefore those weapons and devises, will not prosper. Isaiah 54:17 says, "No weapon that is formed against thee shall prosper; and every tongue that shall rise against thee in judgment thou shalt condemn. This is the heritage of the servants of the Lord, and their righteousness is of me, saith the Lord."

The greatest thing that a Christian can do is to bear fruit, to win lost souls to Jesus Christ. In John 14:6, "Jesus saith unto him, I am the way, the truth, and the life: no man cometh unto the Father but by me." When we lead a soul to Jesus, we are leading them unto the Way to the Father, the Truth about God the Father, and to the Eternal Life, which is the Gift of God.

Acts 4:12 says, "Neither is there salvation in any other: for there is none other name" (other than the name Jesus,) "under heaven given among men, whereby we must be saved." A major problem in the Christian movement is, **not everyone** who says that he or she is a Christian is truly saved; which means that they have not been given in Christ. And if they have not been given in Christ, then they cannot bear fruit; for we cannot bear fruit of ourselves. And yet many of them are convinced that they are Christians.

In Matthew 7:21-23 Jesus said, "Not every one that saith unto me Lord, Lord, shall enter into the kingdom of heaven; but he that doeth the will of my Father which is in heaven. Many will say to me in that day, Lord, Lord, have we not prophesied in thy name? And in thy name have cast out devils?

And in thy name done many wonderful works? And then will I profess unto them, I never knew you: depart from me, ye that work iniquity." **Who are these people?** They are standing in the judgment; and even then, they are convinced that they had,

1. Prophesied, in the name of Jesus,
2. Cast out devils, in the name of Jesus, and
3. Done many wonderful works, in the name of Jesus.

And they are so convinced that they had done so, that they are calling on Jesus, to verify that what they said is true: as though Jesus was with them, when they were doing those things, or as if He was an eye witness to these things. Jesus' response to them is;

1. I **never** knew you,
2. Depart from me,
3. You are the ones that work iniquity.

To me these are some of the **scariest** words in all of the Bible.

Jesus is saying, in response to their question; I don't acknowledge any acquaintance with you, I don't admit to having any relationship with you, not now, or ever. I don't want you near me; and I banish you from my presence, which would have entitled you to my grace. And if you really want to know what I think of you; for the record, you are those people who have been working iniquity. Your work was in opposition to all that I was saying, and doing. You were standing in the way of people who were trying to find their way to me. In other words, *Go to Hell*.

After you are called to the judgment, is not the time to check with Jesus, to see if you are doing the right thing; you need to check with him now, while the blood is still running warm in your veins, and you still have time to get right.

We will do this when we stop trying to be in charge, and let the Lord Jesus be the Lord of our lives. I don't know what it was, that made these people feel that they were doing God a service. They may have had fun doing it, and it may even have been contagious; but whatever it was, **it wasn't worth catching**. Only that which is God given, is worth catching.

The best part of everlasting life, is the beginning; because if you don't have a beginning, you don't have anything else. Everything you do, apart from having everlasting life, means nothing; and Everlasting Life is the Gift of God; you cannot merit it. The only way that you can begin to have everlasting life is to believe on the Lord Jesus, our Savior. In John 6:47 Jesus said, "Verily, verily, I say unto you, He that believeth on me hath everlasting life." You must be born again.

In John 3:6-8 Jesus said, "That which is born of the flesh is flesh; and that which is born of the Spirit is spirit. Marvel not that I said unto thee, Ye must be born again. The wind bloweth where it listeth, (wants to) and thou hearest the sound thereof, but canst not tell whence it cometh, and whither it goeth: so is every one that is born of the Spirit."

You must be baptized into the body of Christ, by the Holy Spirit. In 1 Corinthians 12:12-13 it says, "For as the body is one, and hath many members, and all the members of that one body, being many, are one body: so also is Christ. For by one Spirit are we all baptized into one body, whether we be Jews or Gentiles, whether we be bond or free; and have been all made to drink into one Spirit."

There are those who think that they can work to earn their salvation. There is a work that can lead to everlasting life. John 6:28-29 says, "Then said they unto Him, What shall we do, that we might work the works of God? Jesus answered and said unto them, **This is the work of God, that ye believe on Him whom HE hath sent.**"

PART 4:
THE MYSTERY OF DESTINY,
IN THE HANDS OF A LOVING
GOD:

Chapter 14

God directs the life of my wife Marie:

Whether she was always aware of it or not, the Lord was directing my present wife's life. There were many painful things that she had to endure in life; but those things would serve to make her to be the woman that she is now.

She and her sister had to grow up in a broken home, being pulled from one home, living with her father, aunt, uncle, and grandmother, in Birmingham, Alabama, to another home, living with her mother, stepfather, and half brother and sisters, in Washington Pennsylvania.

When she was very young, this was a very traumatizing experience for her, which caused those who loved her to worry that she would not even live through it. However, she did live through it all, and became a beautiful young lady.

When she was about fifteen years old, she came to Washington Pa. Where she lived with her mother, and where she would eventually meet her first husband, the late Homer Patterson. Her mother owned the local store there, and Marie would tend to the store for her mother. At the age of sixteen, she married Homer, and gave birth to seven children in that union. One of those children died at birth. At the age of twenty four, Marie had given birth to all of her children; and she was separated from her husband, who left her and was living with another woman, who lived next door. But the Lord helped her to raise those children by herself, and yet manage to get her G.E.D., and to become a nurse.

She got saved and the Lord filled her with the Holy Ghost, and she began to lead a life of serving the Lord. She did day work, worked in a halfway house for troubled youth, worked with the city mission, and managed a mission store, in which the Lord used her to touch many lives, through prayer, and counseling. Marie, the woman whom I love as my wife, is by the grace of God, a survivor. She was sixteen, and I was thirteen, when I beheld her face for the first time.

Chapter 15

God directs my life and orders my steps:

In the year 1950, when I was a lad of 13 years of age, I was living in the coal-mining town of Westland, Pennsylvania. I will always have fond memories of that little town, where everybody knew everybody. We raised food in our own gardens, and raised hogs and chickens. Not everyone raised their own food, but I was blessed with parents who knew how to do it, and had enough of get up and go to do it. I never really knew a hungry day in my life; and people with families much smaller than ours would sometimes come to my parents for some food.

After school, and on weekends, we young people would find various ways to amuse ourselves.

Some times we would go up into the woods, and swing on the grape vines like Tarzan, or would spend some time at our log cabin that we built, go swimming in the creek, or the abandoned strip mine that had been flooded with water coming from the many springs that fed it.

Some times we would take a broom handle, or a mop handle, and some soda pop tops and play ball with them. I always loved to pitch, because you could make those tops do some incredible curves, drops, and such; and using a boom handle for a bat made it quite a challenge to get a hit. This is the kind of wholesome environment that I grew up in.

Although I did so many things with my friends, and playmates, I was aware, at a very early age, that there was something different about me, when compared with other boys my age.

When I was quite young, I would daydream about being married, having a job, and having children. To my knowledge, boys my age didn't do that; I was a very serious young lad; but I knew how to have fun.

One evening, when I was coming up the street to my home, I noticed an automobile sitting out in front of our home. As I walked past it to go into my home, I noticed a young girl, who appeared to be about my age, sitting in the back seat of the car , alone; and she was looking back at me. Immediately, something leaped within me, and I began to get excited. I had recognized the car.

Sometimes my future brother in law would come with some of his friends, in that car. Many times I would go places with them, and they would be paired off, and I would be alone. So now I was excited, because I thought that they were bringing her to me.

When I got inside the house, I asked my sister, "Who is that girl sitting outside in the car?" She looked out the window and said, "Ah, that's Homer's wife." When she said that, I felt like someone had stabbed me to the heart. I said to myself, "That girl is my age, what is Homer doing with her? He already has somebody."

I felt like someone had broken up my love affair, with someone whose name I didn't even know. I was a strange kid indeed.

Then my sister scolded Homer for leaving her out in the car, and went out and told her to come on into the house. So she came in; and was sitting in a room by herself, and I continued looking at her, peeping around the corner from time to time.

I did not lay eyes on her again until 1959, when I was 21 years old, married, but was having problems in my marriage, and was the father of one precious daughter, who was the apple of my eye. A friend of mine wanted me to take him someplace in Washington, Pa.; it was in the afternoon, and we ended up at this club. He had come to see a particular person, who came in a little while after we had got there.

She came in, and was accompanied with this tall, attractive woman, who caught my eye, immediately. I knew the woman that he had gone there to meet.

My friend and I were seated at a table together, and his friend and her friend that she came in with were sitting at another table together. He went over to talk with her, as I sat still at our table, listening to the music.

Then I thought that the tall woman that came in with my friend's friend, probably seldom got to dance with someone taller than she; so I went over to her and asked her to dance with me.

She was a quiet woman, and I enjoyed dancing with her. Later I asked my friend's friend to dance with me. While I was dancing with her, I said, "I kind of like your friend, but I feel that I would be robbing the cradle with her. She said, "How old do you think that she is?" I said, "sixteen. How old is she?" She said, "Maybe you better ask her."

The next time that I danced with her, I asked her. To my amazement, she told me that she was twenty four years old, and had given birth to seven children. You could have bought and sold me for a dollar. She told me that she and her husband were separated, and that she had lost one child at birth, and was raising her six children by herself.

We would run into each other three or four times again, after that day just by chance, but whenever I would see her, I would dump whoever I was with, at the time, and would invite her to come and sit with me. She didn't drink, smoke, or curse; so I enjoyed being with her. We had a lot in common; She didn't drink, and I was trying to stop drinking; she didn't smoke, and I was trying to stop smoking. She didn't curse, and I was trying to stop cursing. I felt that it was good for me to be with her.

When I was with her, I didn't drink, smoke, or curse. We talked a lot, and although I found out that she had been married to Homer, it wasn't until later that I realized that she was the same young girl, that had sat out in front of our house, in the back seat of that car, that had stolen my heart, the first time that ever I saw her face.

Though we were with each other those few times, we had never kissed, petted, had sex with each other, or even been alone with each other. She had told me that she didn't want to do to any other woman, what had been done to her.

Nearly a year had gone by, and changes had been made in my life, and so I began to stay away from those places. Most of the times that I would go to them, I would not see her. I was trying to repent; or rather I had repented, and was trying to clean up my life.

I had stopped drinking, smoking, and cursing, but after a long while, I found myself back in Washington, about to get into deep trouble, and then I saw Marie, and I dumped the woman that I was with, and asked Marie to come and sit with me. I later drove her home; and while saying good by to her standing on the sidewalk, I kissed her for the very first time.

This woman, who had given birth to seven children, did not even know how to kiss. I held her in my arms and gave her one of those long kisses. She then pushed back and said, "I can't breathe." I said to myself, " I can't believe that in this day and age, that there could be a woman such as this." At this moment I said to myself, "that's it; I'm never going to leave this woman again. What ever it takes, I'm going to be with her." Then I asked myself, "Would you marry a woman with six children?" After thinking about it for a while, I said, "Yes I would." But God had other plans.

There were times that I would get in my car and go less than two blocks to buy a loaf of bread, and would then drive eight miles, just to drive past her house, hoping that I would catch a glimpse of her on her porch, or something. I never did.

It wasn't very long before I began to be under great conviction, until finally, the Lord saved me. Immediately after the Lord saved me, I was so excited and happy that I told the Lord, "I'm going to share this with Marie." And the Lord spoke to me and said, "No you're not. Pray for her and I will send somebody else." I said, "Ok."

I feared that I might fail the Lord, because of the strong feelings that I had for Marie, but God is faithful. The next thing that I knew, six months had gone by, and I hadn't given one thought to Marie. The next time that I saw her it was at the Nazareth Baptist Church. She was singing in the choir, and I was in the ministry.

It would be five or six years later, before I would see her again. I was pastoring the First Baptist Church, in Gallatin Pa.. I had a car load of young people, which I took with me to a service at the First Baptist Church of Donora Pennsylvania. And to my amazement, I saw someone, sitting in the choir stand, and singing with the choir, who looked just like Marie. After the service, I asked someone who had been singing with the choir, "Do you have someone in your choir named Marie Patterson?" She said, "Yes. She told me that you were her old boyfriend." If my skin color was much lighter, you would have seen my face turn red. Smile!

While we were fellowshipping, she came over to me, and we talked a little. I asked her how her children were doing, none of which I had ever seen. She said that they were all doing fine, and pointed out the two that were sticking pretty close to her.

As we left, while driving the young people back to Gallatin, one of them asked, "Rev Jemison, who was that woman that we saw you talking to?; and she was pretty too." I just said, "Oh you kids are crazy."

I didn't see her again until about 1972, or 1973. Her pastor, whom I knew, had died; and I traveled from Midland Pennsylvania, where I was serving as the pastor of the Mount Olive Baptist Church, to Donora, for his funeral. When the funeral service was over, people were all on the sidewalk, preparing to go to the cemetery. As I was about to get into my car, Marie walked up to me and asked, "Are you going to the cemetery?" I thought about it for a while, and then said no. I felt that my time would be better served talking with her and finding out how she and her children were doing, since I had been praying for them, down through the years.

So we stood on the sidewalk, watching the funeral procession leave without us. We updated each other, about how each of our families were doing, and what was happening in our families.

Then I drove back to Midland. As I went, I felt tears come to my eyes, tears of concern and admiration for her raising those children, all by herself. She had been estranged from her mother, sisters, and brother; and she had no other relatives anywhere near her to even talk to. I prayed for God to take care of them, and to provide for them; because I wasn't there to do for them. I had my own family to provide for. This was not the first time that I had prayed that prayer. I would not see her again until after the first Sunday in August, 1995, and after having lived in Modesto, Ca., then San Francisco, then Palo Alto, California, and while living in Santa Clara California, when the Lord spoke to me concerning her.

On that day, after three broken marriages, and one broken engagement, and after I had told the Lord that if it was his will for me to remain single, and celibate, I will do it; and 45 years after I was smitten, when I laid my eyes on her for the first time; the Lord spoke to me and told me to call Marie. I asked Him, "Where?" And He said, "The last place that you saw her.

What I didn't know was, since the last time that I had seen her, she had left First Baptist, had been a member of several different churches, of different denominations, and had moved to Birmingham, Alabama, with plans of staying there, and all before the Lord had commanded her to go back to the First Baptist Church of Donora.

When I called that Sunday morning, I had forgotten the name of the church, and called the St Paul Baptist Church instead. When the pastor answered, I told him that I was trying to get in touch with Marie Patterson. He said, "You got the wrong church. This is St Paul, she is a member of the First Baptist Church." Then he gave me the telephone number of the First Baptist Church. When I called First Baptist, and asked if I could speak with her, the lady who answered the phone said, "She's right here." Marie was standing six feet away from the phone.

My father was ill, and I knew that I was going to Pennsylvania to see him. When Marie came to the phone, I told her who I was, and thanked her for the positive roll that she had played in my life.

Then I informed her that I was scheduled to come to Pennsylvania to visit my father, and that I would like to see her while I was there, and perhaps meet somewhere for dinner. We agreed to meet at Bob Evans restaurant, in Washington Pa. at four PM Sunday, two weeks from that day.

I didn't tell her that the pastor of the St Paul Baptist Church, when he heard of my coming to the area, invited me to come to their church that Sunday morning to preach: even though she had to drive right past the door of that church to get to her own church. I didn't want to send any wrong signals to her, myself, or anybody else.

So after church service, we would both be driving from the same town to the town and place where we said that we would meet. I was praying that the Lord would be leading me.

I didn't know her, and she didn't know me, and I didn't want to get entangled with something that was not of the Lord. I had made enough mistakes to last a lifetime.

When I got to Washington, I knew that I had about an hour and a half, time to kill; so I went across the street to the mall. I wanted to see if I could find some appropriate gift that I could give her. I ran into my sister at the mall, and spent some time talking with her. I asked her if she had any suggestions, as to what to get for her. She said perfume is always in order, so I bought her some perfume.

I got caught up in the traffic, crossing over the street to get to the restaurant, and got there about five minutes late. I wasn't sure what she looked like, so I asked the hostess if there was a lady there who was waiting for someone to join her.

She said, "yes," but she had told me that she was going to wait only five minutes more, and then she was going to leave. The hostess led me to her table, and I greeted her with an embrace, and then sat down.

She was wearing glasses, so she looked a little different from what I had expected her to look like. I told her, "I'm glad you came." She said, "If you had been another five minutes late, I would have been gone."

I'm sure that is what she believed, but there is one thing that I knew; it wasn't my intention to be late, for even five minutes, but I had it by divine revelation; if I had been one hour late, she would not have left that restaurant, and if she had, she would have returned.

I told her, "You weren't going anywhere." She said, "You don't know me, I would have been gone." I said, "I don't know you, but I know the Lord, and he wasn't going to let you go anywhere." We ordered our food, and talked while we ate. She took off her glasses, and I said, "Oh, there you are, hiding behind those glasses." After we finished eating, we continued to sit and talk.

Then I said, "Lets give up this table, so that someone else can be seated. So we went to my car, and I just drove around while we talked. I drove through the town where my father lived, and kept on driving until we came to this park. I pulled into the park, where we sat and continued to talk.

Then we got out and began to walk around, holding hands. All the time, I was trying to keep the reigns on myself, and to guard my heart.

Then we got back into the car, and I started driving back to Washington, and her car, which was about twenty, or twenty five miles away, stopping only to get some ice cream along the roadside. When we got back to her car, she got in, and drove back to her home in Donora; and I got back into my car, and drove back to my fathers house in Westland. A couple of days later, I got on a plane and went back to my home in California.

We kept in contact with each other by phone, and later in the year, the last of October, I went back to Westland to see my father. Each day while I was there, I went and picked up Marie, after her job as manager of the mission store, and we would come to be at the bed side of my ailing father, and then I would drive her back home, and return to my fathers house.

That was a thirty mile trip, each way; and I did it each day while I was there. I felt that we needed all the time that we could get, to be with each other, and to try to get to know each other. It was during this period that I was led to propose to her, and she said, "yes." We didn't set a date, believing that the Lord would help us to work it out. Again, I got on the plane and flew back to my home in Santa Clara, California, and we stayed in touch by telephone.

Marie shared our engagement with her family and friends; and Karen, a lady friend, with whom Marie had once worked, came to Marie and said that she believed that the Lord was leading her to get an airplane ticket to San Francisco, Ca., and to give it to Marie, to come and visit me.

Karen and her husband had been trying for years, with no success, to have a child. Marie prayed for her, that the Lord would bless their union with a child. On November 18, 1995, Marie flew to California, and we were married in the Genesis Baptist Church, in Sacramento California, on November 24, 1995. Dr. Robert Porter performed the ceremony.

On July 30, 1996, Karen gave birth to a bouncing baby girl, who is the delight of her and her husband's lives. Their daughter Kaitlyn is a sweetheart.

My wife and I are grateful for Karen and her family, and we use this opportunity, to pray God's continued blessing upon Karen and her family. May the salvation, and the blessings of God be upon them, even now. Amen!

Sometimes, you think that you can't get there from here, but if the Lord has planned it as your destiny, all of the devils in hell cannot prevent it from happening. This coming November, we will have been married to each other for ten years.

Chapter 16

Satan means it for evil, but God means it for good:

Being a person of destiny may mean that things won't go the way that you planned, or maybe not even go the way that you think that they should have gone. We are the sum total of our failures and our successes, along with divine intervention.

Whether we like our lives or not, it is our own personal life that we live; and we have to make the best of it. It is too bad that wisdom doesn't usually kick in, until we have gone through so much pain. And we live in a society of people who are generally, just like us; and we have similar struggles all through each of the stages of our lives.

The life of Joseph, the dreamer, is a classic example of destiny in the life of one whose life is being guided by God. Read Genesis 37 through Genesis 50. If you really want to be encouraged, you must read about the life of Joseph. What God has for you, is for you.

Many things that appear to be evil, may invade, or affect your life. Those things were not sent by God, but God did permit them to come. However, the Lord will not allow anything to come into the life of one of His own, but that He believes that thing, or those things, will blend in with all of the other things, to make us better. What a blessing it is to know that we are in the hands of a loving Father.

PART 5:
THE EXCITING, REVEALING, AND UNDENIABLE, RECORD OF GOD:

Chapter 17

What does the Bible say? (Treasures from Heaven) The Word of God, Our Heavenly Treasure

In 2 Timothy 3:16-17 Paul reminds Timothy, "All scripture is given by inspiration of God, and is profitable for doctrine, for reproof, for correction, for instruction in righteousness: That the man of God may be perfect, thoroughly furnished unto all good works." The Word of God is the greatest gift that the Lord has ever given to us.

Think about it. The Creator, and Supreme Ruler of Heaven and Earth has come to Earth, and has communicated with us so that we can enjoy a personal relationship with Him.

He enters into our lives, personally, by means of His Word; and who are we? Each of us are just a speck on the Planet Earth, which is a smaller one of several planets within our solar system revolving one midget star, among the billions of stars scattered throughout the universe.

If the universe was a human body, a grain of sand on the seashore would be thousands of times larger than our solar system. And yet Jesus said in Matthew 10:29-31, "Are not two sparrows sold for a farthing? And one of them shall not fall on the ground without your Father. But the very hairs of your head are all numbered. Fear ye not therefore, ye are of more value than many sparrows." The very fact that He makes me aware of this through His Word, boosts my self esteem beyond measure. Jesus loves me; this I know, for the Bible tells me so.

We are blessed to have a written record of what the Lord has said. Romans 11:29 says, "For the gifts and calling of God are without repentance." As it says in 2 Corinthians 1:20, "For all the promises of God in Him are yea, and in Him Amen." Galatians 3:22 says, "But the scripture hath concluded all under sin, that the promise by faith of Jesus Christ might be given to them that believe." We have the glorious record of our Lord Jesus, praying for us, that we might become one with Him and the Father. He prays in John 17:17, "Sanctify them through thy truth: thy word is Truth."

Every promise that the Lord has made, coupled together with the conditions required to activate the promise, is just as fresh, and valid, as the day that He spoke it. His word ever lives to perform whatever the Lord has promised. Since God cannot lie, everything that He says becomes a law, more sure than the Law of Gravity.

I remember the first time that I flew in a plane; looking out the window, and seeing the clouds below, it seemed as if you could walk on them; but I assure you that you can't, and the reason why you can't, is gravity. If you were flying about 30,000 feet up in a plane, and wanted to get down to ground level in a hurry; you need only to step out the door, and **the Law of Gravity** will take over. All of us know that, and any sane person would not argue with that. Once you did your part, the Law of Gravity took over and did the rest. You would not have to do anything else, in order to make it happen. It would happen, whether you were wearing a parachute or not. Without a parachute, it would be much faster, and falling could even be fun, and exhilarating. Falling won't kill you. It's that sudden stop that will kill you.

Well when the Lord makes a promise, with a condition; it becomes a law. The only thing that we have to do, in order to activate that promise, is to meet the required condition. For example, in John 6:47 Jesus said, "Verily, verily, I say unto you, He that believeth on me hath everlasting life." The promise is, You have everlasting Life. The condition is, You must believe on me. The question is, How long. The answer is, forever. If you have everlasting life for even one second, then you will have it forever; and if you don't have it forever, that is proof that you never had it for even a split second. This also shows that you have not yet met the required condition, Believe on Jesus for your salvation, because Jesus cannot lie.

Romans 8:1-3 says, "There is therefore now no condemnation to them which are in Christ Jesus, who walk not after the flesh, but after the Spirit. For the law of the Spirit of life in Christ Jesus hath made me free from the law of sin and death. For what the law could not do, in that it was weak through the flesh, God sending His own Son in the likeness of sinful flesh, and for sin, condemned sin in the flesh:"

Galatians 2:19 says, "For I through the law am dead to the law, that I might live unto God." Just as when you step out of the plane, you have met the conditions for the Law of Gravity to take over; when you meet the condition of believing on Jesus Christ as your Savior, **the Law of the Spirit of Life in Christ Jesus** takes over from there; the ball is in the Lord's court.

All through the word of God, there are such promises from God, that can be activated, simply by meeting the conditions. Jesus said in John 10:10, "The thief cometh not, but for to steal, and to kill, and to destroy: I am come that they might have life, and that they might have it more abundantly."

John 10:27-30 says, "My sheep hear my voice, and I know them, and they follow me: And I give unto them eternal life; and they shall never perish, neither shall any *man* pluck them out of my hand. My Father, which gave *them* me, is greater than all; and no *man* is able to pluck *them* out of my Fathers hand. I and *my* Father are one."

Methuselah, the man who lived longer than any other man

The Bible itself tends to prove it's own authenticity. The genealogies in particular, are proof that the Bible tells it like it is. Genealogies are history of different peoples.

The birth records of many people in the Bible are so precise, that if it could have been refuted, the people involved would have refuted it long ago; but on the contrary, they have built their lives around the history of their births. The one thing that has set the children of Israel apart from the world, is the fact that they have preserved their history so well. That history includes the beginning of mankind, and their discovery of the living God.

In Genesis 5:21-32 the record says, "And Enoch lived sixty five years , and begot Methuselah: And Enoch walked with God after he begat Methuselah three hundred years, and begat sons and daughters: And all the days of Enoch were three hundred sixty five years: And Enoch walked with God:

and he was not; for God took him. And Methuselah lived a hundred eighty and seven years, and begat Lamech:

And Methuselah lived after he begat Lamech seven hundred eighty and two years, and begat sons and daughters: And all the days of Methuselah were nine hundred sixty and nine years: and he died. And Lamech lived a hundred eighty and two years, and begat a son: And he called his name Noah, This same shall comfort us concerning our work, and toil of our hands, because of the ground which the Lord hath cursed. And Lamech lived after he begat Noah five hundred ninety and five years, and begat sons and daughters:

And all the days of Lamech were seven hundred seventy and seven years: and he died. And Noah was five hundred years old: and Noah begat Shem, Ham, and Japheth."

And in Genesis 7:6, "And Noah was six hundred years old when the flood of waters was upon the earth."

And in Genesis 7:21-24 the word says, "And all flesh died that moved upon the earth, both of fowl, and of cattle, and of beast, and of every creeping thing that creepeth upon the earth, and every man: All in whose nostrils was the breath of life, of all that was in the dry land, died. And every living substance was destroyed which was upon the face of the ground, both man, and cattle, and the creeping things, and the fowl of the heaven; and they were destroyed from the earth: and Noah only remained alive, and they that were with him in the ark. And the waters prevailed upon the earth a hundred and fifty days.

If Methuselah had lived nine hundred and seventy years, instead of 969 years; he would have lived one year beyond the flood; thus the length of his life would be in contradiction with the Biblical account of the flood, in which all flesh was to have died; with the exception of those who were in the ark with Noah.

Neither did any of his sons lived long enough to have lived through the flood. This record helps to prove that the flood did happen. I believe the report of the Lord. His arm has been revealed to me.

A strange preacher, a needy people, and a loving God

There is so much in the Word of God, that reveals the Lord's measureless love, awesome power, and unsearchable wisdom. There is so much in the Word of God about His compassion, that makes me want to believe in Him. Yahweh is my kind of God.

In the book of Jonah, there is a moving story of such a God as that.

JONAH CHAPTER 1

1 Now the word of the LORD came unto Jonah the son of Amittai, saying,

2 Arise, go to Nineveh, that great city, and cry against it; for their wickedness is come up before me.

3 But Jonah rose up to flee unto Tarshish from the presence of the LORD, and went down to Joppa; and he found a ship going to Tarshish: so he paid the fare thereof, and went down into it, to go with them unto Tarshish from the presence of the LORD.

4 ***But the LORD*** sent out a great wind into the sea, and there was a mighty tempest in the sea, so that the ship was like to be broken.

5 Then the mariners were afraid, and cried every man unto his god, and cast forth the wares that were in the ship into the sea, to lighten it of them. But Jonah was gone down into the sides of the ship; and he lay, and was fast asleep.

6 So the shipmaster came to him, and said unto him, What meanest thou, O sleeper? arise, call upon thy God, if so be that God will think upon us, that we perish not.

7 And they said every one to his fellow, Come, and let us cast lots, that we may know for whose cause this evil is upon us. So they cast lots, and the lot fell upon Jonah.

8 Then said they unto him, Tell us, we pray thee, for whose cause this evil is upon us; What is thine occupation? and whence comest thou? what is thy country? and of what people art thou?

9 And he said unto them, I am an Hebrew; and I fear the LORD, the God of heaven, which hath made the sea and the dry land.

10 Then were the men exceedingly afraid, and said unto him, Why hast thou done this? For the men knew that he fled from the presence of the LORD, because he had told them.

11 Then said they unto him, What shall we do unto thee, that the sea may be calm unto us? for the sea wrought, and was tempestuous.

12 ***And he said unto them, Take me up, and cast me forth into the sea; so shall the sea be calm unto you: for I know that for my sake this great tempest is upon you.***

13 Nevertheless the men rowed hard to bring it to the land; but they could not: for the sea wrought, and was tempestuous against them.

14 Wherefore they cried unto the LORD, and said, We beseech thee, O LORD, we beseech thee, let us not perish for

this man's life, and lay not upon us innocent blood: for thou, O LORD, hast done as it pleased thee.

15 So they took up Jonah, and cast him forth into the sea: and the sea ceased from her raging.

16 ***Then the men feared the LORD exceedingly, and offered a sacrifice unto the LORD, and made vows.***

17 Now the LORD had prepared a great fish to swallow up Jonah. And Jonah was in the belly of the fish three days and three nights.

Jonah was a strange prophet, a strange preacher; so strange that it causes one to ask the question, "How did he ever get to become a prophet? He appears to be probably, the most ignorant preacher that I have ever heard of." It seems to me, that some of the most basic and fundamental things that one can know about God are, that He is omnipotent, omniscient, and omnipresent.

In my opinion, if a person did not know these fundamental things, he wasn't qualified to be a prophet of God. You ought to at least know who He is, if you are going to represent Him. But then again, I guess that he didn't get a chance to read Psalm 139:1-12:

1. "O Lord thou hast searched me, and known me.

2. Thou knowest my downsiting and mine uprising; thou understand my thought afar off.

3. Thou compassest my path and my lying down, and art acquainted with all my ways.

4. For there is not a word in my tongue, but, lo, O Lord, thou knowest it altogether.

5. Thou hast beset me behind and before, and laid thine hand upon me.

6. Such knowledge is too wonderful for me; it is high, I cannot attain unto it.

7. Whither shall I go from thy Spirit? Or whither shall I flee from thy presence?

8. If I ascend up into heaven, thou art there: if I make my bed in hell, behold thou art there.

9. If I take the wings of the morning, and dwell in the uttermost parts of the sea;

10. Even there shall thy hand lead me, and thy right hand shall hold me.

11. If I say, Surely the darkness shall cover me; even the night shall be light about me.

12. Yea, the darkness hideth not from thee; but the night shineth as the day: the darkness and the light are both alike to thee."

Despite the fact of how ignorant Jonah appears to be, we see God communicating with him, and commissioning him to do an important task. His task was to give a final warning to a very large, and wicked city. He was to preach a city-wide revival, to turn the people's hearts back to God. Jonah's response was to decide in his heart, not to do it, because of the hatred, and bias in his heart, against Nineveh; and **to get out of Dodge**, far away from the presence of God.

The last thing that he wanted to see, was Nineveh saved and living under the blessings of God. Nineveh was a very large city, in which there was an estimated 500,000 people living, located on the Tigris River, in the country that is now known as Iraq, near Mosul. Nineveh became the capital of the Assyrian Empire, who had made Judah to be slave state.

Jonah would rather live away from the presence, and favor of God, than to help the Ninevites get into favor with God. **Jonah was the evangelist who did not want a revival**. If every person in Nineveh, died and went to hell, it would have been just fine with Jonah.

So Jonah goes down to the dock in Joppa; he found a ship going to where he thought that he wanted to go. **He paid the price**, he thought that he would have to pay, and **he went down** into the ship, that he felt was going from the presence, and influence of God.

There were other people who would be on that ship, destined to go to the city of Tarshish, a place that had the reputation of being a Godless place. Whether it was for business or pleasure, that is where they wanted to go. It is only reasonable for us to believe that there were some of them who wanted to go there, because they were looking forward to, with great anticipation, that which awaited them there. They were people of the world, or worldly people, eager to engage in the commercialism of that area.

We know that Jonah must have felt very comfortable sailing with this group of people; because when he got on board, he began telling them his secrets. He told them that he was getting away from his God, and was going to Tarshish, to hide out. Surely God would never find him there. Jonah, was really, a very strange preacher. Why would God call him to speak for Him?

Why didn't the Lord choose the Right Reverend Sounding Brass, and Tinkling Cymbal? Surely he would have been very proud to have been selected to do such an awesome task, and he wouldn't have spotted himself by fellowshipping with such unsavory characters, like those that were on that ship going to Tarshish.

The people on board the ship to Tarshish, got the chance to become acquainted with the living and true God, who was persistent enough to follow one man out to sea, to demand reverence from His prophet, and who was powerful enough to cause a severe storm, that threatened to destroy the ship that His prophet was on, and all others, who were on board if necessary, to get His preacher off that boat. This great God who was able to cause the storm to stop, immediately, after His preacher was thrown overboard.

This was enough to get these people to start praying to the living God, and to offer up sacrifices to Him. This is when these people began to be wise; because the fear of God is the beginning of wisdom. And you can bet your last dollar, that when they got to Tarshish, they told this amazing story to anyone who would listen, thus evangelizing the region of Tarshish. The Lord needed a Jonah, in order to accomplish this.

Meanwhile, back at the ranch, the Lord had prepared a great whale, which swallowed Jonah, and kept him incarcerated for three days. He had plenty of time to consider the error of his ways.

After those three days had passed, when Jonah came to himself, he prayed to God from out of the whales belly. The whale vomited him up onto the shore, after the Lord spake unto the great fish.

Then the Lord re-commissioned Jonah, he needed that, because when someone has been that rebellious, one would assume that he would have been fired, and someone else would have taken his place. But the Lord did not fire him, but instead confirmed his appointment. The Lord doesn't call great preachers, He makes preachers great.

The sight of this prophet, who had a serious, and determined look on his face, with traces of sea weed in his hair, and smelling like fish, and who told this amazing story of spending three days in the belly of a whale, was enough to get the attention of the people of Nineveh. **They fasted, and prayed to God, and were spared.** This was the greatest revival ever recorded, until most recent times.

Please don't miss the lesson of this great story. It teaches us volumes about the one and only living and true God. This lesson is so important, that Satan has attacked it on every hand. Let me list some of the different attacks.

1. Some preachers teach, that the story of Jonah being swallowed by a whale is only a myth.

2. Satan has caused it to be taught in some of the seminaries, that there was no such prophet named Jonah.

3. Although our Lord Jesus refers to Jonah the prophet, and confirms that Jonah was swallowed by a whale, they deny it; thus **calling Our Lord Jesus a liar**.

4. The Lord likened Jonah's being in the belly of the whale three days and three nights, to His being in the heart of the earth, three days and three nights, and said that it was the only sign that an evil and adulterous generation would ever receive.

So Satan has been very effective in convincing many people that Jesus was crucified on Friday, which would mean that Jesus was only two days, and two nights in the heart of the earth. If this is so, then Jesus would have been wrong, and even if He was resurrected, He would be disqualified to be the Savior of the world. If Jesus was wrong when He prophesied that He would be buried for three days, and three nights; that would have made Him a false prophet.

The Lord is angry about this His church holding up Friday, as the day that Jesus was crucified, putting them on the other side of Jesus and even Himself. The Lord is angry, because man has again fallen for Satan's great lie; and the main problem with this is, many people don't find anything wrong with it. They say, "What difference does it make, what day He was crucified, as long as He rose from the dead? And although many of them know the truth, they are unwilling to correct their error, thus admitting that they had been wrong.

If you are a true believer in Jesus Christ, then you know that He was God, manifest in the flesh; and God can't lie, and He was incapable of being wrong. Who has believed the report of the Lord? **Let God be true, and every man a liar.** Jesus was crucified on Thursday, not Friday, as commonly reported; and He rose as it began to dawn towards the first day of the week, which is Sunday.

Jonah was a strange preacher, but the Lord chose him anyway, and worked with him, in order to make him a much better preacher, the Lord gave him on the job training. The people on that ship which was headed for Tarshish, which is the region, in and around what is now known as Spain, were a pagan people, who were worshiping pagan gods; and they needed to know the truth. The Lord loved them so much, that He let the events happen that would result in their getting to know the living and true God; they began to worship Him.

The Lord loved the people of Tarshish, and the many people who would be coming in and out of their ports to do trade, so very much, that he would use the converts on the ship to spread the word about this great God there. Nineveh was a wicked city that needed to get to know and worship the Lord, but YAHWEH loved them, and had been long suffering with them, because He is not willing that any should perish.

The whole city of Nineveh turned their hearts to the Lord God Almighty, and thus were spared. That was a very successful revival.

Jonah was that strange prophet. The people on that ship, the people of Tarshish, the people of Nineveh, and also Jonah were all needy people. YAHWEH is that loving God, who is so compassionate, and willing to work with a deficient prophet, to help him learn, and to grow. He is that loving God who concerns Himself that a people, such as the people on board that ship with Jonah, might be serving false gods which could not benefit them at all. He took steps that insured that they would get to know of the one and only, living and true God. And the Lord made sure that the people of Tarshish, heard a credible witness about Him.

And the Lord, who is no respecter of persons, did not give up on the people of Nineveh. Our loving God is not about exclusion, but He is about inclusion; that is why He has sent us to go into the entire world, and to share this gospel with all nationalities.

John 3:16 says, "For God so loved the world, that He gave His only begotten Son, that whosoever believeth in Him should not perish, but have everlasting life."

If you are a preacher, servant of God, and you know that the Lord has sent you into the ministry; but you feel that you are so inadequate, don't quit, don't give up, the Lord is with you. Tune your ears to hear the Lord when He speaks to you, and train your heart to be receptive of the Word of the Lord, and remember that your primary mission is,

Matthew 28:19-20, "Go ye therefore, and teach all nations, baptizing them in the name of the Father, and of the Son, and of the Holy Ghost: Teaching them to observe all things whatsoever I have commanded you: and, lo, I am with you always, even unto the end of the world. Amen."

Remember, Peter and John were perceived to be ignorant and unlearned men, but people had to take note of the fact, that they had been with Jesus, the living Word of God. Study, to show yourselves approved unto God, workmen, that needeth not to be ashamed, rightly dividing the Word of God.

Chapter 18

Who is YAHWEH?

The question of the ages is, "WHO IS GOD?" Pharaoh asked that question, and the whole world got the answer. The Lord has since multiplied evidences of who He is. There is a people who the Lord has chosen, in order to introduce himself to the world, the Jewish people.

The Bible says, concerning Abram, whose name was changed to Abraham; Genesis 15:4-7, "And behold, the word of the Lord came unto him, saying, This shall not be thine heir; but he that shall come forth out of thine own bowels shall be thine heir. And he brought him forth abroad, and said, Look now toward heaven, and tell the stars, if thou be able to number them: and He said unto him, So shall thy seed be. And he believed in the Lord; and He counted it to him for righteousness.

And He said unto him, I am the Lord that brought thee out of Ur of the Chaldees, to give thee this land to inherit it." In Genesis 15:13-14, the Lord makes a promise to Abram, about 463 years before He brought the children of Israel out of the land of bondage; "And He said unto Abram, Know of a surety that thy seed shall be a stranger in a land that is not theirs, and shall serve them; and they shall afflict them four hundred years; And also that nation, whom they shall serve, will I judge: and afterward shall they come out with great substance."

I recall someone saying about Moses; that if he would have had faith in God, and stood strong, he could have been able to deliver the children, forty years earlier than he did. God help us to be more careful about this kind of theology. It can be very harmful to the spiritual growth of those who receive it.

In the first place, it was not Moses that delivered the people of Israel from the Egyptian bondage, it was YAHWEH. Secondly, the children of Israel were not going to be delivered, until all had been fulfilled. They were destined to be there for four hundred years, not three hundred and sixty years. God cannot lie. It was to be just as the Lord had said that it would be.

We must be careful to give weight to the Word of the Lord. God will do just what He said that He would do. Furthermore, the job of delivering the children of Israel, had not yet started, and Moses had not yet been hired for the job of leading the children of Israel, and for the job of being the chosen ambassador of God. No one takes this honor upon himself. Hebrews 5:4 says, "And no man taketh this honor unto himself, but he that is called of God, as was Aaron."

Exodus 5:1-2 records, "And afterward Moses and Aaron went in and told Pharaoh, Thus saith the Lord God of Israel, Let my people go, that they may hold a feast unto me in the wilderness. And Pharaoh said, Who is the Lord, that I should obey His voice to let Israel go? I know not the Lord, neither will I let Israel go."

YAHWEH introduces Himself to Pharaoh, and to the World

Pharaoh was the head of the nation of Egypt, the most powerful nation in the world at this time, and he had began to see himself as a god, who needed to submit to no one. Many nations have become powerful, and the heads of those nations begin to believe that they don't have to submit to anyone. The junk piles of fallen nations, are filled with those nations that felt that way, and the junk pile for kings are filled with the heads of states who also, felt that way.

No nation rises to greatness, without the blessing of God. And no king, prime minister, chairman, or president, rises to that level, but that the Lord God lifts him. The Bible teaches in Psalms 33:12, "Blessed is the nation whose God is the Lord (YAHWEH), and the people whom He hath chosen for His own inheritance." Psalms 40:4 says, "Blessed is the man that maketh the Lord his trust, and respected not the proud, nor such as turn aside to lies." If God be for you, who then can be against you?

The Lord began to introduce Himself to Pharaoh through the ten plagues:

1. The plague of blood; turning the water into blood

2. The plague of frogs; bringing the frogs upon the land, until they were everywhere, in beds, kneading troughs, everywhere.

3. The plague of lice; smiting the dust, turning it into lice, upon both man and beast, throughout the land of Egypt.

4. The plague of flies, bringing swarms of flies into the homes, upon the ground, throughout the land of Egypt, corrupting the land.

5. The plague on livestock, bringing a pestilence upon the cattle of Egypt, and all the cattle died.

6. The plague of boils, Moses takes the dust of the furnace, and throws it into the air, in the presence of Pharaoh; and it spreads through out all the Land of Egypt, and becomes boils, and sores upon the skin of both man and beast of the Egyptians.

7. The plague of hail, the Lord told Moses to stretch out his rod toward heaven, and the Lord sent thunder, and hail, mingled with fire, that ran along the ground.

It was a severe storm, and everything, and every man that was out in it died. And for all of these plagues, there was none in the land of Goshen, where the children of Israel lived. They were spared of all of these plagues.

In Exodus 9:13-17, "And the Lord said unto Moses, Rise up early in the morning, and stand before Pharaoh, and say unto him, Thus saith the Lord God of the Hebrews, Let my people go, that they may serve me. For I will at this time send all my plagues upon thine heart, and upon thy servants, and upon thy people; that thou mayest know that there is none like Me in all the earth. For now I will stretch out My hand, that I may smite thee and thy people with pestilence; and thou shalt be cut off from the earth. And in very deed for this cause have I raised thee up, for to show in thee my power; and that my name may be declared throughout the earth.

As yet exaltest thou thyself against my people, that thou will not let them go? Isn't it amazing, that the Lord raised up Egypt, to become a great world power, in order to show His own power.

I am an American, and I am glad to be an American; but my prayer to God is that we, as a powerful nation, will remember who it is that made this nation great. YAHWEH is the God of the United States of America, just as He was the God of Egypt, as well as the God of Israel; whether we like it or not. There may be things that are wrong in our country; things that may be pulling our country down. But the Lord has given us a formula that will result in the healing of our land. The Lord said in 2 Chronicles 7:14, "If my people, which are called by my name, shall humble themselves, and pray, and seek my face, and turn from their wicked ways; then will I hear from heaven, and will forgive their sin, and will heal their land."

I was meeting with the ministers of our city, and we broke off into small groups to pray for each other, the churches, our city, state, and our nation and it's rulers. In my prayer, I was recalling these words of our Lord. I acknowledged that we were His people, and that too many of us are unwilling to humble ourselves, and many of the people of God don't pray enough, and tend to lean to their own understanding, and often, instead of seeking the Lords face for His approval, some of us seek the approval of each other, and the hand of God instead of His face, and too many of us, His people, are not even willing to admit that we have some wicked ways. When I finished praying, another preacher began his prayer by saying, "I don't receive that." Herein lies the problem; although I mentioned these things in my prayer, I was not the one who was making these accusations.

These were the words of our Lord; and if we are to be blessed, it is Imperative that we agree with God.

8. The plague of locust, God sends an east wind that brought the locust, that that covered the land until it appeared to be black, and ate every green thing in the land of Egypt.

9. The plague of darkness, the Lord brought darkness over the land of Egypt, for three days, a darkness that you

could feel. But all of the children of Israel had light in their dwellings.

10. The plague on the firstborn, the Lord destroys the first born of all of the Egyptians at midnight, on the fourteenth day of the first Jewish month, at midnight. The month that the Lord destroyed the firstborn of the Egyptians, but spared the Hebrew children, who were protected by the blood of the unblemished lamb, was their beginning of months.

This time is called the time of the Passover, for when the death angel saw the blood on the lintels, and the doorposts, the Lord did not allow him to go in and destroy anyone who was covered by the blood. The Word of God said in Exodus 11:7, "But against any of the children of Israel shall not a dog move his tongue, against man or beast: that ye may know how that the Lord doth put a difference between the Egyptians and Israel."

What kind of God is it, that when He has destroyed you and your country, can again cause you to harden your heart, so that you would be stupid enough to threaten the people of God, who He is protecting. It must be a terrible thing to be blinded by Satan, to your own destruction.

This is what Pharaoh did. He threatened Moses in Exodus 10:28-29, "And Pharaoh said unto him, Get thee from me, take heed to thyself, see my face no more; for in that day that thou seest my face thou shalt die. And Moses said, Thou hast spoken well, I will see thy face again no more." Exodus 11:1-3, "And the Lord said unto Moses, Yet I will bring one plague more upon Pharaoh, and upon Egypt; afterward he will let you go hence: when he shall let you go, he shall surely thrust you out hence altogether. Speak now in the ears of the people, and let every man borrow of his neighbor, and every woman of her neighbor, jewels of silver, and jewels of gold. And the Lord gave the people favor in the sight of the Egyptians.

Moreover Moses was very great in the land of Egypt, in the sight of Pharaoh's servants, and in the sight of the people." Thus the promise that the Lord would bring them out with great substance, was fulfilled. God was suing the Egyptians, for restoration of what had been taken, and for punitive damage, pain and suffering.

Other things that God did, that we might know who He is:

There were other things that the Lord did, so that we can know who He is, and how He provides for the people that He calls His own.

1. The pillar of cloud by day, and pillar of fire by night that led them:

Exodus 13:17-18, "And it came to pass, when Pharaoh had let the people go, that God led them not through the land of the Philistines, although that was near; for God said, Lest peradventure the people repent when they see war, and they return to Egypt.

But God led the people about, through the way of the wilderness of the Red Sea: and the children went up harnessed out of the land of Egypt."

2. The pillar that protected them:

Exodus 13:21-22, "And the Lord went before them by day in a pillar of a cloud, to lead them the way; and by night in a pillar of fire, to give them light; to go by day and night: He took not away the pillar of cloud by day, nor the pillar of fire by night, from before the people."

3. The parting of the Red Sea:

Exodus 14:15-20, "**And the Lord said unto Moses, Wherefore criest thou unto me? Speak unto the children of Israel, that they go forward: But lift thou up thy rod, and stretch out thine hand over the sea, and divide it**: and the children of Israel shall go on dry ground through the midst of the sea.

And behold, I will harden the hearts of the Egyptians, and they shall follow them: and I will get me honor upon Pharaoh, and upon all his host, upon his chariots, and upon his horsemen. And the Egyptians shall know that I am the Lord, when I have gotten me honor upon Pharaoh, and upon his chariots, and upon his horsemen. And the angel of God, which went before the camp of Israel, removed and went behind them; and the pillar of the cloud went from before their face, and stood behind them: And it came between the camp of the Egyptians and the camp of Israel; and it was a cloud and darkness to them, but it gave light by night to these: so that the one came not near the other all the night."

4. The destruction of Pharaoh's army:

Exodus 14:24-28, "And it came to pass, that in the morning watch the Lord looked unto the host of the Egyptians through the pillar of fire and of the cloud, and troubled the host of the Egyptians, And took off their chariot wheels, that they drove them heavily: so that **the Egyptians said, Let us flee from the face of Israel; for the Lord fighteth for them against the Egyptians.**

And the Lord said unto Moses, Stretch out thine hand over the sea, that the waters may come again upon the Egyptians, upon their chariots, and upon their horsemen. And Moses stretched forth his hand over the sea, and the sea returned to his strength when the morning appeared; and the Egyptians fled against it; and the Lord overthrew the Egyptians in the midst of the sea.

And the waters returned, and covered the chariots, and the horsemen, and all the host of Pharaoh that came into the sea after them; there remained not so much as one of them."

5. God feeds the children of Israel:

Exodus 16:11-15, "And the Lord spake unto Moses, saying, I have heard the murmurings of the children of Israel: speak unto them saying, At even ye shall have flesh, and in the morning ye shall be filled with bread; and ye shall know that I am the Lord your God. And it came to pass, that at even the quails came up, and covered the camp: and in the morning the dew lay round about the host. And when the dew that lay was gone up, upon the face of the wilderness there lay a small round thing, as small as the hoar frost on the ground. And when the children of Israel saw it, they said one to another, It is manna: for they wist not what it was.

And Moses said unto them, **This is the bread which the Lord hath given you to eat.**"

6. The Lord gives them water from a rock:

Exodus 17:1-7, "And all the congregation of the children of Israel journeyed from the wilderness of Sin, after their journeys, according to the commandment of the Lord, and pitched in Rephidim: and there was no water for the people to drink. Wherefore the people did chide with Moses, and said, Give us water that we may drink. And Moses said unto them, Why chide ye with me? Wherefore do ye tempt the Lord? And the people thirsted there for water; and the people murmured against Moses, and said, Wherefore is this that thou hast brought us up out of Egypt, to kill us and our children and our cattle with thirst? And Moses cried unto the Lord, saying, What shall I do unto this people? They be almost ready to stone me.

And the Lord said unto Moses, Go on before the people, and take with thee of the elders of Israel; and thy rod, wherewith thou smotest the river, take in thine, and go. Behold I will stand before thee thereupon the rock in Horeb; and thou shalt smite the rock, and there shall come water out of it, that the people may drink. And Moses did so in the sight of the elders of Israel. And he called the name of the place Massah, and Meribah, because of the chiding of the children of Israel, and because they tempted the Lord, saying, Is the Lord among us or not?"

7. The defeat of Jericho: Joshua 6:16-21, "And it came to pass at the seventh time, when the priests blew with the trumpets, Joshua said unto the people, Shout; for the Lord hath given you the city. And the city shall be accursed, even it, and all that are therein, to the Lord: only Rahab the harlot shall live, she and all that are with her in the house, because she hid the messengers that we sent.

And ye, in any wise keep yourselves from the accursed thing, lest ye make yourselves accursed, when ye take of the accursed thing, and make the camp of Israel a curse, and trouble it. But all the silver, and gold, and vessels of brass and iron, are consecrated unto the Lord: they shall come into the treasury of the Lord.

So the people shouted when the priest blew with the trumpets: and it came to pass, when the people heard the sound of the trumpet, and the people shouted with a great shout, that the wall fell down flat, so that the people went up into the city, every man straight before him, and they took the city. And they utterly destroyed all that was in the city, both man and woman, young and old, and ox and sheep, and ass, with the edge of the sword."

All of these things, that the Lord has done, help us to know who God is. And infinitely more than these things did He do; And the Lord is still doing great things.

Explaining the Ubiquitous God of the Universe

Once Oliver B. Green came to the Pittsburgh area for a Crusade, about 40 miles from where I lived in Canonsburg Pa., and I volunteered to be one of the counselors, who would pray with the people who would come forward during the invitation; and we would lead them to a saving knowledge of Jesus Christ. We were trained by the Gospel Hour team, in the art of leading a soul to Christ.

One night as Reverend Green was about to preach, the service was interrupted by three or four young men, who wanted to ask questions. They wanted to steal the platform from Reverend Green, and to be in the lime light, before that crowd of about 1500 people who were gathered in that large tent. The ushers came and ushered them out to the parking lot.

I was moved with compassion for these young men, because I thought that they might have a sincere desire to know; so I followed these men to the parking lot and said to them; "You young men must know that you can't just break into the service, to ask questions. If you really want to know something, you could have waited until the service was over and asked. These people have come from all over the tri-state area to hear Oliver Green preach. He preaches on the radio, every day, and they are here to hear from him. You can't just come and steal the audience that he has gone through great time, effort, and expense, to bring to this place. Now, if you have any questions, perhaps I can answer them for you."

They said, "Yes we have some questions. We are students at Pitt University, and we have questions about God." I said, "You guys probably believe in evolution, as the means of creation, don't you?" They said, "Yes." I said, "Since they teach that the species had to evolve, in order to survive; tell me why then is it that every species that they had to evolve from, is still here? And since all life evolved from the Amoeba, Can you tell me where did the Amoeba come from?

Since there can be no creation without a creator, and since there can be no design without a designer, and since there can be no law without a law giver; Who created the Amoeba? Have you ever thought of yourself as a creation? As a matter of fact, everything that you see has been created. And everything has a design. Someone had to design these things, and someone had to create them.

And then there are the different laws of nature, the natural scheme of things, such as the Law of Gravity, The Law of Inertia, The Law of Motion, The Law of Conservation of Energy, and The Law of Thermodynamics; Who made these laws?

I know that you have questions like, Where did God come from?" They said, "Yeah, where did God come from?"

I said, "He didn't come from anywhere. The Bible says that God is a Spirit. And since God is a spirit, He did not have to be created, and if He were created, then he would not be the Maker and Supreme Ruler of Heaven and Earth; The one who created **Him**, would be **that** God.

The Bible teaches that God has always existed; He has no beginning, and He has no ending. I know that you are wondering, How can that be? But look up." We were standing out in the field that was being used for a parking lot, on a fairly clear moonlit night.

As we all looked up I asked them, "What do you see?" They began to answer, "Stars, clouds, the moon, probably some planets." I said, "What else do you see?" They said, "I don't know, maybe a satellite." "What else do you see?" I asked. One of them said, "Nothing, just space." I said, "Space? And you can see it?" They said, "Yes, we can see it." I said, "Just think about it; there is all that space, and you can see it with your naked eye.

Tell me, How far does that space extend? A million light years away, a billion light years, a million billion light years? Lets just say that it extends a billion zillion light years away. Now my next question is, What is at the end of that space? Are we living in an egg like shell? Lets just suppose that we are. Now our next question is, How thick is that shell? Is it a million light years thick, a billion light years thick? Lets just suppose that it too is about a billion zillion light years thick. That brings us to another question; What is on the other side of the shell?

Do you see my point? That thought process can go on forever. If there is to be more space on the other side of the shall, the shell is not needed. Space has no beginning, and it has no ending, and yet you can see it with the naked eye, and although you cannot see all of space, yet you do see it.

You can look at a forest, and although you cannot see all of it, yet you do see it. That's the way that God is, He has no beginning, and He has no ending."

These young students were visibly impressed, and I said to them, "I will have to go back in, but before I go, I would like to have a word of prayer for you all." One of them said, "Yes please pray for us, because we tried our own way, and it has not helped." So I prayed with them, and then went back inside the tent.

If you have been wondering about YAHWEH, who He is and where He came from, you must remember that the living and true God is Ubiquitous. He exists in every place at the same time, and in every time, at the same place. I know that you don't fully understand; but if you did, I guess that you would be God. That's just a view of how awesome our God is. There is none like Him.

Chapter 19

Who is IMMANUEL?

There are two prophesies concerning the name of the Messiah, before His birth.

1. Isaiah 7:14, "Therefore the Lord himself shall give you a sign; Behold a virgin shall conceive, and bear a son, and shall call his name Immanuel."

2. Luke 1:26-35, "And in the sixth month the angel Gabriel was sent from God unto a city of Galilee, named Nazareth, To a virgin espoused to a man whose name was Joseph, of the house of David; and the virgin's name was Mary. And the angel came in unto her, and said, Hail, thou art highly favored, the Lord is with thee: blessed art thou among women. And when she saw him, she was troubled at his saying, and cast in her mind what manner of salutation this should be. And the angel said unto her, Fear not, Mary: for thou hast found favor with God.

And behold thou shalt conceive in thy womb, and bring forth a son, and shalt call his name JESUS. He shall be great, and shall be called the Son of the Highest: and the Lord shall give unto Him the throne of His father David;

And He shall reign over the house of Jacob for ever; and of His kingdom there shall be no end. Then said Mary unto the angel, How shall this be, seeing I know not a man? And the angel answered and said unto her, The Holy Ghost shall come upon thee, and the power of the Highest shall overshadow the: therefore also that holy thing which shall be born of thee shall be called the Son of God."

The Bible says in Proverbs 23:7, "As he thinketh in his heart, so is he." This saying is confirmed by Jesus, when He said in Matthew 15:18, "But those things which proceed out of the mouth come forth from the heart;" This saying is also true of our God; the God who has a mouth, and does speak. Did He not say, Let there be light, and it was so? Light was in God's heart, and it came to be, because He spoke it.

All of the things that was necessary to make light was incorporated within God's word, when He spoke it. As He spoke it, it became a command, a work order. Incorporated in that spoken word was the design, and the creation of that light. Since nothing else existed, everything had to come from within the heart of God. We know who God is, by the things that He said. What the Lord YAHWEH said, is an extension of Himself.

John 1:1-5 says, "In the beginning was the Word, and the Word was with God, and the Word was God. The same was in the beginning with God. All things were made by Him; and without Him was not anything made that was made. In Him was life; and the life was the light of men. And the light shineth in darkness; and the darkness comprehended it not." The omnipresent God, the God who exists everywhere, decided to exist also as the Word of God.

The Word of God is God in action.

Genesis 1:1 says, "In the beginning God created the heaven and the earth."

John 1:10-14 says, He was in the world, and the world was made by Him, and the world knew Him not. He came unto His own, and His own received Him not.

But as many as received Him, to them gave He power to become the sons of God, even to them that believe on His name: Which were born, not of blood, nor of the will of the flesh, nor of the will of man, but of God. And the Word was made flesh, and dwelt among us, (and we beheld His glory, the glory as of the only begotten of the Father,) full of grace and truth.

When Mary conceived of the Holy Ghost, the child within her womb was God in action, which is the Word of God, bonding with Adam's race, but without the contaminated blood of Adam, who had sinned, and the life of the body is in the blood; and forming the first and only God man; possessing all of the attributes of the living God, and also possessing all of the attributes of man, but yet without sin.

Because He was to be born in the same manner as any other man, there has to be, for the record, the explanation of His birth, since Mary had not had any sexual relations with any man. "Who was the Father?" That is what every body wants to know. Man that is born of a woman is a son. People want to know, "Who is the boy's father? What is his name going to be?"

Since YAHWEH is His Father, his name shall be called Jesus. (Y@howshuwa), which means YAHWEH to save. And what is this son to be, what will He do? He will not be a carpenter, so we will not call Him Jesus Carpenter. He is not going to make wheels, so we will not call Him Jesus Wheelwright. He is not the son of Joseph, so we will not call Him Jesus Josephson.

The God of the Universe is His Father, and that God is connected to mankind in Jesus, who is our salvation, and He has come to gather, shelter, and to bring us back to the Father; So His name shall be Jesus Immanuel; Y@howshuwa Immanuw'el; which means YAHWEH to save, God with us for the purpose of being our refuge, our dwelling place of rest, and our way to escape. That is who Immanuel is, and I believe on His name; YHWHshua Immanuel. All who believe on that name has the power to become the sons of God.

PART 6:
FROM SALVATION TO REST, FROM REST TO POWER, FROM POWER TO BEARING MUCH FRUIT: (LIFE AND THAT MORE ABUNDANTLY)

Chapter 20

What does God want from us?

In Luke 13:34-35 Jesus said, "O Jerusalem, Jerusalem, which killest the prophets, and stonest them that are sent unto thee; how often would I have gathered thy children together, as a hen doth gather her brood under her wings, and ye would not!

35. Behold, your house is left unto you desolate: and verily I say unto you, Ye shall not see me, until the time come when ye shall say, Blessed is he that cometh in the name of the Lord.

In Luke 19:41-44 it says, "And when he was come near, he beheld the city, and wept over it,

42 Saying, If thou hadst known, even thou, at least in this thy day, the things which belong unto thy peace! but now they are hid from thine eyes.

43 For the days shall come upon thee, that thine enemies shall cast a trench about thee, and compass thee round, and keep thee in on every side,

44 And shall lay thee even with the ground, and thy children within thee; and they shall not leave in thee one

stone upon another; because thou knewest not the time of thy visitation."

In John 3:16-18 Jesus said, "For God so loved the world, that he gave his only begotten Son, that whosoever believeth in him should not perish, but have everlasting life.

17 For God sent not his Son into the world to condemn the world; but that the world through him might be saved.

18 He that believeth on him is not condemned: but he that believeth not is condemned already, because he hath not believed in the name of the only begotten Son of God."

Simply put, the Lord has gone out of His way, to see that provisions were made for man to be in a right relationship with Him, and would have shelter, and an abundant, and eternal life. That is what the Lord wants for everybody.

The Lord has given us His word of promise, and simply wants us to believe it, and receive it, so that we might live, and that things may be well with us.

When people begin to accept the reality of God, the next thing that want to know is, what does God want from me. Of course, the answer to that question depends of where you are spiritually.

1. You may not be saved:

If you are one of those people who are not saved, The Lord wants you to hear what He has to say to you. He wants you to believe what He tells you, and He wants you to believe on His only begotten Son, Jesus, in order to receive the life that was prepared for you, from the foundation of the world.

2. You may be saved, but not committed to the work of God: If you are one of those people who are saved, but have not committed yourself to the work of the Lord, You are asking for trouble; because you are living a life without purpose, and have made yourself a perfect target for Satan.

You are going to have an awful time trying to get the victory over sin. You are living a life of defense, and not a life of offense. In order to gain the victory, we must be an offense to the devil. Those on offense score, and they win. He who winneth souls is wise.

Being a soul winner will strengthen your life in four different ways. When you begin witnessing,

A. It will cause you to watch the way you live. You will want to be a credible witness for God.

B. It will cause you to increase your Bible study time, because you will get tired of saying, "I don't know, but I'll look it up." You will want to have some of the answers to the questions that people will ask you.

C. It will intensify your prayer life, because people that we go to will drive us to pray, and then again, we will want to ask the   Lord's assistance in our efforts to win souls. God gives the increase.

D. It will cause us to find others who are like minded. When we began to have experiences in our soul winning, we will want to share those experiences with others; but only those who are in Christ Jesus, and are committed to the work of God can rejoice with you. Forget not the assembling of yourselves together.

And all the while, you will have the blessing of knowing that you were pleasing God, and that He is going with you, all the way.

3. You may be saved, but still have much learning to do:

If you are one of those people who are saved, but still a babe in Christ, don't get discouraged; your brothers and sisters in Christ were all babes in Christ. Take the strongest Christian that you know; they too were once a babe in Christ. But study the Word of God, and commit it top heart. David said in Psalm 119:11, "Thy word have I hid in my heart, that I might not sin against thee."

When you read the Word of God, settle it in your heart, get the intended understanding. If you don't understand the Word, it is very difficult to hide it in your heart, and to commit it to memory. But the Lord has so fixed it, that we can win other souls to Christ, on the very same day that He saved us; because, it's not by might, nor by power, but by my spirit, saith the Lord.

4. You may be saved, and God is calling you to a higher level:

If you are one of those people who are saved, and you believe that the Lord is calling you to a higher calling; I say to you, be sure that it is the Lord who is calling you, and not just a member of your church, or a friend, or relative, who see great potential in you. If you have great potential, you already know that; but if you are going to be the preacher, or the prophet of God, you must be sure that it is the Lord calling you, because, all that you give, you must get from him.

And when things get rough for you, and they will, only God will stick with you, and will help you. Friends will leave you hanging.

5. You may be saved, and on a higher level:

If you are one of those people who are saved and serving on a higher level, I say praise the Lord for you. The Lord no doubt, has been using you, and He will use you. Be encouraged, and don't look for validation from your peers.

Seek the Lord's face, because He, and He alone can fully appreciate the thing that He has told you to do, and you were faithful to do those things. Seek the Lord's face, and be sure to let people know who deserves the glory. You are that one who is always in my prayers. Always remain faithful to God, and committed to the Gospel of Jesus Christ, no matter who it offends.

6. You may have a higher position, but are not saved:

If you are one of those people who are occupying positions in high places, of church, who have come to grips with the fact that you are not saved, I say to you, find someone in Christ, who is at least on your level, ecclesiastically speaking, and confess this to them, and get some direction, immediately. Not only are you in jeopardy, because you are not saved, but you are in a position where you can be the cause of many people going to hell, thinking that they are going to heaven.

You are among those people that Jesus talked about, to whom He would say, "I never knew you." In Matthew 7:21-23 Jesus said, "Not every one that saith unto me Lord, Lord, shall enter into the kingdom of heaven; but he that doeth the will of my Father which is in heaven.

Many will say to me in that day, Lord, Lord, have we not prophesied in thy name? And in thy name have cast out devils? And in thy name done many wonderful works? And then will I profess unto them, I never knew you: depart from me, ye that work iniquity." I suggest that you go forward to the **_INSTRUCTIONS ON HOW TO BE SAVED,_** in Chapter 24 of this book, and follow the instructions. I pray that the Lord will save you, and that you may have the blessing of going back, and helping those that you may have led astray.

7. You may be saved, sanctified, and filled with the spirit:

To you my brother, and my sister, I say pray for me, that I may be strengthened in the Spirit, and in the inner man, and that the Lord will give free course to His gospel in me, and that I may preach and teach with great power; the Lord bearing witness with signs and miracles following.

Please don't be satisfied with that infilling, that you received many years ago. We are the vessels of God, and I would like to think that we are growing. If this is true, what filled us many years ago, is not filling us now, so we need to be refilled again, and again. May the Lord God be with you, and you be found faithful in Him.

Chapter 21

Walking in the Spirit, and not in the flesh: Jesus said, John 3:6-8:

6. "That which is born of the flesh is flesh; and that which is born of the Spirit is spirit.

7. Marvel not that I said unto thee, Ye must be born again.

8. The wind bloweth where it listeth, and thou hearest the sound thereof, but canst not tell whence it cometh, and whither it goeth: so is every one that is born of the spirit."

A person cannot be expected to walk in the Spirit, if he or she have not been born of the Spirit.

ROMANS CHAPTER 8

1. There is therefore now no condemnation to them which are in Christ Jesus, who walk not after the flesh, but after the Spirit.

2. For the law of the Spirit of life in Christ Jesus hath made me free from the law of sin and death.

3. For what the law could not do, in that it was weak through the flesh, God sending his own Son in the likeness of sinful flesh, and for sin, condemned sin in the flesh:

4. That the righteousness of the law might be fulfilled in us, who walk not after the flesh, but after the Spirit.

5. For they that are after the flesh do mind the things of the flesh; but they that are after the Spirit the things of the Spirit.

6. For to be carnally minded is death; but to be spiritually minded is life and peace.

7. Because the carnal mind is enmity against God: for it is not subject to the law of God, neither indeed can be.

8. So then they that are in the flesh cannot please God.

9. But ye are not in the flesh, but in the Spirit, if so be that the Spirit of God dwell in you. Now if any man have not the Spirit of Christ, he is none of his.

10. And if Christ be in you, the body is dead because of sin; but the Spirit is life because of righteousness.

11. But if the Spirit of him that raised up Jesus from the dead dwell in you, he that raised up Christ from the dead shall also quicken your mortal bodies by his Spirit that dwelleth in you.

12. Therefore, brethren, we are debtors, not to the flesh, to live after the flesh.

13. For if ye live after the flesh, ye shall die: but if ye through the Spirit do mortify the deeds of the body, ye shall live.

14 For as many as are led by the Spirit of God, they are the sons of God.

15 For ye have not received the spirit of bondage again to fear; but ye have received the Spirit of adoption, whereby we cry, Abba, Father.

16 The Spirit itself beareth witness with our spirit, that we are the children of God:

17. And if children, then heirs; heirs of God, and joint-heirs with Christ; if so be that we suffer with him, that we may be also glorified together.

18. For I reckon that the sufferings of this present time are not worthy to be compared with the glory which shall be revealed in us.

19. For the earnest expectation of the creature waiteth for the manifestation of the sons of God.

20. For the creature was made subject to vanity, not willingly, but by reason of him who hath subjected the same in hope,

21. Because the creature itself also shall be delivered from the bondage of corruption into the glorious liberty of the children of God.

22. For we know that the whole creation groaneth and travaileth in pain together until now.

23. And not only they, but ourselves also, which have the first fruits of the Spirit, even we ourselves groan within ourselves, waiting for the adoption, to wit, the redemption of our body.

24. For we are saved by hope: but hope that is seen is not hope: for what a man seeth, why doth he yet hope for?

25. But if we hope for that we see not, then do we with patience wait for it.

26. Likewise the Spirit also helpeth our infirmities: for we know not what we should pray for as we ought: but the Spirit itself maketh intercession for us with groanings which cannot be uttered.

27. And he that searcheth the hearts knoweth what is the mind of the Spirit, because he maketh intercession for the saints according to the will of God.

28. And we know that all things work together for good to them that love God, to them who are the called according to his purpose.

29. For whom he did foreknow, he also did predestinate to be conformed to the image of his Son, that he might be the firstborn among many brethren.

30. Moreover whom he did predestinate, them he also called: and whom he called, them he also justified: and whom he justified, them he also glorified.

31. ¶ What shall we then say to these things? If God be for us, who can be against us?

32. He that spared not his own Son, but delivered him up for us all, how shall he not with him also freely give us all things?

33. Who shall lay any thing to the charge of God's elect? It is God that justifieth.

34. Who is he that condemneth? It is Christ that died, yea rather, that is risen again, who is even at the right hand of God, who also maketh intercession for us.

35. Who shall separate us from the love of Christ? Shall tribulation, or distress, or persecution, or famine, or nakedness, or peril, or sword?

36. As it is written, For thy sake we are killed all the day long; we are accounted as sheep for the slaughter.

37. Nay, in all these things we are more than conquerors through him that loved us.

38. For I am persuaded, that neither death, nor life, nor angels, nor principalities, nor powers, nor things present, nor things to come,

39. Nor height, nor depth, nor any other creature, shall be able to separate us from the love of God, which is in Christ Jesus our Lord.

Walking in the Spirit, **the born again child has accepted his own execution,** as payment for his own sin, through Jesus, our proxy in death, and our source of new life. The old account is settled, and the new man, who is that new creature in Christ Jesus, will never be charged for the sins of the old man. The old man is reckoned as dead, and the new man is invisible, eternal, and sinless. So walk in the spirit, and you will be walking by faith; and you will be pleasing God.

PART 7:
THE CONCLUSION

Chapter 22

Where does guilt come from?

There was a time when men never experienced guilt. Without the Law, there is no knowledge of sin. If you admit to being a sinner, then you are agreeing with the Bible which said in Romans 3:23, "For all have sinned, and come short of the glory of God."

The original plan of God was for man not to have to concern himself about good and evil, but to simply trust Him. That wasn't such a bad idea, since we are so dependent on Him for all things; "Without Him was not anything made that was made." John 1:3

Guilt entered into the world because Adam and Eve wanted to know, what was good and what was evil. In Genesis 3:1-7 the Word of God says, "Now the serpent was more subtile than any beast of the field which the Lord God had made. And he said unto the woman, Yea, hath God said, Ye shall not eat of every tree of the garden? And the woman said unto the serpent, We may eat of the fruit of the trees of the garden: But the fruit of the tree which is in the midst of the garden, God said, Ye shall not eat of it, neither shall ye touch it, lest ye die.

And the serpent said unto the woman, **Ye shall not surely die**: For God doth know that in the day ye eat thereof, then your eyes shall be opened, and ye shall be as gods, knowing good and evil. And when the woman saw that the tree was good for food, and that it was pleasant to the eyes, and a tree to be desired to make one wise, she took of the fruit thereof, and did eat, and gave also unto her husband with her; and he did eat.

And the eyes of them both were opened, and they knew that they were naked; and they sewed fig leaves together, and made themselves aprons."

If Adam and Eve had never eaten of the forbidden fruit, they would have never experienced guilt.

When it comes to guilt, we should feel guilty for our prayerlessness. The Word of the Lord says in 1 Thessalonians 5:17, "Pray without ceasing."

Chapter 23

Surrounded by things that we don't understand

1. Have you noticed that there are so very many things all around us that we don't understand?

2. There is gravity, the tendency of two bodies to be attracted to each other:

3. Magnetic power, the ability of iron, nickel, cobalt, etc., and their alloys to have their molecules to line up so as to attract and hold iron: Like magnetic poles repel each other, while unlike poles attract each other; how this happens by the orderly flow of electrons through a metal.

4. Pain, what is it? You can't see it, and you can't show it to anyone.

5. Intuition, what is it, and where does it come from? Sometimes you just know what is going to happen.

6. The placebo effect, why does it work? Sometimes when a person is in pain they will give him morphine until the final day, when instead they give him a placebo, saline solution, which takes the pain away. How does this happen?

7. Ultra-energetic cosmic rays, detected on Earth: For more than a decade some physicists in Japan have been seeing these cosmic rays that are particles, mostly protons, but sometime heavy atomic nuclei, that travel through the universe at close to the speed of light; according to Einstein's special theory of relativity dictates that these cosmic rays, reaching Earth from a source outside our galaxy will have suffered so many energy shedding collisions, that their maximum possible energy is 5 x 1019 electron volts. This is known as the Greisen-Zatsepin-limit. We don't know where these came from, although they are above the 1020 electron volt limit. Where did they come from?

8. Homeopathy, how and why does it work? A pharmacologist at Queen's University, Belfast, set out to prove that homeopathy, the claim that a chemical remedy could be diluted to the point where a sample was unlikely to contain a single molecule of anything but water, and yet still have a healing effect. Her study, looked at the effects of ultra-dilute solutions of histamine on human white blood cells involved in inflammation. The solution worked just like histamine. This study was replicated in four different labs, and found to work.

9. What holds the galaxies together, and conserves their spin, Astronomers claim that there is not enough mass in the galaxies, to produce the observed spin. There is something at work that we cannot see nor understand.

10. Why does tests on Mars indicate that there is life there, and yet our instruments, designed to identify organic molecules considered to be essential signs of life, has found none; we may be hung up on the phrase, "Life as we know it." I wouldn't be a bit surprised at how little we know. But the creator knows.

11. The detection of six particles that should not exist, four years ago, in a particle accelerator in France, tetra neutrons, which are four neutrons that are bound together in a way that defies the laws of physics: The laws of God governs the laws of physics. The universe is Yahweh's invention.

12. What is causing the two space craft, Pioneer 10, and 11 to speed up, rather to slow down? There is another force at work.

13. Why is our universe expanding at ever increasing speeds? If our universe got started with the "Big Bang," shouldn't it be slowing down? And beside this where did the energy come from, to cause such a bang?

14. What created the 37 second signal from outer space in the direction of Sagittarius at 1420 megahertz, on the radio frequency?

15. Why is it that more and more researchers believe in the possibility of cold fusion, due to successful experiments? What power is at work that caused successful results in those experiments?

16. Some people who had died, after prayer they were raised from the dead, even after rigor mortis had set in. What power was able to make this happen?

Think the excellence of all of creation around us. Consider, if you will, these wonderful bodies in which we live. Aren't these bodies of ours incredible? David said in Psalm 139:14, "I will praise thee; for I am fearfully and wonderfully made: marvelous are thy works; and that my soul knoweth right well."

Before work can be done, there must be the ability to do work. Before there can be design, there must be a designer. Before there can be creation, there must be a creator. And before there can be laws, there must be a law giver, and a law enforcer; otherwise those laws are meaningless.

The Bible gives us a step by step account of how all things came into being, and backs it up with history, and experiments that has been performed by many of those who have gone before us, and that are now still being performed by those of us today, who believe what he said. What the Bible says is not a theory, that must be changed because experiences, and experiments have proved otherwise. What God says is truth, which is eons beyond facts. Facts are our proven conclusions, as we have found them to be true, in our relative state of being, from our point of view.

1. Man saw a heavy stone, that he could not move, rolling down a hill, being pulled by the gravity that our God created, and began to think about a wheel.

2. Man saw fruit that the Lord had spoke into existence, fall from the tree to the ground, and decided that he didn't have to climb the tree, in order to get the fruit at top; he could that he could throw something and knock it loose, or take a stick and knock it loose, and the gravity that the Lord had created would bring it down to him.

3. He saw the birds that our Lord spoke into existence, flying through the air, but whenever he jumped into the air, to try to do the same, he found that he couldn't, because something would pull him back down again.

4. Eventually, his mind suggested that perhaps he could find a way to do the same.

5. Man studied the operation of the eye that the Lord created, and thought of the camera lens.

6. Man studied the brain that our Lord had made, and thought of making a computer.

7. Man discovered the electrons that our lord had created, and found a way to harness it to do work for him.

And of all the things that man has invented, he was inspired by the things that the Lord had made, and he had to use only the things that the Lord had created. There is nothing new under the sun. Even the food that we eat is the same food that the Lord God spoke into existence, in the beginning. There is no new food. All food comes from the original food. The Lord created every living thing with the ability to reproduce, after it's own kind.

This is the journal of the Lord. Clear records were kept, and no one has been able to disprove any of it since it was first given.

The Lord's Bookkeeping, Scientific, and Legislative Journals

The book of Genesis serves as YAHWEH'S bookkeeping journal that shows the acquisition of all things, and which records and lists all of His discernable assets, and which explains how and when these assets came into His possession. It is also a maintenance record, which documents the purging of Earth.

Genesis and Exodus is the Lord's journal that recorded the proof of His administrative powers, and absolute authority and ruler ship over the Earth.

Genesis, Exodus, Leviticus, Numbers, and Deuteronomy is the Lord's legislative journal, that provides a comprehensive record of the laws that the Lord passed to rule over his earthly kingdom, the constitution by which the people would be governed, and the covenants that He had established with His subjects, the people of Earth.

The New Testament is the record of the Lord's constitutional amendment, which has updated, and replaced the old constitutional record. And all through the Bible, there are checks and balances, to validate the word of God, and to prove that which is good. We hear the Lord saying, "prove me", or "try me", or "try the spirits." There are prophesies from the Lord, from time to time, that validate, and verify the effectiveness of His ruler ship. He rules sovereign, and supreme.

The Bible also serves as an ancestral record of the first families of Earth, the first families of the Old Covenant, and the first families of the New Covenant. It is also a genealogical record that traces the different family groups, where they settled, and informs us of some of their contributions to mankind. Therefore the Lord has provided, for all to see:

1. An Accounting Journal
2. A Scientific Journal
3. A Legislative Journal
4. An Ancestral Journal; (family tree)
5. A Genealogical Journal
6. A Chronological Journal of the different kingdoms
7. A Prophetic Journal of how it will all end

I would like to see Scientist, Biologists, Physicists, and Philosophers top that. The world is very diligent to find the way to provide cold fusion; that is to harness the powers that power the Sun, safely, and economically. They have been working on it for many years. They keep on trying, because the rewards of such an accomplishment would be enormous. They are not sure that they can accomplish it; but they really want to, so they never stop.

Just think what a blessing it would be, if scientists, biologists, physicists, archaeologists, paleontologists, and philosophers really wanted to know the truth about God. They would find Him, and take a quantum leap forward in their respective fields. The Word of God say's, Jeremiah 29:13 *"And ye shall seek me and shall find me when you shall search for me with all your heart."* Dear Lord, I pray that you make it so.

Genesis Chapters 1 through 4, creation, the foundation of True Science

GENESIS CHAPTER 1

1 In the beginning God created the heaven and the earth.

2 And the earth was without form, and void; and darkness was upon the face of the deep. And the Spirit of God moved upon the face of the waters.

3 And God said, Let there be light: and there was light.

4 And God saw the light, that it was good: and God divided the light from the darkness.

5 And God called the light Day, and the darkness he called Night. And the evening and the morning were the first day.

6 And God said, Let there be a firmament in the midst of the waters, and let it divide the waters from the waters.

7 And God made the firmament, and divided the waters which were under the firmament from the waters which were above the firmament: and it was so.

8 And God called the firmament Heaven. And the evening and the morning were the second day.

9 And God said, Let the waters under the heaven be gathered together unto one place, and let the dry land appear: and it was so.

10 And God called the dry land Earth; and the gathering together of the waters called he Seas: and God saw that it was good.

11 And God said, Let the earth bring forth grass, the herb yielding seed, and the fruit tree yielding fruit after his kind, whose seed is in itself, upon the earth: and it was so.

12 And the earth brought forth grass, and herb yielding seed after his kind, and the tree yielding fruit, whose seed was in itself, after his kind: and God saw that it was good.

13 And the evening and the morning were the third day.

14 And God said, Let there be lights in the firmament of the heaven to divide the day from the night; and let them be for signs, and for seasons, and for days, and years:

15 And let them be for lights in the firmament of the heaven to give light upon the earth: and it was so.

16 And God made two great lights; the greater light to rule the day, and the lesser light to rule the night: he made the stars also.

17 And God set them in the firmament of the heaven to give light upon the earth,

18 And to rule over the day and over the night, and to divide the light from the darkness: and God saw that it was good.

19 And the evening and the morning were the fourth day.

20 And God said, Let the waters bring forth abundantly the moving creature that hath life, and fowl that may fly above the earth in the open firmament of heaven.

21 And God created great whales, and every living creature that moveth, which the waters brought forth abundantly, after their kind, and every winged fowl after his kind: and God saw that it was good.

22 And God blessed them, saying, Be fruitful, and multiply, and fill the waters in the seas, and let fowl multiply in the earth.

23 And the evening and the morning were the fifth day.

24 And God said, Let the earth bring forth the living creature after his kind, cattle, and creeping thing, and beast of the earth after his kind: and it was so.

25 And God made the beast of the earth after his kind, and cattle after their kind, and every thing that creepeth upon the earth after his kind: and God saw that it was good.

26 And God said, Let us make man in our image, after our likeness: and let them have dominion over the fish of the sea, and over the fowl of the air, and over the cattle, and over all the earth, and over every creeping thing that creepeth upon the earth.

27 So God created man in his own image, in the image of God created he him; male and female created he them.

28 And God blessed them, and God said unto them, be fruitful, and multiply, and replenish the earth, and subdue it: and have dominion over the fish of the sea, and over the fowl of the air, and over every living thing that moveth upon the earth.

29 And God said, Behold, I have given you every herb bearing seed, which is upon the face of all the earth, and every

tree, in the which is the fruit of a tree yielding seed; to you it shall be for meat.

30 And to every beast of the earth, and to every fowl of the air, and to every thing that creepeth upon the earth, wherein there is life, I have given every green herb for meat: and it was so.

31 And God saw every thing that he had made, and, behold, it was very good. And the evening and the morning were the sixth day.

GENESIS CHAPTER 2

1 Thus the heavens and the earth were finished, and all the host of them.

2 And on the seventh day God ended his work which he had made; and he rested on the seventh day from all his work which he had made.

3 And God blessed the seventh day, and sanctified it: because that in it he had rested from all his work which God created and made.

4 These are the generations of the heavens and of the earth when they were created, in the day that the LORD God made the earth and the heavens,

5 And every plant of the field before it was in the earth, and every herb of the field before it grew: for the LORD God had not caused it to rain upon the earth, and there was not a man to till the ground.

6 But there went up a mist from the earth, and watered the whole face of the ground.

7 And the LORD God formed man of the dust of the ground, and breathed into his nostrils the breath of life; and man became a living soul.

8 And the LORD God planted a garden eastward in Eden; and there he put the man whom he had formed.

9 And out of the ground made the LORD God to grow every tree that is pleasant to the sight, and good for food; the tree of life also in the midst of the garden, and the tree of knowledge of good and evil.

10 And a river went out of Eden to water the garden; and from thence it was parted, and became into four heads.

11 The name of the first is Pison: that is it which compasseth the whole land of Havilah, where there is gold;

12 And the gold of that land is good: there is bdellium and the onyx stone.

13 And the name of the second river is Gihon: the same is it that compasseth the whole land of Ethiopia.

14 And the name of the third river is Hiddekel: that is it which goeth toward the east of Assyria. And the fourth river is Euphrates.

15 And the LORD God took the man, and put him into the garden of Eden to dress it and to keep it.

16 And the LORD God commanded the man, saying, of every tree of the garden thou mayest freely eat:

17 But of the tree of the knowledge of good and evil, thou shalt not eat of it: for in the day that thou eatest thereof thou shalt surely die.

18 And the LORD God said, It is not good that the man should be alone; I will make him an help meet for him.

19 And out of the ground the LORD God formed every beast of the field, and every fowl of the air; and brought them unto Adam to see what he would call them: and whatsoever Adam called every living creature, that was the name thereof.

20 And Adam gave names to all cattle, and to the fowl of the air, and to every beast of the field; but for Adam there was not found an help meet for him.

21 And the LORD God caused a deep sleep to fall upon Adam, and he slept: and he took one of his ribs, and closed up the flesh instead thereof;

22 And the rib, which the LORD God had taken from man, made he a woman, and brought her unto the man.

23 And Adam said, This is now bone of my bones, and flesh of my flesh: she shall be called Woman, because she was taken out of Man.

24 Therefore shall a man leave his father and his mother, and shall cleave unto his wife: and they shall be one flesh.

25 And they were both naked, the man and his wife, and were not ashamed.

GENESIS CHAPTER 3

1 Now the serpent was more subtile than any beast of the field which the LORD God had made. And he said unto the woman, Yea, hath God said, Ye shall not eat of every tree of the garden?

2 And the **woman said** unto the serpent, *We may eat of the fruit of the trees of the garden:*

3 But of the fruit of the tree which is in the midst of the garden, God hath said, Ye shall not eat of it, neither shall ye touch it, lest ye die.

4 And the serpent said unto the woman, Ye shall not surely die:

5 For God doth know that in the day ye eat thereof, then your eyes shall be opened, and ye shall be as gods, knowing good and evil.

6 And when the woman saw that the tree was good for food, and that it was pleasant to the eyes, and a tree to be desired to make one wise, she took of the fruit thereof, and did eat, and gave also unto her husband with her; and he did eat.

7 And the eyes of them both were opened, and they knew that they were naked; and they sewed fig leaves together, and made themselves aprons.

8 And they heard the voice of the LORD God walking in the garden in the cool of the day: and Adam and his wife hid themselves from the presence of the LORD God amongst the trees of the garden.

9 And the LORD God called unto Adam, and said unto him, Where art thou?

10 And he said, I heard thy voice in the garden, and I was afraid, because I was naked; and I hid myself.

11 And he said, Who told thee that thou wast naked? Hast thou eaten of the tree, whereof I commanded thee that thou shouldest not eat?

12 And the man said, The woman whom thou gavest to be with me, she gave me of the tree, and I did eat.

13 And the LORD God said unto the woman, What is this that thou hast done? And the woman said, The serpent beguiled me, and I did eat.

14 And the LORD God said unto the serpent, Because thou hast done this, thou art cursed above all cattle, and above every beast of the field; upon thy belly shalt thou go, and dust shalt thou eat all the days of thy life:

15 And I will put enmity between thee and the woman, and between thy seed and her seed; it shall bruise thy head, and thou shalt bruise his heel.

16 Unto the woman he said, I will greatly multiply thy sorrow and thy conception; in sorrow thou shalt bring forth children; and thy desire shall be to thy husband, and he shall rule over thee.

17 And unto Adam he said, Because thou hast hearkened unto the voice of thy wife, and hast eaten of the tree, of which I commanded thee, saying, Thou shalt not eat of it: cursed is the ground for thy sake; in sorrow shalt thou eat of it all the days of thy life;

18 Thorns also and thistles shall it bring forth to thee; and thou shalt eat the herb of the field;

In the sweat of thy face shalt thou eat bread, till thou return unto the ground; for out of it wast thou taken: for dust thou art, and unto dust shalt thou return.

20 And Adam called his wife's name Eve; because she was the mother of all living.

21 Unto Adam also and to his wife did the LORD God make coats of skins, and clothed them.

22 And the LORD God said, Behold, the man is become as one of us, to know good and evil: and now, lest he put forth his hand, and take also of the tree of life, and eat, and live for ever:

23 Therefore the LORD God sent him forth from the garden of Eden, to till the ground from whence he was taken.

24 So he drove out the man; and he placed at the east of the garden of Eden Cherubims, and a flaming sword which turned every way, to keep the way of the tree of life.

GENESIS CHAPTER 4

1 And Adam knew Eve his wife; and she conceived, and bare Cain, and said, I have gotten a man from the LORD.

2 And she again bare his brother Abel. And Abel was a keeper of sheep, but Cain was a tiller of the ground.

3 And in process of time it came to pass, that Cain brought of the fruit of the ground an offering unto the LORD.

4 And Abel, he also brought of the firstlings of his flock and of the fat thereof. And the LORD had respect unto Abel and to his offering:

5 But unto Cain and to his offering he had not respect. And Cain was very wroth, and his countenance fell.

6 And the LORD said unto Cain, Why art thou wroth? and why is thy countenance fallen?

7 If thou doest well, shalt thou not be accepted? And if thou doest not well, sin lieth at the door. And unto thee shall be his desire, and thou shalt rule over him.

8 And Cain talked with Abel his brother: and it came to pass, when they were in the field, that Cain rose up against Abel his brother, and slew him.

9 And the LORD said unto Cain, Where is Abel thy brother? And he said, I know not: Am I my brother's keeper?

10 And he said, What hast thou done? the voice of thy brother's blood crieth unto me from the ground.

11 And now art thou cursed from the earth, which hath opened her mouth to receive thy brother's blood from thy hand;

12 When thou tillest the ground, it shall not henceforth yield unto thee her strength; a fugitive and a vagabond shalt thou be in the earth.

13 And Cain said unto the LORD, My punishment is greater than I can bear.

14 Behold, thou hast driven me out this day from the face of the earth; and from thy face shall I be hid; and I shall be a fugitive and a vagabond in the earth; and it shall come to pass, that every one that findeth me shall slay me.

15 And the LORD said unto him, Therefore whosoever slayeth Cain, vengeance shall be taken on him sevenfold. And the LORD set a mark upon Cain, lest any finding him should kill him.

16 And Cain went out from the presence of the LORD, and dwelt in the land of Nod, on the east of Eden.

17 And Cain knew his wife; and she conceived, and bare Enoch: and he builded a city, and called the name of the city, after the name of his son, Enoch.

18 And unto Enoch was born Irad: and Irad begat Mehujael: and Mehujael begat Methusael: and Methusael begat Lamech.

19 And Lamech took unto him two wives: the name of the one was Adah, and the name of the other Zillah.

20 And Adah bare Jabal: he was the father of such as dwell in tents, and of such as have cattle.

21 And his brother's name was Jubal: he was the father of all such as handle the harp and organ.

22 And Zillah, she also bare Tubalcain, an instructor of every artificer in brass and iron: and the sister of Tubalcain was Naamah.

23 And Lamech said unto his wives, Adah and Zillah, Hear my voice; ye wives of Lamech, hearken unto my speech: for I have slain a man to my wounding, and a young man to my hurt.

24 If Cain shall be avenged sevenfold, truly Lamech seventy and sevenfold.

25 And Adam knew his wife again; and she bare a son, and called his name Seth: For God, said she, hath appointed me another seed instead of Abel, whom Cain slew.

26 And to Seth, to him also there was born a son; and he called his name Enos: then began men to call upon the name of the LORD.

The Father, the Son, and the Holy Ghost

Matthew 28:19 says, "Go ye therefore, and teach all nations, baptizing them in the name of the Father, and of the Son, and of the Holy Ghost:"

Many people are confused by this. They ask, "How can there be one God, and yet be manifest in three different persons?" Some people even try to accuse those of us, who believe in the Father, the Son, and the Holy Ghost, of believing in three gods; but I am convinced that they don't really believe that; they are just trying to make fun of our beliefs. People who really want to know the truth, will receive the truth, when they see it, or hear it.

The Spirit of the Lord came upon me to write a poem, that would explain the concept of the Holy Trinity. The name of it is; "IF YOU DON'T KNOW THE FATHER, YOU DO NOT KNOW THE SON."

IF YOU DON'T KNOW THE FATHER, YOU DO NOT KNOW THE SON.

By David L. Jemison

People seem so puzzled,
When you say 'TRINITY'.
One God manifest in three persons,
Seems very simple to me.

One God, whose name is Yahweh,
Who created everything,
Who laid the foundations of the earth,
And caused the morning stars to sing
A God who is eternal,
Must be known by everyone.
Because if you don't know the Father,
You cannot know the Son.

The only living and true God has attributes,
That are unique to Him alone you see.
And because He is an omnipresent Spirit,
He can be there with you, and here with me.

Spirit is what God is,
And how God is, is Holy.
Everlasting is when He was born, And how long He lives.
But how God is, is Holy.

A Father is a male person,
Who has begotten a child

And without a child is not.
Yahweh became a Father when,
The virgin conceived, Christ Jesus was born,
And the Son of God was begot.

The God who is Omnipresent,
Must be clear to everyone.
Because if you don't know the Father,
You can not know the Son.

Because God is omnipotent,
There is nothing that He cannot do.
There is no power, situation, or circumstance,
That can keep Him from blessing you.
Satan is real, and a strong influence.
And there are things that he leads us to do.
But before you waste all of that fear on him,
you need to remember, that God made him too.

God is so powerful, in His own right,
There is nothing, with Him to compare.
He parts the sea, and rolls back the night,
and delivers His people everywhere.

The Lord God Yahweh is omnipotent,
Since before the world had begun.
And if you don't know the Father,
You just can't know the Son.

It is so good to know, that God is omniscient.
And that there is nothing that He does not know:
Everything that was, is, and is to come

Everything in the heavens above,
Everything in the Earth below.

There is no pain I have, That God cannot feel,
No problem of mine, He cannot see,
No obstacle that has been blocking my path,
And no habit or fault, that is hindering me.

When God does not provide, Some things that I want,
Some things that I've been praying for,
I may be disappointed, because I love Him so,
But He doesn't give, because He loves me more.
If you never know the omniscient God,
I'm afraid that you'll never come.
Because if you don't know the Father,
There is no way that you can know the Son.

In a world that is ever changing,
Among people who keep changing too,
It's great to know that God is immutable.
The God that was, He will always be,
And what He has done He will always do.

God is Holy, Just, and Good.
Full of grace and mercy is He.
He is for the right, and against the wrong.
And we can know, that He will always be.
What would it be like, if the Lord our God,
Was like the many fickle people we know?
And just when we understand that He said yes,
He changes His mind and says no.

Some people say that God does not do
The things that He used to do.
But not only does God do what He has always done,
He now wants to do these things through you.

If you do not know, that God will not change,
You will never know the Holy One.
Because if you don't know the Father,
You will never know the Son.

Yahweh is the God who cannot tell a lie.
Everything that He says is true.
No one can refute Anything that He has said.
All that He promises, He'll do

Despite all that you see, that is bad in this world,
Control is still in God's hand.
He made all that you see, And declared that it is good.
But since then, it's been corrupted by man.

God is the Creator and Supreme Ruler of Heaven and
Earth.
He makes countries great, at His will.
He knows every king from the time of their birth.
And uses them, His will to fulfill.

God rules this world, and He cannot lie,
When all is said and done.
And if you fail to get to know the Father,
You will never get to know His Son.

Our Lord is the God, who walks and talks with man,
And takes time to show us the right way.
He has made so many great promises to us,
And He hears and answers, each time we pray.

You cannot know Jesus until He is introduced to you.
This is just the way that it's done.
You need to get to know the Father,
If you hope to get to know His Son.

The character of God revealed through His Law,
Makes us know, we haven't been so nice.
It shows us our sin, that we have committed against him.
It's our schoolmaster, to bring us to Christ.

When you get to know the Father,
You know that He loves you.
And has for your life, a great plan
And He has provided for you,
A Way back to Him, Through Jesus,
The only Way, the Son of Man.

So When you know the Father,
And believe all that He has done..
You will be glad that you know the Father
And you will be saved because you know the Son.
A son is a male child,
born of a Father and Mother, for sure.
Because of the blood, flowing through His veins,
Jesus was without blemish and pure.

Jesus Immanuel is His name,
And Son, is what He is to His Dad.
All that God is, was placed into Him,
And He got all that His Mother Mary had.

His flesh, feelings, and appetites, came from His Mom.
His blood, life, and power from above:
Blood and life, to give for our sins,
And power, to raise us by His love.
So Jesus is the gift that God gives to man,
To pay for all of our sins.
Whoever it is that believes on this Gift,
Is forgiven, and new life begins.

And since our Savior Is now gone above,
He wants us to live just like He.
The Holy Ghost, that He gives to his church,
Is His Spirit, to dwell in us eternally.

Jesus went to Calvary, Bled, died, and refused to fuss.
But it was God the Father,
who so loved the World
And gave this Son for all of us.
So come to the Bible and learn of this Great God.
And see all that He has done.
Study His word, and eat all of it.
Because this is how you get to know the Father.
And this is how you get to know the Son.

There is no greater love, than what the Father has for me.
That He should send such a blessed Son, to die in agony.
Jesus' blood, to pay for our sin,

He died for everyone.
But if you don't meet this gracious Father
You will never get to meet His wonderful Son.

Chapter 24

What will believing in Christ Jesus Immanuel do for you?

Believing in Christ Jesus Immanuel will do for us just what the Lord said that believing in Him will do. The moment that the Lord speaks, His word becomes activated. It is destined to perform it's purpose, and will be relentless, until it had produced all for which it has been sent. Believing in Jesus Christ, is to take Him at His Word; after all, it will be His word that will judge us in that day.

1. Power to become the sons of God:

John 1:12, "But as many as received Him to them gave He power to become the sons of God, even to them that believe on His name."

2. He gives us the ability to die, without going to the grave:

Galatians 2:20, "I am crucified with Christ: nevertheless I live; yet not I, but Christ liveth in me: and the life that I now live in the flesh I live by the faith of the Son of God, who loved me, and gave Himself for me."

3. Our sins are carried away:

John 1:29, "The next day John seeth Jesus coming unto him, and saith, Behold the lamb of God, which taketh away the sin of the world."

4. We are imputed with the righteousness of Jesus Christ:

Romans 4:3-8, "For what saith the scripture? Abraham believed God, and it was counted unto him for righteousness. Now to him that worketh is the reward not reckoned of grace, but of debt. But to him that worketh not, but that believeth on Him that justifieth the ungodly, his faith is counted for righteousness. Even David also describeth the blessedness of man, unto whom God imputeth righteousness without works, Saying, Blessed are they whose iniquities are forgiven, and whose sins are covered. Blessed is the man to whom the Lord will not impute sin."

5. We become new creatures in Christ: 2 Corinthians 5:17, "Therefore if any man be in Christ, he is a new creature: old things are passed away; behold, all things are become new."

6. The Holy Ghost comes into us to stay:

1 Corinthians 3:16-17, "Know ye not that ye are the temple of God, and that the Spirit of God dwelleth in you? If any man defile the temple of God, him shall God destroy; for the temple of God is holy, which temple ye are."

Matthew 28:18-20, "And Jesus cams and spake unto them, saying, All power is given unto me in heaven and in earth. Go ye therefore, and teach all nations, baptizing them in the name of the Father, and of the Son, and of the Holy Ghost: Teaching them to observe all things whatsoever I have commanded you: and, lo, I am with you always, even unto the end of the world. Amen.

7. We have reservations for our heavenly home:

1 Peter 1:3-5, "Blessed be the God and Father of our Lord Jesus Christ, which according to His abundant mercy hath begotten us again unto a lively hope by the resurrection of Jesus Christ from the dead, To an inheritance incorruptible, and undefiled, and that fadeth not away, reserved in heaven for you, Who are kept by the power of God through faith unto salvation ready to be revealed in the last time.

God gives a prayer for his children

The Lord woke me up one morning, and inspired me to write this prayer for His little children. Many children now say, "Now I lay me down to sleep, I pray the Lord, my soul to keep. If I should die before I wake, I pray the Lord, my soul to take." This prayer has been a blessing down through the years; but it speaks about death. This new prayer speaks about life, as we live it.

(A CHILD'S PRAYER)

by David L. Jemison

"LORD I'M SO GLAD THAT YOU ARE HERE WITH ME"

Dear Heavenly Father I know you are here
I have learned from the Bible That you are everywhere

You have always been And you always will be
That's why I'm so glad that You are here with me

I thank you for Jesus Who died for our sin
And I open my heart's door To let Him come in

I pray for my family Friends and enemies too
Would you please send someone To lead them to you

Please watch over me Lord While I'm sleeping tonight
And if I have done wrong Lord Please help me do right

The night is so long Lord And its hard to see
That's why I'm so glad that You are here with me

AMEN

My hope and prayer to God is that those who read this book might receive the "Gift of God," and be saved. I pray that the faith of the believer in Christ may be strengthened; and that the servants of God may be inspired to be the soul winners that the Lord would have them to be. Anyone who is saved can show someone else how to be saved. It is the eleventh hour, the Lord is hiring. See Matthew 20:1-16:

<u>INSTRUCTIONS ON HOW TO BE SAVED
HERE IS THE INFORMATION</u>

EVERY SINNER WHO IS SEEKING GOD, WANTS TO KNOW.
There are many people praying for you to be SAVED, many of whom you don't even know.
If you follow these direct instructions, you will be SAVED
<u>today</u>, and <u>you will know </u>that you are saved.
For Your Information

Salvation has nothing to do with denominations, but it has everything to do with our personal relationship with the Lord God YAHWEH, and His Son Jesus Immanuel, the Christ.

You don't have to be in a church in order to be saved. You can be at work, on a street, in a house, on a train, bus, or airplane. You may be even in an automobile.

You might be in a hospital, in a jail, prison, or on the battlefield; it doesn't matter. If you follow these instructions *you* will be saved.

If you are a gang member, fornicator, thief, murderer, lesbian, homosexual, or an adulterer, if you follow these instructions, you will be **saved**.

It doesn't matter what your background is: If you are Muslim, Hindu, Scientologist, Evolutionist, atheist, or whatever, it doesn't matter. If you follow these instructions, you **will** be saved.

THESE ARE THE INSTRUCTIONS FROM THE BIBLE

1. Hebrews 11:6; But without faith it is impossible to please Him: for he that cometh to God must believe that He is, and that He is a rewarder of them that diligently seek Him.

When you come to God, you must believe that He exists, and that He will respond to you when you are serious in your search for Him. You will be rewarded.

2. Jeremiah 29:13; *And ye shall seek me and shall find me when you shall search for me with all your heart.*

You must make a sincere effort to get to know and please the Lord.

3. 1 John 1:8-10; *If we say that we have no sin, we deceive ourselves, and the truth is not in us. If we confess our sins, he is faithful and just to forgive us our sins, and to cleanse us from all unrighteousness. If we say that we have not sinned, we make him a liar, and his word is not in us.*

It is of the utmost importance that we agree with God, and admit that we have sinned.

4. Mark 1:14-15; *Now after that John was put in prison, Jesus came into Galilee, preaching the gospel of the kingdom of God,*

And saying, The time is fulfilled and the kingdom of God is at hand: repent ye, and believe the gospel.

Matthew 3:1-2; *In those days came John the Baptist, preaching in the wilderness of Judea,*

And saying, Repent ye: for the kingdom of heaven is at hand.

Before you can be saved, you must repent of your sins. You must change your mind about what you think about sin, and see it as offensive to God and ruinous to your soul. God hates sin.

If you know that it is sin, then make a decision to stop doing it, and to live to please God.

5. 1 Samuel 16:7; *But the Lord said unto Samuel, Look not on his countenance, or on the height of his stature; because I have refused him: for the Lord seeth not as man seeth; for man looketh on the outward appearance, but the Lord looketh on the heart.*

You must be sincere with the Lord because He can see what is in your heart.

6. Acts 2:21; *And it shall come to pass, that whosoever shall call on the name of the Lord shall be saved.*

Romans 10:13; For whosoever shall call upon the name of the Lord shall be saved.

If you want God to save you, then ask Him to save you. Invite Him into your heart. He will do it.

Stop right now and pray this prayer

Oh Lord, be merciful unto me. I am a sinner. I have broken your laws and I am so sorry. Please forgive me. Come into my heart and save me. AMEN

7. *Mark 16:16; He that believeth and is baptized shall be saved*

John 3:16; For God so loved the world that He gave His only begotten Son, that whosoever believeth in Him should not perish, but have everlasting life.

John 3:18; He that believeth on Him is not condemned: but he that believeth not is condemned already, because he hath not believed in the name of the only begotten Son of God.

John 3:36; He that believeth on the Son hath everlasting life: and he that believeth not the Son shall not see life; but the wrath of God abideth on him.

John 5:24; Verily, verily, I say unto you, He that heareth my word and believeth on him that sent me, hath everlasting life, and shall not come into condemnation; but is passed from death unto life.

John 6:40; And this is the will of Him that sent me, that everyone that seeth the Son and believeth on Him, may have everlasting life: and I will raise him up at the last day.

John 6:47; Verily, verily, I say unto you, he that believeth on me hath everlasting life.

John 14:6; Jesus saith unto him, I am the way, the truth, and the life: no man cometh unto the Father but by me.

Acts 4:12; Neither is there salvation in any other: for there is none other name under heaven given among men, whereby we must be saved.

Ephesians 2:8-10; For by grace are ye saved through faith; and that not of yourselves: it is the gift of God

Not of works, lest any man should boast.

For we are His workmanship, created in Christ Jesus unto good works, which God hath before ordained that we should walk in them.

The information is overwhelming, and the instructions are emphatically clear; if one is to be saved, He must believe in Jesus Christ. You must believe God's promise of eternal life.

8. Romans 10:9; *That if thou shalt confess with thy mouth the Lord Jesus, and believe in thine heart that God hath raised Him from the dead, thou shalt be saved.*

Right now, pray this prayer with me.

Dear Lord, thank you for loving me, and thank you for the promise of everlasting life. I believe your promise, that if I believe on your Son Jesus, I do have eternal life.

Right now I do declare that according to your word, I do have everlasting life, and I welcome you into my life as my Lord and Savior. Thank you for saving me. From now on, my life belongs to you. AMEN!

You must open your mouth and declare that you have eternal life, because you believe in Jesus, and because He has saved you.

Romans 10:11; For the scripture saith, whosoever that believeth on Him shall not be ashamed.

Now that you are truly saved, you won't be ashamed to tell others that the Lord saved you; because you believe on Jesus. That witness inside you that tells you that you are saved, is the Holy Spirit, who is now inside you. This is the evidence that you do believe God's Word.

There is the first literary work that the Lord inspired me to write, which led to the formation of GOOD NEWS EVANGELISM INC. of Canonsburg, Pennsylvania, which has since been dissolved. That literary work is the gospel tract called "SAVED." I believe that I would be remiss, if I didn't include it in this book. I believe that the words still have power.

"SAVED"

Saved! This is one little word that seems to confuse so many when talking about **SALVATION.** However, ordinarily we use it every day and have no trouble understanding it.

This word in Webster's Dictionary means: rescued, delivered from Danger, preserved or (kept); or having avoided.

Spiritually speaking, what does one need to be saved from, rescued from, delivered from, or kept from? What does he need to avoid? The Word of God says "The soul that sinneth, it shall SURELY DIE." (Ezek. 18:4) "The wages of sin is death." (Rom. 6:23) Whosoever is not written in the Book of Life will be cast into the Lake of fire. (Rev. 20:15)

If you can't say right now that you are saved, beloved, you are on your way to hell.

The Lord has inspired me to write this tract so that you will know the truth, and so that the TRUTH will make you free.

If you had a bottle of poison in your hand, clearly marked poison, the label was put there that you might be aware of the danger and so that you could avoid a tragedy. When you believe that warning, it will save you from dying a tragic death.

If you had accidentally or purposely taken the poison into your body; then having decided that you did not want to die; you read on the label that it will kill you in ten minutes and that the only antidote is five raw eggs; If you take the only antidote, you will not die, but you will surely live. Any sane and wise person would take the antidote.

You have been poisoned by Satan's bite: that Old Serpent called 'the Devil'. "For all have sinned and come short of the

Glory of God" (Rom. 3 :9,23,1 John 1 :8) . "The soul that sinneth it shall SURELY DIE" (Ezek. 18:4).

If You have not and will not take the only antidote **(JESUS CHRIST)** as your savior, **YOU WILL** die and burn in Hell. For He says "I am the Way, the Truth, the Life, no man cometh unto the Father, but by Me." (John 14 :6) I am just as sure of this fact as I am that there is a God and that the Bible is His Word.

But you need not go to Hell; because **JESUS LOVES YOU** and is not willing that any should perish, but that all should come to repentance. (2 Peter 3 :9) 'For God so **loved** the world, that He GAVE His only begotten Son, that whosoever **believeth** in Him should not perish but have everlasting LIFE.' (John 3:16) **Whosoever** includes you: No matter how great your sins are.

He has **an AMAZING LOVE** for us. 'He came to seek and to save we who are lost.' (Luke 19: 10) If you are a lost sinner, then the coming of Jesus and His death, burial, and resurrection is for you.

So confess your sins to Him; for 'If we confess our sins, he is faithful and just to forgive us our sins and to cleanse us from all unrighteousness'.

(1 John 1 :9) Be sorry for your sins and turn from them to God. (This is true repentance)

Sin is so terrible in the eyes of God, that His Holiness and Justice demands the death penalty. But His **Love** and **Mercy** is so great that He sent Jesus, His only begotten Son to pay the **sin debt** and to receive the wages of sin; **(DEATH).** He died for us that we would not have to die. 'Without the shedding of blood there is no forgiveness for sin. (Heb. 9:22) Jesus suffered and shed His blood for our forgiveness.

But we must, as individuals; receive (accept) Him as our savior. 'As many as received Him, to them gave He power to become the Sons of God. Even to those that believe on His name; **(JESUS)** (John 1 : 12).

To accept Him as our savior, means to abandon all trust in anything else for salvation. Don't trust in your own righteousness, good works, church membership, good feelings, water baptism, church attendance, or any thing other than the unshakable, True Word of God. **If God tells us that we are SAVED, then we ARE saved. 'God cannot lie.'** Titus 1 :2

Simply close your eyes right NOW and tell God that you know that you are a sinner and that you are sorry. Invite Him to come into your heart and save you, and He Will, because His Word; that cannot lie, says "For *whosoever* shall call upon the name of the Lord; shall be SAVED." (Rom. 10: 13) Then just by **FAITH**, accept Jesus Christ as **your own** personal savior and BELIEVE His Word; for He cannot lie.

Jesus said "Verily, verily, I say unto you, He that BELIEVETH on Me hath everlasting life."

Do you **believe on Jesus**, BELIEVE that He was born of a virgin, BELIEVE that He died and was buried and rose up on the 3rd day? Do you BELIEVE that He was God's Son, and that He paid for all your sins with his own life?

If the answer to all these questions is yes, then when Jesus said "He that BELIEVETH on Me", He was talking about you. He described you perfectly, although He did not call your name, because **YOU** are the one that **believeth** on Him, and He says that you **HATH** (present tense) right now **everlasting LIFE.** He did not say that you probably have ,or will have everlasting life, but **HATH definitely,** right now, everlasting life.

If you believe that the Bible is the Word from **GOD,** and that Jesus; **HIS SON,** did not tell you a lie, you have **JUST NOW,** gotten **SAVED** from death and Hell and will be kept by the **power** of GOD, until the day of redemption. (John 6:39, 10:27-30, Eph. 4:30)

'For by **GRACE** (unearned favor) are ye saved through **FAITH** (believing God) and that not of yourselves, it's the **GIFT** of God, not of works, lest any man should boast. (Eph. 2:8,9)

If you really do believe God's Word and have just been saved, then prove it to yourself. God sees your heart and knows if you **TRULY** believe, but you must prove it to yourself by confessing **JESUS as YOUR** savior, to anyone near you, as soon as possible. For God's Word says 'That if thou shalt confess with thy mouth, the Lord Jesus, and shalt **BELIEVE** in thine heart that God has raised Him from the dead, thou **shalt** be saved.

For with the Heart man **BELIEVETH** unto righteousness and with the mouth confession is made into salvation. For the scripture saith, Whosoever believeth on Him shall not be ashamed.' (Rom. 10:9-11)

When you are not ashamed to tell anyone that **God has SAVED you by His GRACE**, through nothing more than **FAITH,** then you are *SAVED*.

There is a Bible lesson that I once taught; that I believe will be a tremendous blessing to you. There are some things that should be settled in our hearts, so that we can move on to do the work that the Lord has assigned to our hands to do. That lesson is, "FIVE BIBLE IMPOSSIBLITIES", things that the Bible teaches is impossible. If some things are impossible, we can save ourselves much heartache, and heart break, if we know what those things are.

"FIVE BIBLE IMPOSSIBILITIES"

"The Lesson Aim"

1. This lesson should convince you, that we can depend on anything that God has promised us.

2. This lesson should teach you what God requires of us.

3. This lesson should teach you, how secure we are in Jesus.

4. This lesson should teach you, who we, the children of God, are and what the New Birth does for us.

5. This lesson should teach you to expect troubles and problems.

"FIVE BIBLE IMPOSSIBILITIES"

I. It is impossible *for God to lie.*

Hebrews 6:17-18: "Wherein GOD, willing more abundantly to shew unto the heirs of promise the immutability of His counsel, confirmed it by an oath: That by two immutable things, in which it was impossible for GOD to lie, we might have a strong consolation, who have fled for refuge to lay hold upon the hope set before us.

Titus 1:1-3: "Paul, a servant of GOD, and an apostle of Jesus Christ, according to the faith of God's elect, and the acknowledging of the truth which is after godliness; In hope of eternal life, which God that cannot lie, promised before the world began; But hath in due times manifested his word through preaching, which is committed unto me according to the commandment of God our Savior."

Numbers 23:19-20: "God is not a man, that He should lie; neither the son of man, that He should repent: hath He said and shall He not do it? Or hath He spoken, and shall He not

301

make it good? Behold I have received commandment to bless: and He hath blessed: and I cannot reverse it."

II. It is impossible *to please God without faith.*

Hebrews 11:1: "Now faith is the substance of things hoped for, the evidence of things not seen."

Hebrews 11:6: "But without faith it is impossible to please Him: for they that cometh to GOD must believe that He is, and that He is a rewarder of them that diligently seek Him."

III. It is impossible *to be saved the second time.*

Hebrews 6:4-6: "For it is impossible for those who were once enlightened, and have tasted of the heavenly gift, and were made partakers of the Holy Ghost, And have tasted the good word of God, and the powers of the world to come, if they shall fall away, to renew them again unto repentance; seeing they crucify to themselves the Son of God afresh, and put Him to an open shame."

John 10:25-30: "Jesus answered them, I told you, and ye believed not: the works that I do in my Father's name, they bear witness of me. But ye believe not, because ye are not of my sheep, as I said unto you. My sheep hear my voice, and I know them, and they follow me: And I give unto them eternal life; and they shall never perish; neither shall any man pluck them out of my hand. My Father, which gave them me, is greater than all; and no man is able to pluck them out of my Father's hand. I and my Father are one."

Matthew 7:21-23: "Not every one that saith unto me, Lord, Lord, shall enter into the kingdom of heaven; but he that doeth the will of my Father which is in heaven. Many will say to me in that day, Lord, Lord, have we not prophesied in thy name? And in thy name have cast out devils? And in thy name done many wonderful works? And then will I profess unto them, I never knew you: depart from me, ye that work iniquity.

IV. It is impossible *for the person who is 'Born of God' to sin.*

John 3:3-8: "Jesus answered and said unto him, Verily, verily, I say unto thee, Except a man be born again, he cannot see the kingdom of GOD. That which is born of the flesh is flesh; and that which is born of the Spirit is spirit.

Marvel not that I said unto thee, Ye must be born again. The wind bloweth where it listeth, and thou hearest the sound thereof, but canst not tell whence it cometh, and whither it goeth: so is every one that is born of the Spirit."

1 John 3:9: "Whosoever is born of GOD doth not commit sin; for His seed remaineth in him: and he cannot sin, because he is born of GOD."

2 Corinthians 5:17: "Therefore if any man be in Christ, he is a new creature: old things are passed away; behold all things are become new."

Galatians 2:19-21: "For I through the law am dead to the law, that I might live unto GOD. I am crucified with Christ: nevertheless I live; yet not I, but Christ liveth in me: and the life that I now live in the flesh I live by the faith of the Son of GOD, who loved me, and gave Himself for me. I do not frustrate the grace of God: for if righteousness come by the law, then Christ is dead in vain."

Romans 4:5-8: "But to him that worketh not, but believeth on him that justifieth the ungodly, his faith is counted for righteousness. Even as David also describeth the blessedness of the man, unto whom God imputeth righteousness without works, Saying, Blessed are they whose iniquities are forgiven, and whose sins are covered. Blessed is the man to whom the LORD will not impute sin."

V. It is impossible *for a Christian <u>not</u> to have offenses*.

Luke 17:1: "Then said He unto the disciples, It is impossible but that offences will come: but woe unto him, through whom they come!"

FINALLY

We are **SAVED and <u>SAFE</u>;** *not as a result of what we do for God*, but because of what the Lord God has done for us. Ephesians 2:8-10: "For by grace are ye saved through faith; and that not of yourselves: it is the gift of GOD: Not of works, lest any may should boast. For we are His workmanship, created in Christ Jesus unto good works, which God hath before ordained that we should walk in them.

Proverbs 18:10: "The name of the LORD is a strong tower: the righteous runneth into it and is safe."

Titus 3:3-8: "For we ourselves also were sometimes foolish, disobedient, deceived, serving divers lusts and pleasures, living in malice and envy, hateful, and hating one another. But after the kindness and love of God our Savior toward man appeared, not by works of righteousness which we have done, but according to His mercy He saved us, by the washing of regeneration, and the renewing of the Holy Ghost; Which He shed on us abundantly through Jesus Christ Our Savior; That being justified by His grace, we should be made heirs according to the hope of eternal life. This is a faithful saying, and these things I will that thou affirm constantly, that they which have believed in GOD might be careful to maintain good works. These things are good and profitable unto men."

1 John 5:10-13: "He that believeth on the Son of GOD hath the witness in himself: he that believeth not hath made

him a liar; because he believeth not the record that GOD gave of his Son. And this is the record, that GOD hath given to us eternal life, and this life is in His Son. He that hath the Son hath life; and he that hath not the Son of GOD hath not life. These things have I written unto you that believe on the name of the Son of GOD; that ye may know that ye have eternal life, and that ye may believe on the name of the Son of GOD.

Romans 6:23: "For the wages of sin is death; but the gift of GOD is eternal life through Jesus Christ our Lord."

John 6:37-47: "All that the Father giveth me shall come to me; and him that cometh to me I will in no wise cast out. For I came down from heaven, not to do mine own will, but the will of Him that sent me.

And this is the Father's will which hath sent me, that of all which He hath given me I should lose nothing, but should raise it up again at the last day. And this is the will of Him that sent me, that every one which seeth the Son, and believeth on Him, may have everlasting life: and I will raise him up at the last day.

The Jews then murmured at him, because he said, I am the bread which came down from heaven. And they said, Is not this Jesus, the son of Joseph, whose father and mother we know?

How is it then that he saith, I came down from heaven? Jesus therefore answered and said unto them, Murmur not among yourselves. No man can come to me, except the Father which hath sent me draw him, and I will raise him up at the last day. It is written in the prophets, And they shall all be taught of GOD.

Every man therefore that hath heard, and hath learned of the Father, cometh unto me. Not that any man hath seen the

Father, save he which is of GOD, he hath seen the Father. Verily, verily, I say unto you, he that believeth on me hath everlasting life."

Philippians 2:13: "For it is God which worketh in you both to will and to do of His good pleasure."

THESE THINGS WE KNOW

We can depend on GOD, because it is impossible for Him to lie.

The LORD requires that we please Him, and this is impossible to do without faith.

When we receive the Lord Jesus as our Savior and put all of our trust in Him for salvation, we are safe from condemnation and Hell. If it were possible for a person who has experienced all that a saved person experiences to get lost, that person could never be saved a second time.

The person who is born again is spirit, like the wind, invisible, and they possess attributes of God; invisible, everlasting, and sinless, thus it is impossible for them to sin, because they are the seed of GOD.

The Lord makes it clear that it is impossible for us to live in this world without having offences; so we might as well get ready.

Don't be surprised.

"I BELIEVE BECAUSE"

Because of the day that I prayed with Oral Roberts, for the Lord to save me, and He answered my prayer, by planting within me, a great hunger for the Word of God; it made me know that He was ordering my steps.

Because of the day that the Lord turned the pages of my Bible, so that I would know the truth about His love, mercy, and grace, I learned that He cared for me.

Because of the day that God spoke to me, brought salvation scriptures back to my memory, and then saved me, and also verified the certainty of my salvation; it made me certain that the Lord is real, and He loves me.

Because of the night that the Lord gave me a dream, to let me know that I wasn't ready to become a preacher, and that I needed to know much more, and needed to study much more; He made me know that He wants His preachers to know His Word, and to be sure of His message.

Because of the day that the Lord carried me away in the spirit, and commanded me to go and preach His gospel, it made me know that God uses ordinary people.

Because of the day when the lord threw me across the room onto my face twice, He made me know that He was not just a metaphysical God, which only had the power that you let him have, and that he cared about me and my spiritual growth, a particular Jewish man in New York, named Stanley, and the people of Nigeria.

Because of the day that the Lord paid a special visit to Margaret, a woman whose heart had been so hard, that she said to me that she didn't want to hear about God, to save her personally; It made me know that God doesn't just care for groups of people; He loves and cares for the individual person.

Because of the week of revival in Midland, Pennsylvania, during which we had a Holy visitation, and during which thirty two people came to the Lord, and were saved, I've come to know that any people, who are hungry, and praying for revival, can and will have it.

Because of the day when the vision of fire that appeared over the pulpit, and that arched over seven of us, who were seated in the middle, while the Reverend Herman Gore was preaching; I found out that God was still bearing witness, with signs, and wonders; and that He had a greater work for me to do.

Because of the day that the Lord caused a church to plan week of street evangelistic services, especially so that a certain prostitute could be saved, and that a young rebellious man, might get his last chance to be saved, He taught me that He is not willing that anyone should perish, but is long suffering.

Because of the day that I got fed up with the way that things were going in the church of which I was a member; and I prayed to God saying, "Lord, you've got to get me out of here," and He answered immediately, within a half an hour of my prayer, when I got a call to go to preach, a church where the pastor had just resigned, that same morning. And that church kept me, changed the name of their church, so that I would come and be their pastor; and I would not have to go back to the church that I asked the Lord to get me out of. Because of this I know that the Lord God is with me.

Because of the day when I came within two inches of dying, and the Lord kept me alive, I was reminded that God will take care of me.

The End of the Beginning

This is the end of this book; but it is just the beginning of a life of serving The Lord, in the power of the Holy Ghost, because the Lord has led you to this book, so that you might know Him, and the power of His resurrection. He wants to use you to get the harvest in, during these last and evil days. Some of you are they who were standing around in the market place, at the eleventh hour; and the Lord is asking you, "Why are you standing around?" and some of you are saying, "Because no one has hired us." But, can't you hear the Lords voice, saying unto you, "Go and work, and whatever is right, I will pay?" So child of God, this is your chance.

Go in the name of the Lord, knowing that all power in heaven and earth is in His hands, and that Jesus will go with you, and that He will never leave you or forsake you.

And to those of you who haven't yet made up your minds to accept the Lord Jesus as your Lord and Savior; you must remember:

The Word of God is despised, and God's Word is God's Grace